DESERT W[...]

BEING THE CHRONICLE OF

THE EASTERN SOUDAN CAMPAIGN

Published in 1988 by Ken Trotman Ltd,
Booksellers & Publishers,
Unit 11 135 Ditton Walk, Cambridge CB5 8QD

This edition © Ken Trotman Ltd
All rights reserved. No part of this publication
may be reproduced, stored in a retrieval system or
transmitted in any form by any means electrical,
mechanical or otherwise without first seeking the
written permission of the copyright owner and
of the publisher.

ISBN 0-946879-43-5

Printed by Antony Rowe Ltd.,
Chippenham, Wiltshire.

DESERT WARFARE

BEING THE CHRONICLE OF

THE EASTERN SOUDAN CAMPAIGN.

BY

BENNET BURLEIGH,

WAR CORRESPONDENT, NOW OF THE LONDON "DAILY TELEGRAPH;"
FORMERLY "CENTRAL NEWS."

WITH OFFICIAL MAPS.

LONDON: CHAPMAN AND HALL,
LIMITED
1884.

INTRODUCTORY.

In July, 1882, I first visited Egypt, going out as War Correspondent, in order to chronicle the incidents in the campaign that terminated in the victory at Tel-el-Kebir. Since then I have seen a good deal of that country, having revisited the land of the Pharaohs three times, on the last occasion going to what was probably their remotest boundary, the Eastern Soudan, as War Correspondent with the little army commanded by Major-General Sir Gerald Graham, V.C., etc. The ostensible and proclaimed object of the expedition was the relief of the Egyptian garrison, beleaguered at Tokar by Osman Digna. In attempting to rescue them two Egyptian commands had come to grief, namely, that which Consul Moncrieff accompanied, and the one Baker Pasha led. It will perhaps assist the reader in comprehending more clearly what follows in these pages if I introduce a few notes, borrowed from various sources, respecting the Mahdi, Baker Pasha's defeat, and the geography of the Soudan.

In the portion of this book which treats of the operations of Major-General Graham's force, I have preserved and presented to the reader my telegrams and letters in the form in which they were cabled and appeared in the columns of the London *Daily Telegraph*. Even the dates and names of places whence they were despatched are preserved, with the view to distinctly mark the days as well as the hours they were sent. In none of the telegrams has there been the slightest attempt at alteration, either for compositional improvement or in order to modify and trim expressions of opinion. As they were they are, except in the few instances where a printer's or telegraphist's error has crept in, or explanatory passages have been added.

This course I have adopted because I believe that the public, as well as the soldiers and sailors who took part in the expedition, will prefer reading the telegrams precisely as they were written, whether in the advance on the road, in the bivouac by night, in the midst and hurry of battle, or on the return to quarters. Most of the officers and men are familiar with the fact, that on foot or horseback my note-book and pencil were seldom out of my hand, if any movement was taking place; and that the record of the event, whatever it may have been, was there and then inscribed. The record of the moment, nowadays, is not only indispensable, but for many purposes is better than the narrative of a month after, or the memory that jogs a year behind the event. I know many gentlemen, of high literary attainments, whom I most unqualifiedly admire, that bewail the death of the letter-writing and essayist-chroniclers of war, avowing the telegraph and the "specials" have killed all these grand writers of history. I cannot share in their lamentations, for it seems to me that accuracy is of as much value to humanity as well-turned sentences. Whilst the progress of modern science has evolved the "specials," the same necessity still operates that produced the finished letter-writers; so let their admirers take heart, their epitaphs need not be written yet.

With this preamble, and apologising for the many defects of my narrative, I present to the readers my record of the battles of February and March, 1884, and the campaign in the Eastern Soudan.

BENNET BURLEIGH.

London, *June*, 1884.

Note.—The regiments are designated by their old numbers, instead of the new territorial names: the 65th is the 1st York and Lancaster; the 75th, the 1st Gordon Highlanders; the 60th, the 3rd Battalion King's Royal Rifles; the 89th, the 2nd Royal Irish Fusiliers; the 42nd, or Black Watch, the 1st Royal Highlanders.

CONTENTS.

CHAPTER I.
GEOGRAPHICAL AND DESCRIPTIVE 1

CHAPTER II.
THE MAHDI, OSMAN DIGNA, AND HICKS PASHA 6

CHAPTER III.
BAKER PASHA'S DISASTER 12

CHAPTER IV.
STEAMING FOR SUAKIM 20

CHAPTER V.
AT TRINKITAT 26

CHAPTER VI.
THE ADVANCE TO FORT BAKER 34

CHAPTER VII.
THE BATTLE OF EL TEB 41

CHAPTER VIII.
AFTER THE BATTLE 57

CONTENTS.

CHAPTER IX.
EL TEB TO TOKAR 63

CHAPTER X.
TOKAR, DUBBA, AND AFAFEET 77

CHAPTER XI.
OFFICIAL DESPATCHES—TEB AND TOKAR 89

CHAPTER XII.
CHANGE OF BASE TO SUAKIM 113

CHAPTER XIII.
EVENTS AT SUAKIM 123

CHAPTER XIV.
ADVANCING TO ATTACK OSMAN DIGNA 130

CHAPTER XV.
THE NIGHT BEFORE THE BATTLE 145

CHAPTER XVI.
THE BATTLE OF TAMAAI 152

CHAPTER XVII.
INCIDENTS AT TAMAAI 164

CHAPTER XVIII.
GENERAL COMMENT ON TEB AND TAMAAI . . . 178

CHAPTER XIX.
CONTINUATION OF GENERAL COMMENT 190

CONTENTS.

CHAPTER XX.
BACK TO SUAKIM 209

CHAPTER XXI.
OFFICIAL DESPATCHES, TAMAAI 216

CHAPTER XXII.
SUAKIM TO HANDOUK 234

CHAPTER XXIII.
ANOTHER FORWARD MOVEMENT 249

CHAPTER XXIV.
THE SKIRMISH AT TAMANIEB 257

CHAPTER XXV.
THE END OF THE CAMPAIGN 269

CHAPTER XXVI.
THE FINAL OFFICIAL REPORTS 284

SUPPLEMENTAL 314

MAPS AND PLANS.

	PAGE
GENERAL MAP OF SOUDAN . . . . *facing*	1
THE DEFENCES OF THE PORT OF SUAKIM	21
THE SQUARE AT EL TEB	42
THE EARTHWORKS AT EL TEB	55
OFFICIAL MAPS OF EL TEB AND TOKAR	89
OFFICIAL PLAN OF EL TEB	113
ADVANCE OF THE TWO SQUARES TOWARDS TAMAAI . .	138
OFFICIAL PLAN OF TAMAAI	152
PLAN OF THE BATTLE OF TAMAAI	171
POSITIONS OF 1ST AND 2ND BRIGADES AND THE LOST GUNS .	202
HAMBUK TO ES SIBIL	248

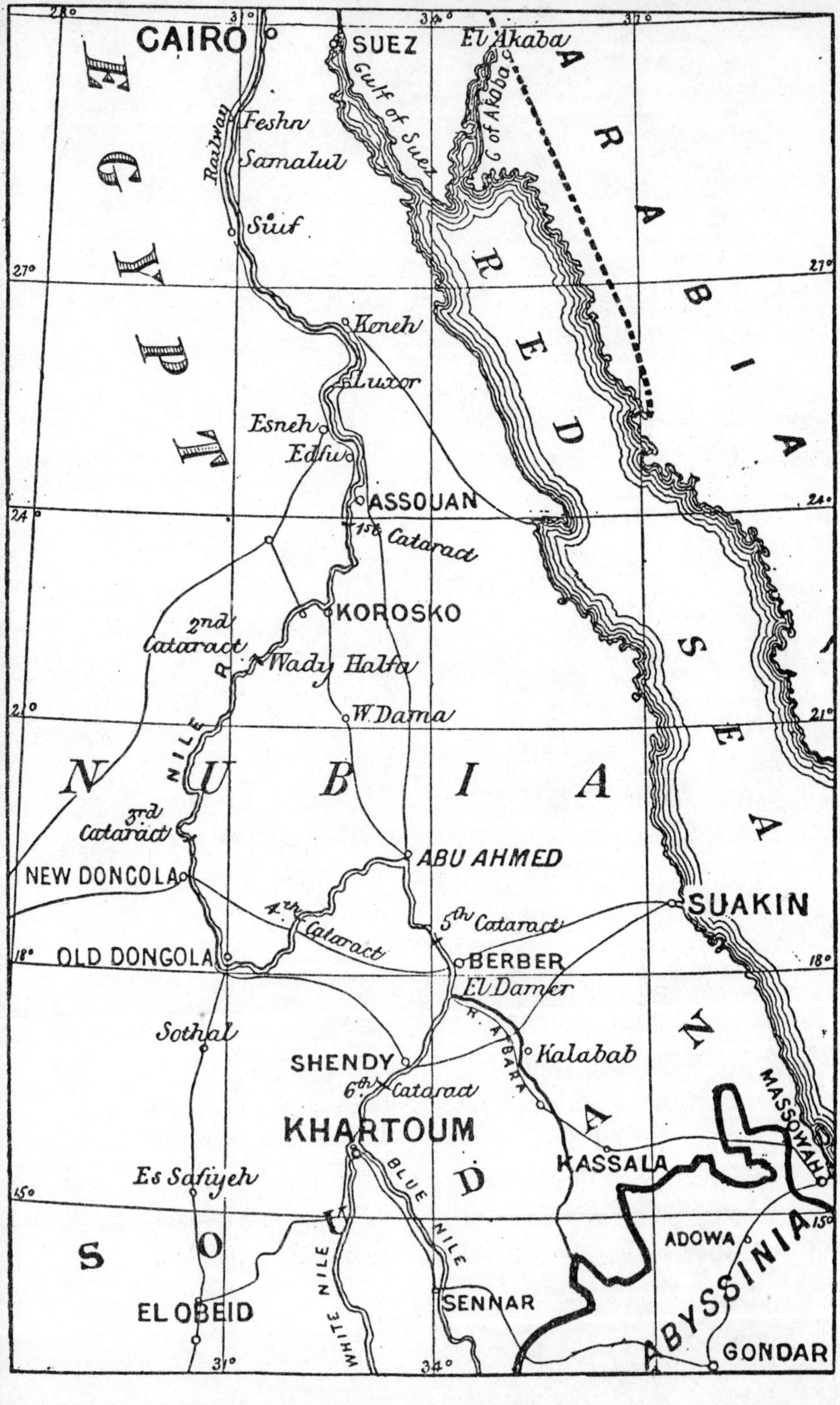

CAIRO
SUEZ
El Akaba
EGYPT
ARABIA
RED SEA
NUBIA
SOUDAN
Gulf of Suez
G. of Akaba
Railway
Feshn
Samalut
Siuf
Koneh
Luxor
Esneh
Edfu
ASSOUAN
1st Cataract
KOROSKO
2nd Cataract
Wady Halfa
W. Dama
NILE
3rd Cataract
NEW DONGOLA
ABU AHMED
4th Cataract
5th Cataract
SUAKIN
OLD DONGOLA
BERBER
El Damer
R. ATBARA
Sothal
Kalabab
SHENDY
6th Cataract
KHARTOUM
MASSOWAH
KASSALA
Es Safiyeh
BLUE NILE
WHITE NILE
ADOWA
ABYSSINIA
EL OBEID
SENNAR
GONDAR

DESERT WARFARE:

BEING THE CHRONICLE OF

THE EASTERN SOUDAN CAMPAIGN.

CHAPTER I.

GEOGRAPHICAL AND DESCRIPTIVE.

THE Soudan, or "Country of the Blacks," nominally includes that region of Eastern and Central Africa between the twentieth and tenth degrees of North latitude, extending on the east from the Red Sea far into the great unexplored deserts and wastes of Central Africa.

The following enumeration of places and distances is taken from the pamphlet, "The Soudan and the British Ministry."

The Egyptian territory, south of the Nubian Desert, may be divided as follows:

1. Upper Nubia.
2. Lower Nubia [embracing the eight departments of (*a*) Dongola; (*b*) Berber—chief town, Berber, on Nile; (*c*) Taka—chief town, Kasala, on the Mareb; (*d*) Khartoum—chief town, Khartoum (this province has been divided into the two

districts of Dar Halfiyeh and Dar Shendy); (e) Kordofan—chief town, El Obeiyad, west of White Nile; (f) Sennar—chief town, Sennar, on Blue Nile; (g) Fazokl—chief town, Kiri, on Blue Nile; (h) Bogos—chief town, Keren, seized by Munziger Bey, from Abyssinia, in 1874.]
3. Darfur.
4. The Equatorial Province, *i.e.*, all south of about latitude 9 deg. N., below the Rivers Sobat and Bahr-el-Ghazal.
5. The Red Sea Littoral, from Suakim to Formosa Bay.
6. Harrar, and the Gallas Tribes.

* * * * * *

Khartoum is the capital and trade mart of the Soudan. It was established by Mehemet Ali in 1838. Planted at the junction of the two Niles, whence the united stream flows northwards in an immense volume of water, Khartoum commands all the trade routes of the surrounding territories, as well as the great waterway of Eastern Africa. The population, according to Sir Samuel Baker, is about 25,000, but this is probably an under-estimate. There are in the place Arabs, Syrians, Egyptians, Blacks, and even some Europeans. The town lies chiefly along the left bank of the Blue Nile, at a height of 1,450 feet above the sea. The governor's house, hospital, mosque, barracks, magazines, and the residences of the principal merchants are spacious and well built, but most of the houses are poor, and made of sun-dried brick. The bazaar is large, and well supplied with Manchester goods, cutlery, etc.

THE EGYPTIAN TERRITORIES.

The map herewith contains the whole of the territories that have been under the rule of the Khedive, from Alexandria on the north to Lake Victoria Nyanza on the extreme south—*i.e.*, from the Equator to latitude 32 deg. North.

The British Cabinet decided, early in January, 1884, that all south of the line drawn across by Wadi Halfa should be abandoned.

The principal rivers, provinces, towns, and desert routes are marked, as well as the chief Arab tribes.

A special map is given of Khartoum, and also of the country round Suakim.

The district of Suakim has been the scene of three disastrous defeats to the Egyptian arms. On November 6th an Egyptian force marching to the relief of Tokar was annihilated, and Commander Moncrieff, British Consul at Suakim, was killed. A month later a battalion of black troops, rashly sent out by Mahmoud Tahir Pasha from Suakim, under Chaggia, to relieve Sinkat, was annihilated. The third defeat was the terrible disaster to General Baker's army on February 4th. It took place just south-west of Trinkitat.

Kashgil, close to Melbeis, in the heart of Kordofan, was the scene of the destruction of General Hicks' army on November 7th, 1883. He had marched from Khartoum by the White Nile to El Duoim, just south of Rumela. Thence his army had struck across the waterless desert to attack the Mahdi at El Obeiyad, the chief town of Kordofan, just north of Melbeis.

There are still some 15,000 to 20,000 Egyptian

soldiers scattered in garrisons throughout the Soudan. Sennar, on the Blue Nile; Kasala, near Abyssinia; Fashoda; Lado, and many other equatorial towns; El Fasher and other stations in Darfur all hold troops and large stores of ammunition, food, and merchandise. Slatin Bey, Governor of Darfur, and Dr. Emin Bey, Governor of the Equatorial Provinces, are both distinguished and high-toned officials. They, as well as the soldiers and a civilian population of some 40,000, are left to the mercy of the Mahdi's barbarians.

ROUTES.

	MILES		MILES
Khartoum to Cairo	1250	Suakim to Berber	280
,, Berber	200	,, Khartoum	480
,, Abou Hamed	350	,, Kasala	300
,, Korosko	510	,, Massowah (by sea)	300
,, Debbeh (by desert)	220	,, Massowah (by land)	500
,, Wadi Halfa (*viâ* Debbeh)	450	,, Tokar	50
,, Suakim (*viâ* Berber)	480	,, Sinkat	30
		Massuah to Keren	120
,, Sennar	180	Keren to Kasala	160
,, Fashoda	500	Kasala to Kedaref	120
,, El Obeiyad (by Nile)	230	Sennar to Abu-Haraz	50
		Obeiyad to Foga	140
,, El Obeiyad (across desert) about	180	Foga to Omchanga	50
		Omchanga to Fasher	60
		Omchanga to Towaisha	80
,, El Fasher (capital of Darfur)	550	Towaisha to Darra	80
		Darra to Kalaka	90
		Kalaka to Shakka	120
,, Lado (by river)	1000	Berber to Merowa	150
,, Albert Nyanza Lake	1300	Khartoum to Debbeh	220
		Zeila to Harrar	200

THE EGYPTIAN TERRITORIES.

ROUTES (*Continued*).

	MILES		MILES
Khartoum to Fashoda (as crow)	490	Murchison's Falls to Anfina's Isle	42
Fashoda to River Sobât	60	Anfina's Isle to Foweira	10
Sobât to Lado	450	Foweira to Mruli	73
Lado to Gondokoro	10	Mruli to Nyamyongo	80
Gondokoro to Regâf	16	Nyamyongo to Urundogani	14
Regâf to Bedden	13	Urundogani to Ripon Falls	40
Bedden to Kerri	28	Dufli to Fatiko	54
Kerri to Dufli	85	Fatiko to Foweira	76
Dufli to Magungo	135	Dufli to Fashelie	9
Magungo to Murchison's Falls	18	Magungo to Keroto	54
		Keroto to Masindi	44

CHAPTER II.

THE MAHDI, OSMAN DIGNA, AND HICKS PASHA.

WHEN in Cairo, in the early part of 1883, I was favoured by Brigadier-General Dormer with a perusal of the following account of the Mahdi, who was then attracting the attention of Europeans in Egypt. It was written by Lieut.-Colonel Stewart, who was in the Soudan in 1882-3, and who has since returned there as aide-de-camp to General Gordon.

"THE MAHDI.

"Mahomet Achmet, the Mahdi, is a Dongolawdi, or native of the province of Dongola. His grandfather was called Fahil, and lived on the island of Naft Arti (Arti—Dongolawi for 'Island') opposite Dongola. His father was Abdullahi, by trade a carpenter. In 1852 this man left and went to Shindi (Shendy), a town on the Nile south of Berber. At that time his family consisted of three sons and one daughter, called respectively Mahomed, Hamid, Mahomet Achmet (the Mahdi), and Nur-el-Sham (Light of Syria). At Shindi another son was born, called Abdullah.

"As a boy, Mahomet Achmet was apprenticed to Sherif-ed-deen, his uncle, a boatman, residing at Shakabeh, an island opposite Sennar. Having one day received a beating from his uncle, he ran away to Khartoum, and joined the free school or 'Medressu' of a faki (learned man, head of a sect of dervishes), who resided at Hoghali, a village east of Khartoum. This school is attached to the tomb of Sheikh Hoghali, the patron saint of Khartoum, and who is greatly revered by the inhabitants of that town and district. (The sheikh of this shrine claims to be a descendant of the original Hoghali, and through him of Mahomet.)

"Here Achmet remained for some time studying religion, the tenets of his sheikh, etc., but did not make much progress in the more worldly accomplishments of reading and writing. After a time he left and went to Berber, where he joined another free school kept by a Sheikh Ghubush, at a village of that name situated nearly opposite to Mekherref (Berber). This school is also attached to a shrine greatly venerated by the natives. Here Mahomet Achmet remained six months completing his religious education. Thence he went to Aradup (Tamarind Tree) village, south of Kana. Here in 1870 he became a disciple of another faki—Sheikh Nur-el-Daim (Continuous Light). Nur-el-Daim subsequently ordained him a sheikh or faki, and he then left to take up his home in the island of Abba, near Kana, on the White Nile. Here he began by making a subterranean excavation (khaliva—retreat) into which he made a practice of retiring to repeat for hours one of the names of the deity, and this accompanied by fasting, incense-burning, and prayers. His fame and sanctity by degrees spread far and wide, and Mahomet Achmet became wealthy, collected disciples, and married several wives, all of whom he was careful to select from among the daughters of the most influential Baggara sheikhs (Baggara—tribes owning cattle and horses) and other notables. To keep within the legalised number (four), he was in the habit of divorcing the surplus and taking them on again, according to his fancy.

"About the end of May, 1881, he began to write to his brother fakis (religious chiefs), and to teach that he was the Mahdi foretold by Mahomet, and that he had a divine mission to reform Islam, to establish a universal equality, a universal law, a universal religion, and a community of goods ('beyt-ul-mal'); also that all who did not believe in him should be destroyed, be they Christian, Mahommedan, or Pagan. Among others, he wrote to Mahomet Saleh, a very learned and influential faki of Dongola, directing him to collect his dervishes (followers) and friends, and to join him at Abba. This sheikh, instead of complying with his request, informed the Government, declaring the man must be mad. This information, along with that collected from other quarters, alarmed His Excellency Réouf Pasha, and the result was the expedition of the 3rd of August, 1881.

"In person, the Mahdi is tall, slim, with a black beard and light brown complexion. Like most Dongolawis, he reads and writes with difficulty. He is local head of the Gheelan or Kadrigé Order of dervishes, a school originated by Abdul Kader-el-Ghulami, whose tomb is, I believe, at Bagdad. Judging from his conduct of affairs and policy, I should say he had considerable natural ability. The manner in which he has managed to merge the usually discordant tribes together denotes great tact. He had probably been preparing the movement for some time back."

Osman Digna, the Mahdi's lieutenant in the Eastern Soudan, is a native of that country, having been born near Tokar. His parents were Hadendowas, but his grandfather, it is said, was a Turk. He claims to be a pure Arab, and by tribal custom is one. Osman is now about forty-eight years of age, tall, gaunt, rather inclined to stoop, and lacking the upright graceful bearing of the Arabs. His features are of the ordinary Hadendowa type, chocolate-coloured skin, full high forehead, shaggy crimpy hair, dark and (in repose) rather melancholy eyes, prominent nose, lips firm and not too large, with a dark brown beard turning slightly grey.

For nearly twenty years he has been known in Suakim as a quiet reticent man, who, having begun in a humble way to deal in fruit, feathers, etc., gradually advanced himself into some dignity as an Arab trader. Like the rest of his countrymen, he was fond of slave-dealing. He was not held in high esteem by the Europeans of Suakim, being looked upon as inclined to sharp traders' practices. The stoppage of the open slave traffic in the Soudan, and the liberation of kidnapped slaves found with Osman's caravans, inflamed him so that in 1878 he assembled a number of sheikhs and slave dealers near Suakim, and tried to incite them to rebel. Failing in rousing the Arabs, he quietly resumed more honest trading. In 1883, whilst buying native articles in the interior, he saw the Mahdi in El Obeid, professed conversion, acknowledging him as the Messiah. Osman was received in due course, and sent forth with his commission to the Eastern Soudan. Letters and commands to the sheikhs and people were given him, that they should obey the Mahdi and his lieutenant Osman. By his reputation for piety, fervour, and eloquence, Osman soon attracted followers. The accession of his old partner, Sheikh Tahir, enabled him to take the field, and threaten the garrisons of Tokar and Sinkat. Sheikh Tahir commanded the Arabs at the battle of El Teb, for Osman himself never engages in the fray, preferring to let the sheikhs lead their men whilst he retires to pray for their success and safety.

Osman selected for his headquarters the well-watered khors and valleys of Tamaai, which is among the foothills twenty miles south-west of Suakim. Here the rebels had their communal camp of dirty tents and gipsy-like huts formed of sticks, reeds, and matting. Grimy and greasy the rebels all were, but happy enough, no doubt, with their share of the common dole from the general store and the twice-repeated daily exhortations of Osman, the Mahdi's inspired disciple, from the Koran. Osman dresses in a sheikh's loose robe, on which is braided in yellow and green, words from the Koran.

In February of 1883, whilst on my way to Egypt,

I was a fellow-passenger with Colonel Hicks, a retired Indian officer, who was then going out to take service under the Khedive for the purpose of fighting the Mahdi. The acquaintanceship I formed at that time with him led me to conclude that no more gallant soldier or energetic officer could have been selected to send against the fanatics led by the False Prophet. He certainly did not underrate his enemy, nor the work before him; and it must have been because of some exceptional wrench of circumstances that any command under his leadership was forced to accept destruction at the hands of an uncivilised foe. I knew several members of Hicks Pasha's Staff, and a more efficient body of officers never accompanied any Egyptian force afield. What the real cause was of the fate that befel Hicks Pasha's army near El Obeid, we shall possibly never know. Perhaps it was due to the one fatal defect that pertains to all Egyptian troops composed of fellaheen—want of courage, or martial ardour. There is no disguising the fact, that as a soldier the Egyptian fellah is worthless. He cowers at alarms, and shrinks from a contest involving physical suffering to himself. For any practical purpose an Egyptian army is useless, and their maintenance is but a waste of money. No amount of personal example and European officering will prevail upon them to offer stubborn and desperate battle even in a situation where their lives are the forfeit.

CHAPTER III.

BAKER PASHA'S DISASTER.

IT was about the end of February, 1884, before I got to Trinkitat. General Baker's (or Baker Pasha's) force had lost their battle with the Arabs on the 5th of that month. The harbour above mentioned is termed on the Admiralty charts "Tring-hatah," and is large enough to accommodate thirty or forty big steamers. It is completely land-locked, and there is good anchorage and deep water close inshore. There being no fresh water near, and the route to the interior difficult, the port is very little used even by the Arabs, and neither house nor hut marks the place. The nearest wells are at El Teb, eight miles inland. It was on Trinkitat's coral sands that General Baker and his force disembarked. What occurred to them has been well told by Mr. John Macdonald, the special correspondent of the London *Daily News*. The following are his telegrams describing that defeat :

"Advance Camp, four miles south of Trinkitat.
"Sunday.

"On the 2nd February three battalions occupied this post, constructing a strong fort with outworks in three hours.

"To-day, February 3, the whole of the army reached the fort, and will advance to-morrow towards the wells at Teb, five miles distant.

"The troops appear in fairly good spirits.

"There is no news of the friendly tribes between this place and Massowah, nor of the fate of Sinkat, except that two days back Mahomed Ali Bey, at the head of only 1,000 of the friendly tribesmen, was still within nine miles of the garrison; but reports brought in by spies here and at Suakim are often sensational and contradictory. Two spies sent out from here four days since have not returned. They have probably been massacred."

The advance camp, or Fort Baker as we came to call it, that Mr. Macdonald speaks of, was a strong earthwork, crowning the crest of the ridge where the seashore flats ended and the mimosa bush-covered plain began. It had a deep trench all around, and a thick parapet, which would have rendered it impregnable, if held by three hundred good troops, against hordes of savages. It was probably not more than two-and-three-quarter miles from Trinkitat, but much of the route was vile, leading through sea-ooze and mud; and like the negro who answered how far it was to Tappahannock, "Dat depends on circumstances, sah," one can easily comprehend why anybody who crossed from Trinkitat to Fort Baker might estimate the distance at from two to ten miles.

"Trinkitat, Feb. 5.

"The battle of Teb has been fought and lost, and 2,000 men of our army have been annihilated.

"At 6.30 yesterday morning we marched with 3,500 men from our advanced fort three miles distant from this place. Our formation was as follows :—Three infantry battalions in échelon, and marching in columns of companies; the artillery and cavalry on the front and flanks, and cavalry vedettes extending all round at points at a mile distance from the main body.

"About nine o'clock shots were heard from the vedettes on our left front, where a number of the enemy were soon visible. The enemy were dispersed by three rounds of Krupps. Bands of rebels then appeared on the ridges in front and towards the right. In the latter direction a small body of the rebel cavalry suddenly came in sight.

"Clearly the enemy's intention was to rush upon us on all sides. Major Giles, commanding the Turkish cavalry, received orders to charge the Arab horse, which he did in capital style, but was nearly caught in a trap; for after a pursuit of upwards half a mile he was confronted by spearmen, who jumped out of the brushwood. Here the enemy had the best of the tactics. Major Giles then retreated towards our front, and a musketry fire from the rebels was opened on all sides, the rear excepted.

"By the time the cavalry returned the battle was raging. We had been taken by surprise, but warnings of the coming catastrophe might have been detected previously. The vedettes on our left had for some time been drawing closer to the main body. They were getting out of order, and it seemed as if the responsible officers had forgotten their very existence.

"Meanwhile also the infantry had been gradually re-forming, for the [purpose of getting into a single large square in front and on the left flank, as also on part of the right; but in the remaining part and along the whole of what was intended to be the rear side of the square the companies were a noisy confused rabble. The sight filled one with dismay.

This was the state of things when the enemy, numbers of whom, in spite of the vigilance of the cavalry vedettes and scouts, had concealed themselves in the brushwood, rushed down with loud yells, delivering their chief attack upon the left side of the square and the left portion of the front line.

"The frantic efforts of the Egyptians to get into proper formation, the confused din of orders, and the chaos in the rear, where 300 camels, with the whole of the transport and commissariat, were struggling to force their way inside the square, defies description. As a matter of fact, what should have been the rear side was an irregular out-bulging mass of horses, mules, camels, and men tightly wedged together, and extending towards the centre of the square. The Soudani Blacks, who composed both the left side of the square and a portion of the front, stood well for a short time, but were soon demoralised by the inrush of fellow-soldiers and the camel men behind.

"The Egyptian cavalry were the first to run. One of their native officers at full gallop struck against my horse. He was thrown, and doubtless butchered, as most were when once dismounted. The Egyptian cavalry, with many riderless horses, rushed past in a stream. They were wild with terror. In their panic the infantry in their so-called square fired anywhere and anyhow. Baker Pasha, outside the square, narrowly escaped being shot by his own men. An Egyptian soldier within three yards of me fell by a shot from his own comrades. Captain Cavalieri was killed in the same way. Finally the scene became one of pure savage massacre. The Egyptian infantry, throwing away their weapons, knelt down, raised their clasped hands, and prayed for mercy. The Arabs seized them by the neck, speared them through the back, and then cut their throats; and this frightful carnage lasted most part of the pursuit, upwards of five miles, to the fort which we left early in the morning. The yells of the Arabs and the cries of their Egyptian victims were appalling.

"In eight minutes from the beginning of the Arab rush the whole force was in hopeless flight. Of the Soudani regiment of 400 from Sanheet, on the Abyssinian frontier, only 70 returned. Of the Turkish battalion only 30 are known to survive. The European company of 36 was all but destroyed.

"Baker Pasha was the last to return to Trinkitat. More than once an Arab spearman was within a foot of him. He, with his Chief of Staff, Colonel Hay, escaped death by charging through a group of them, who intercepted his way to the last remnants of the square. Baker Pasha tried to rally at the base fort already named, and draw a cordon across the path to Trinkitat with the object of stopping the fugitives, but the attempt was fruitless. The Egyptians reaching the beach of Trinkitat made for the boats, which might have been sunk were it not that the English officers fired their revolvers at the crowd following.

"Six Englishmen are missing, among them being Morice Bey, Doctor Leslie, Major Watkins (who had newly arrived from home), and Lieutenant Carrol. The first four were standing inside the left front corner of the square beside the guns, where I left them a few moments before. They were cut off from the main body by the inrush of the Arabs, and were defending themselves with their revolvers and swords. They directed the working of the guns to the last. Their quiet demeanour was as a ray of light and of Divine hope in that hell of fierce triumph and clinging despair. Among other European officers killed were Captain Palioka, of the Albanian Company, Yussuf Bey, Captains Bertan and Morisi, and Abdul Rosack. Baker Pasha's native Chief of Staff was killed near the General.

"By midday the rebels were in possession of the base

fort. All last night they prowled about our camp here, but fortunately for us did not attack. During the night our men and horses were being shipped, but no Egyptian officers assisted. They were in bed or skulking elsewhere. The whole of the work had to be done by Baker Pasha, Colonel Hay, and Mr. Bewley, who is chief of the transport. No more rascally set of cowards ever existed than these native officers. There is more excuse for their men, who, thanks to their agricultural practice and tradition, can dig and delve to perfection, as is shown by their splendid entrenchments, but their employment in battle is sheer crime and idiocy.

"This disaster proves once more the futility of attempting to subjugate a strong, brave race by a weak and timid one. It was a good fortune we were attacked so soon. Had the enemy allowed us to reach Tokar, not one of us would have returned. There is no English officer here who has not escaped, in spite of, as well as because of his coolness and daring, and who has not been in repeated peril between the fire of his own men and the spears of the Arabs."

"Suakim, Feb. 5, Later.

"I have arrived with 500 troops on board. Baker Pasha, with the rest of the force, follows. He fears an Arab rush upon Suakim. Our defeat near the wells of Teb, the scene of Consul Moncrieff's massacre, may possibly incite the Mahdi's followers to attack Upper Egypt. Eastern Soudan is now severed from the Egyptian dominions. The rebels between Trinkitat and Tokar and Sinkat are now well supplied with the spoils of yesterday's fighting, including five guns, with thirty-six thousand pounds of cannon ammunition, besides a large quantity of rifle cartridges. This morning we could clearly see them removing the booty from the front. They must also have picked up 3,000 rifles, which our troops in their flight threw away."

"Suakim, Wednesday Morning.

"Admiral Hewett has just landed 150 Blue-jackets and Marines for the purpose of defending the town, if attacked, and preserving order among the inhabitants.

"Osman Digna is now strengthened in his resolution of destroying Sinkat, and then assaulting Suakim."

The three consecutive successes gained by Osman Digna and his followers over the forces of Consul Moncrieff, Baker Pasha, and Chaggia, secured to the rebels an abundance of stores and munitions of war; and the flush from such a succession of victories may help the reader to understand the character and disposition of the bold and resolute men whom General Graham was sent to overawe.

CHAPTER IV.

STEAMING FOR SUAKIM.

ELEVEN days ago, or to be exact, on Friday, February 15th, I set out, express haste, from London for the Soudan. I have said "Express haste," for though, nowadays, "post-haste" means more in England than it ever did, yet even there one can sometimes continue to outstrip Her Majesty's mails. Out of England it is an easier matter still. Strangely enough, the further home was left behind the worse the weather became. In France it rained, and in Switzerland the snow fell so thickly that the first real anxiety was occasioned—that was lest the railway should be blocked, and the mail steamer should leave before our arrival. It was quite an English train that ran through from Calais to Brindisi that day, for between forty and fifty of the passengers were British officers bound for Egypt. They were chiefly under orders to proceed to Cairo. Four of them— Lieutenant-Colonel Colville, Grenadier Guards, Mr. St. Leger Herbert, Major E. A. Groves, West Kent Regiment, and Lieutenant Probyn, Bengal Cavalry—were,

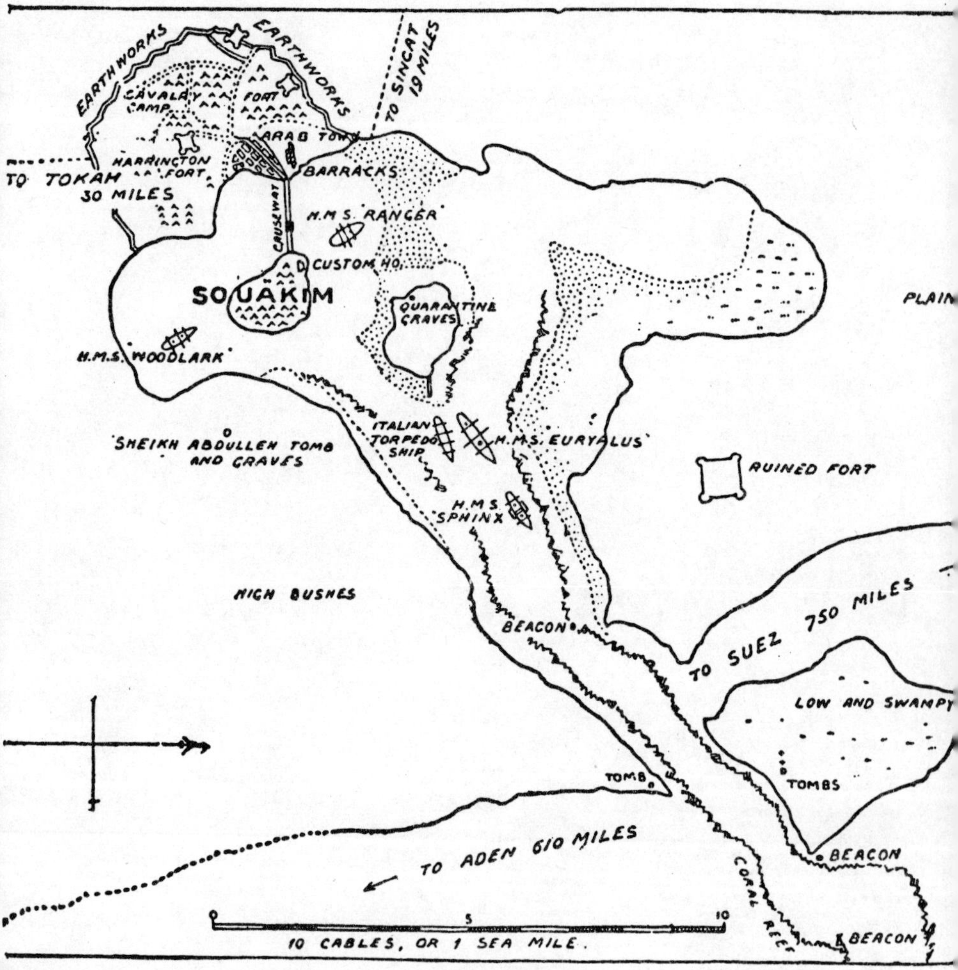
EARTHWORKS
EARTHWORKS
CAVALRY CAMP
FORT
TO SINCAT 19 MILES
ARAB TOWN
HARRINGTON FORT
TO TOKAH 30 MILES
BARRACKS
CAUSEWAY
H.M.S. RANGER
CUSTOM HO.
SOUAKIM
QUARANTINE GRAVES
PLAIN
H.M.S. WOOLARK
ITALIAN TORPEDO SHIP
H.M.S. EURYALUS
SHEIKH ABDULLEH TOMB AND GRAVES
RUINED FORT
H.M.S. SPHINX
HIGH BUSHES
BEACON
TO SUEZ 750 MILES
LOW AND SWAMPY
TOMB
TOMBS
TO ADEN 610 MILES
BEACON
CORAL REEF
BEACON
0
5
10
10 CABLES, OR 1 SEA MILE.

THE DEFENCES OF THE PORT OF SUAKIM.

The above plan or chart of the Port of Suakim is from a sketch by the special artist of the *Illustrated London News*. It is from a drawing of official authority, and shows the facilities for defence by the naval and military forces. This plan is in such a position that the upper side represents the west quarter towards the mainland in the direction of Sinkat, while Tokar or Tokah, which lies beyond the limit of the sketch, would be approached by a route to the south, marked on the left; and the Red Sea, with the maritime routes northward to Suez and southward to Aden, is shown at the bottom. The harbour of Suakim is entered from the sea by a long and narrow inlet or strait, which is shut in by the land on both sides, and at the mouth of which is a long and swampy island. The depth of the channel allows steamers of heavy tonnage to anchor within less than one hundred yards of the beach. It will be seen that the principal portion of the town is situated on an island connected with the mainland by a narrow causeway. On the island are the Custom House, Government offices, and stores for merchandise. On the mainland is the bazaar with the Arab town, consisting of rude huts, in many cases mere sunshades of tree branches and matting, the more permanent buildings being square, flat-topped mud structures. The camp outside the Arab town, covering the roads from Sinkat and Tokar, is enclosed by a semi-circular line of earthworks which have a length of nearly two miles. Inside the camp are several forts—one named after Colonel Harrington, who was in command of the garrison in General Baker's absence on his ill-fated expedition to relieve Tokar. The batteries were then mounted with twelve guns, but this armament was very considerably increased by Admiral Hewett, and both forts were held by British troops, who had ample stores of food and ammunition. They cannot possibly be captured by the enemy. When the sketch was made, Her Majesty's ships *Ranger* and *Woodlark* had taken up positions which enabled them to sweep the causeway. It may be assumed with confidence that Admiral Hewett has a sufficient force at his disposal to hold Suakim against any assault which the rebels may make.

[N.B.—The land on the north of Suakim, where our words "Quarantine graves" appear, is really part of the mainland, the dotted space being firm ground. There was plenty of room for vessels to swing inside the harbour, the size of vessels shown being relatively out of proportion with width of channel. The British tents and camp were on the south side of Suakim, latterly near where words "High bushes" are.]

like myself, going to the Soudan. We were following in the wake of, and striving to overtake, Sir Redvers Buller, V.C., Colonel Herbert Stewart, and Colonel Tuson, R.M., who had left London on the previous Tuesday evening, to assist General Graham. They had not only a good start, but the Admiralty had arranged for their rapid transport to Egypt by the despatch steamer *Helicon*. Through Italy we sped, a biting cold rain rattling down the while. We reached Brindisi on Sunday night. The steamer, the *Tanjore*, of the Peninsular and Oriental line, did not start till 5.0 a.m. Monday, two hours behind her usual time. The mails were bulkier than usual, hence the delay. I availed myself of the interval to wire to Port Said for a steam launch to meet the steamer on her arrival there to take us through the Suez Canal. I hoped by so doing to gain twenty-four hours on Buller's party, as small launches go full speed in the Canal. Time was to me more than money. Had it been as coin, I might have negotiated a loan of one week. Head-winds, gales, and rain-squalls tossed us about all the voyage. It was half-past five on Thursday evening, the 21st inst., before we got into Port Said harbour. The little steam launch came alongside before the *Tanjore* had lost way, and with bag and baggage I bundled aboard her, accompanied by the gentlemen I have already named, as they were equally anxious to push onward. Wistfully the brave fellows on the *Tanjore* saw us steam away, and gladly would most of the seniors as well as the subalterns, under orders to report to General Stephenson or General Wood at Cairo, have changed places with us. Envious as they felt, they showed their goodwill by cheering our "Good-bye!" shouts. The weather was still cold, with a head-wind and rain showers. It was near midnight when we entered Lake Timsah. There we got such a facer of a squall that the Maltese crew made the launch fast to one of the beacon-boats. We, the poor passengers, sought shelter in the little fore-cabin, lying down upon our angular portmanteaus and valises. Most of us still carry about the impressions made upon us that night. At this moment I feel what it is to have lain too long upon the penetrating edge of a Gladstone bag. After an hour or so of waiting, Major Groves and I forced the three Maltese and an Arab boy, who composed the launch's crew, to start ahead. It was pitch dark, but we were anxious to "move on." We "pottered" about for another hour, going aground twice, and getting off with difficulty, till at length we found the Canal entrance on the opposite side of the lake. Day was breaking when we got to the large Bitter Lake, where quite a sea was running. We dashed across, shipping water at every wave, and entered upon the last cutting or reach. As our craft was using fresh water in her boiler we were compelled to stop for a few minutes at four of the Canal Company's stations on the journey to fill the tanks. This was done by attaching a canvas hose to the end of the 6-in. service pipe (supplied from the Sweet Water Canal) which is carried out to every wharf. Then a valve was turned, and we soon had all we needed of yellow Nile water. As the day advanced we feared that the Egyptian mail steamer which was to leave Suez that morning (Friday) at ten o'clock for Suakim, would sail before we got there. We, therefore, telegraphed first from one and then from another of the way stations of the Canal Company, to the captain to wait our arrival— the arrival, as we put it, of several cabin passengers. It seemed an age before we got to Suez, a strong current, as well as a head-wind, setting against us. On reaching that place we made a tour of the ships in the offing, to ascertain if any were leaving for Suakim. Next we made for the docks and boarded the Egyptian mail steamer. She had just got in that morning from Suakim, whence she had brought about 200 Arabs and Soudanese, misnamed soldiers. They were the remnants of Baker Pasha's force, and many of them were supposed to be wounded. Neither physically nor mentally, so far as I could see, were any of them much hurt. They looked shabby and frowsy, and their weapons were rusty, but in these respects they were no worse than the average Egyptian soldier. They chattered like magpies, or Arabs, and gambolled like kittens the moment they found themselves safe ashore in their own beloved Delta once more. How glad our fellows must have been to have seen their backs for the last time at Suakim! There were a few utterly wretched-looking women and children brought back with them. The whole party were that evening packed off with their rag-pickers' belongings to Cairo.

We soon learned the mail steamer would not be ready to return to Suakim for two or three days. There was a pleasant offset to this news, however. The *Helicon*, like the *Tanjore*, had been delayed by storms in crossing from Brindisi, and Sir Redvers Buller and his party had only sailed for Suakim the previous evening (Thursday) on board the Egyptian steamer *Damanhour*. Now as the *Damanhour*, like everything Egyptian, was a slow goer, hope whispered we would yet be in time to see the relief of Tokar. Those professing to be in the secret of Horse Guards and War Office mysteries said General Graham would never attack the rebels till Buller arrived. A few minutes later, without waiting an invitation, with all our baggage, we boarded the hired transport steamship *Northumbria*, of Hull. She was to sail for Suakim that evening at six o'clock. The captain looked aghast, and wondered where we were to sleep, as there was no cabin accommodation, except for himself and the two or three officers. When we ventured to say the deck would do, he relaxed, and, sailor-like, welcomed us. One of the naval transport officers shook a little red tape before us; but as he saw it had not the slightest effect he walked off, and left us in possession of the deck. There were three large gangs of Arab stevedores at work completing the loading of the *Northumbria*. The vessel's hold was packed with mules, and her decks were piled high with sutlers' and army stores. Mingled among the boxes and barrels were waggons, ambulances, machinery for condensers, and other things. Amid all this there rose a babel of sound—the rattle and whirr of the steam winches, the shouting of men, and the snorting of horses and mules as these were slung aboard being lifted the while high in mid-air. As a weird accompaniment to all the noise and confusion, there ran through it the sing-song of the Arab stevedores hurrying about in groups of four to six, and bearing on their shoulders huge boxes and bales. At last we got off, leaving at the dock the steamer *Abydos*, the last of the hired transports ordered on the expedition. She was to follow on the morrow, or whenever her loading was finished. As her complement included 95 obstreperous camels, the hour of sailing was, with commendable wisdom, not fixed.

On Saturday morning the steamship *Northumbria* had run down nearly to the mouth of the Gulf of Suez. On our left hand stretched the peninsula of Sinai. The hoar and sacred mountain tops were capped with snow, and the clefts and crevices far down the slopes were full of it; an unusual phenomenon here, proving how far south the cold wave has swept. Perhaps as remarkable a feature as any about the recent inclement weather in this region is that the winds chiefly set from the south-east. The next and following days we coasted down by the Red Sea littoral, getting occasional glimpses of the mountain ranges. Our sailing orders were to make for Hind Kadam, an island thirty-five miles east of Suakim. If we did not receive further directions there, we were to go on to Suakim. Hind Kadam was sighted before daybreak, and the only craft in sight being a few native boats and two transports which had got ashore on the outer reefs, the captain of the *Northumbria* steamed direct for that port.

CHAPTER V.

AT TRINKITAT.

WE were inside the outer reef at Suakim, and had not actually entered the harbour, when there came bearing down on the steamship *Northumbria*, one of those smart little steam launches that it needed no flag to tell belonged to a British man-of-war. In a quarter of an hour she was alongside, and a naval lieutenant stepping aboard our vessel told us all the latest news, for which some of us were feverishly anxious. Possibly it is because a sailor nearly always likes to spin a yarn, that he did not show the faintest sign of being bored or put out by our hundred and one questions. Hurrah! we felt inclined to cheer, the daily-expected battle between General Graham and the rebels had not yet taken place, and we were ahead of Generals Buller and Stewart, for no sign of the Egyptian steamer *Damanhour* had been seen at Suakim. Without anchoring, the *Northumbria*, by Admiral Hewett's orders, started on full steam for Trinkitat, being piloted by the naval lieutenant, who took the steamer by the short cut inside the outer reefs.

After five hours' steaming we entered the harbour of Trinkitat, coming to an anchor close to the shore about 2 p.m., Tuesday, February 26th. A town of white tents of all shapes and sizes lined the strand for about a mile. Soldiers and sailors were going about in hundreds; all was life and bustle. It was plain the little army was still quartered there, snugly enclosed and secured with the clear blue water of the harbour and the gunboats on one side, and on the other a long earthwork, four to five feet high, protected by a trench of moderate depth and width, which at either end ran down to the beach. The many steamers in the harbour were mostly hard at work unloading stores, which were being sent ashore in lighters, pontoon boats, horse boats, launches, and all sorts of nondescript craft. Jack was clearly in his element. Here were ship and shore duties to be done, and everything in a great hurry. Captain Andoe, R.N., of the *Orontes*, as senior transport officer, directed and hastened the disembarking of men, animals, and stores. Pulling and hauling from earliest morn till long after nightfall, slaving at all sorts of jobs, as if each man were making a rapid fortune, the untiring Blue-jackets bundled everything upon the beach in quick methodical fashion. A number of little jetties had been built of timbers and sand-bags, and alongside of these the disembarkation boats were run. Now came the turn of the soldiers, told off on "fatigue duty," to assist in unloading. With his coat off and sleeves rolled up, Tommy Atkins was rivalling Jack's industrious energy. They laboured as if their very lives depended upon their exertions, and not as if to them the result was a shilling or so a day, with possibly death and a nameless grave in a strange land thrown into the scale. The latter fate befel a good many before we left the Soudan.

Yet with some people an old soldier is a nobody, and patriotism and honour are meaningless phrases when applied to anyone below the rank of lieutenant. How the brave fellows toiled, carrying innumerable boxes, bags, and bales to pile upon the beach, or at the places assigned for the Ordnance and Commissariat stores. Glad enough they looked when the noon-meal hour, or better still, when eventide fell, to cool themselves and disport with their comrades at bathing parade in the rippling blue water of Trinkitat. For half-an-hour each evening the army revelled in its sea-bath, the men dressing and undressing on the sand close to the water's edge. What pranks they played, what shouts and laughter bespoke their enjoyment!

To the east of our steamer, the *Northumbria*, lay a little Egyptian tug paddle steamer called the *Tor*, which was employed to condense salt water into fresh, for the use of the army. A three-inch service pipe ran from the *Tor* to the shore, and the fresh water was delivered therefrom in a steady stream into reservoirs of iron tanks and barrels. The other steamers in the harbour were also required to condense water daily for the troops. According to Acting Surgeon-General McDowell and the other medical officers, the low percentage of sickness during the campaign was solely on account of the men having condensed, and therefore pure, water to drink. The one thing that above all else incessantly troubled the troops was the water question. Had we been all ardent—if one may say that of us—teetotallers, we could not have taken more interest in the subject, or better testified to our faith in water, tepid as it often was, by deeds, when opportunity presented itself. The "charges" that were wont to be made at distribution time on the march or in bivouac on the water-barrels was a sight worth seeing. How the dry air and dust parch tongue and throat, only those who have been in the Soudan can form an idea. We drank water whenever it was procurable, and at Tamaai and Tamanieb, where there were tiny rivulets, we literally soaked ourselves in the delicious beverage.

To return to the s.s. *Northumbria*, from the deck of which I had been observing much that was taking place in the harbour and ashore. My first object was to get landed somehow, and quickly. Before the good ship was moored I was off in a small boat with Lieutenant Probyn, who was burning with anxiety for an opportunity to go forward with the expedition. I had telegraphed from London to a friend to secure me two horses. This he had wired me had been done, and I now wished to inspect them, take them over, and put my servant in charge. By one of those odd coincidences, whilst at Suez I met on the gangway of the *Northumbria* my old servant whom I had in the first Egyptian campaign, a Greek named Mekali. He was going to Suakim as an interpreter or mule cicerone, but as ours was a mutually pleasant recognition he threw up his post and instantly re-entered my service, journeying with me to Trinkitat. I found the Arab horses were all right, and placed them under Mekali's care. My next business was to see the camp, and report myself to the General Commanding and his Staff. General Graham's tent was easily distinguishable at the west end of the camp by a red flag which flaunted from a pole placed on a sand-mound close by it. I was told all correspondents were required to carry a pass which could be got from the Commandant of Police and Provost-Marshal Captain G. W. Freeman. This I soon secured—(may all police officers be as courteous and obliging as Captain Freeman that I may have to deal with!)—after explaining my mission, and on the payment of one shilling. For that sum, as had been ordered by Chief of Staff, Colonel Clery, he granted me my passport or license to accompany the expedition. The pass, which was printed on a yellowish card and more like a pedlar's license than aught else, after describing my personality, read as follows:

"INSTRUCTIONS.

"This pass must be always produced when required by any one acting under the orders of the Provost-Marshal, or any officer attached to the troops near whom the bearer is. The pass will be withdrawn for misconduct. If lost, the loss to be at once reported to the Provost-Marshal. The bearer is specially cautioned against buying or receiving any clothing, equipment, or stores from soldiers."

I never could quite understand why passes were deemed necessary, for there were less than half-a-dozen correspondents who sought to accompany the army. Besides all of us were more or less well known to many of the officers, and there was little likelihood that we would stray far out of the fold of the British square or camp. None of us in the least resembled the swarthy Hadendowas, but it was whispered foreign spies were about, and might, unless a vigorous passport system were instituted, "carry aid and comfort to the enemy." Perhaps so, but how and in what shape? No matter, I never was called upon, from first to last, to show my shilling cardboard.

That night I slept on board the ship again, preferring the deck and a fresh tub in the morning to the soft sands of Trinkitat sea-shore. The long earthwork surrounding the camp, which was previously mentioned, had been thrown up with commendable promptitude by Baker Pasha's Egyptians. It not only protected the camp, but kept the horses, mules, and camels from straying off towards Fort Baker and El Teb. General Graham had disembarked a few days earlier in order to make his final arrangements for the advance. With him was Baker Pasha, who had been appointed to the Intelligence Department, and whose skill was to be called upon to guide the force by the best route to the wells at El Teb, where, as everybody knew, the enemy had determined to fight before we could taste of the water there. Brief telegrams had announced all these facts, so there is no need to repeat them at more length. Nominally we were going forward to relieve Tokar, but we all knew well enough that place had capitulated to the enemy, and it was more to administer a drubbing and lesson to the Arabs than aught else that inspired our march.

The following telegram briefly described the situation on my arrival :

"Trinkitat, Feb. 26 (9.35 P.M.)

"The troops now on shore are the 89th (350 strong), 75th (700), 42nd (700), 60th Rifles (500), Marines (250), sailors (135), with six machine guns; cavalry, 19th (315), 10th (250); Mounted Infantry, (120); Engineer company (150); expected from Aden, the 65th (500); total strength, 3,970.

"Deducting the necessary force for garrisoning Trinkitat, and for commissariat, transport, and baggage guards, this leaves a fighting force of 3,500 in the front line.

"This morning the 42nd and 89th, with a camel battery and two squadrons of the 19th Hussars, executed a reconnaissance here and occupied Baker's advanced fort. The cavalry advanced until they saw the enemy, to the number of about 1,000, and then retired, according to orders.

"The spies all report that large forces are gathered at Teb, where they fought before. They probably amount to 6,000 men, and certainly intend to fight.

Osman Digna is at Tamanieb, near Suakim. In order to make the business complete we must turn him out after fighting a battle between Trinkitat and Tokar.

General Graham and Colonel Clery, Chief of the Staff, are doing everything in first-rate style, the staff and navy affording all possible help. Everybody is enthusiastic, and no doubt is entertained of success.

CHAPTER VI.

THE ADVANCE TO FORT BAKER.

On Wednesday morning, the 27th February, I went ashore at an early hour, mounted one of my horses, and set out alone to have a look at the outposts at Fort Baker. It is always of great use in many ways to know the ground well beforehand on which any operations are likely to occur. The route to Fort Baker was conspicuously marked by the *flotsam* and *jetsam* from the tides of transport animals and men that had so often traversed it. Here and there were bales of hay, sacks of corn, ammunition boxes, water tins and barrels, and discarded saddles and trappings from camels, mules, and horses, not to mention the inevitable empty glass bottles, corned beef and sardine tins, that invariably mark the way traversed by any civilised force. In due course Fort Baker was reached, without either having to dismount from getting bogged in the mud, or floundering in some of the deep water-holes. The officers at that post, some of whom were old acquaintances I had met in the campaign against Arabi Pasha, gave me a cup of *tea* as a refresher, whilst they assisted my inquiries by pointing out the direction of El Teb and the ground occupied by the enemy's scouts. I observed that Fort Baker was well provisioned, and had a large store of barrels of condensed water, whilst the approaches to the work were defended by a wire entanglement. Riding forward about half a mile to where our Mounted Infantry vedettes kept watch, I had a chat with the men, saw for the first time our Arab foemen, stealthily moving about among the bushes eight hundred yards away; heard the ping of their rifles, as they took a crack at some of the members of our little party; and handled one of their Remington bullets, which struck within ten yards of the vedettes. Half-a-crown a word for telegraphing chokes off gush, bars detailed description in small matters, and it is only when big events happen that one feels justified in telling the whole story without curtailment or abridgment.

In this way I summed up my first day's trip to the front :

Trinkitat, Feb. 27 (2.20 p.m.)

General Graham expects to advance on Thursday or Friday.

The camp is well protected by earthworks. The sailors are getting stores ashore rapidly. Major-General Buller has arrived. Admiral Hewett had sent in search of the steamer, fearing it had shoaled.

Spies report that Osman Digna is threatening Suakim. Admiral Hewett returned thither yesterday.

Trinkitat, Feb. 27 (6 p.m.)

Major-General Sir Redvers Buller and party have arrived.

Large numbers of the enemy have been observed a mile from Fort Baker.

They fire at our vedettes, but do no damage.

A Krupp gun has just been mounted at Fort Baker.

The Krupp gun was one of the sort we had all become familiar with in the first Egyptian campaign. A heliograph and a look-out station had also been established at Fort Baker, and two machine guns occupied angles of the work, and would have made it hot for any force to have attempted to enter the place in other than a friendly spirit.

Colonel Redvers Buller, V.C., and Colonel Herbert Stewart, acting as General of Cavalry, disembarked at Trinkitat, on the morning of the 27th February. Horses were led down to one of the jetties for them, and, mounting these, off they went on a tour of inspection of their commands. Their voyage in the *Helicon*, Admiralty despatch steamer, which was to go fourteen knots an hour, had been a series of disappointments and delays. The storm in the Mediterranean, which had little affected the P. & O. steamer *Tanjore*, had compelled the *Helicon* to run for shelter, first to Corfu, then Navarino Bay, next hugging Crete, and again anchoring in Marsara Bay all day long. Their coal supply had nearly given out, so the captain abandoned the idea of steaming to Port Said, re-coaling and running through the Suez Canal, and down to Suakim; making instead direct for Alexandria. Glad enough all his military passengers were to be landed there safely on Thursday morning, after the week's cruise among the Grecian isles. A special train was prepared for them, and they were run through to Suez the same evening, and had, for us, the good luck to be sent by the Egyptian steamer *Damanhour*. Her captain, like all his countrymen, was anything but rash. So he invariably slowed down or anchored at night to avoid running on the coral reefs. Hence their delay in getting to Trinkitat.

On my return to Trinkitat on the afternoon of the 27th February, I elicited the unwelcome information that there was usually but one steamer a day sent to Suakim with letters and telegrams. This was ordinarily Admiral Hewett's despatch boat, the *Sphinx*, and her time of setting out was from noon till 2 p.m. No vessels going to Suakim sailed after the latter hour, because, to enter that harbour, it was necessary to get through the reefs before sundown. As the nearest telegraph station was at Suakim, and all our messages had to go there before being sent on to London, the situation vexed me considerably. A new element was imported into my work, and that was to make arrangements for the prompt transmission of telegrams to Suakim and getting them taken instantly to the telegraph office on their arrival there. What was done would hardly interest the unprofessional reader, except to know that I made the best alternative arrangements I could think of. My next telegram was as follows:

Trinkitat, Feb. 28 (2.5 p.m.)

Three new jetties have been built by the Engineers to facilitate the landing of stores.

Yesterday and to-day a stream of mules and camels flowed, without intermission, from Trinkitat to Fort Baker, carrying water and ammunition. The animals floundered through the muddy marsh separating us from the high ground of the fort. The interval of morass resembles Essex Flats.

Here the soldiers, divested of their shoes and stockings, helped the tired animals along.

Last night's orders direct the expedition to start for Fort Baker this afternoon and bivouac there, advancing upon El Teb on Friday.

Our strength is under 4,000. The unmounted troopers, the sick, a company of the King's, and the Rifles guard Trinkitat. The men carry 100 rounds each.

The road from Trinkitat to Fort Baker was a difficult one at the best of times, but what little bottom there was in it had long been trodden out by the countless hoofs of horses, mules, and camels going over it. Oddly enough, the small-hoofed mules and the big-footed camels had more difficulty in making their way across than the horses. Over and again have I seen baggage-mules stuck fast, their legs embedded far past the girths. The soldiers unloaded the packs when they were in this plight and, pulling and pushing at the for once docile and terrified brutes, rolled them upon the firmer ground, where they got upon their legs, thickly swathed with clayey mud and looking utterly dejected. The camels groaned at every step they drew along—I think they tried to weep, but a camel's tears are of the crocodile order. When the ground got too soft and sticky, they used to sink steadily down, making hideous noises before finally settling on their stomachs. Their Egyptian drivers then unloaded them, carried the burdens across to dry solid ground, and then stirred the brutes out of their muddy beds. Why a double row of inch boards was not put flatly down on the mud to bear the animals over the bad three quarters of a mile of the route, one cannot imagine. I have seen that done in Canada and the States, and had boards been laid much time would have been saved in going to or coming from Fort Baker by the transport. A feeble attempt was made at improving the worst places by putting bushes down and making a raised way, but that soon got trodden into a series of pitfalls. It was not so difficult for one on foot to cross, although the state of things depended very much on the direction of the wind. If it blew the sea-water over the ground then the march was most trying. Our men, with praiseworthy thoughtfulness, often found it advisable to strip off not only shoes and stockings, but trousers or kilts, to save these from getting covered with mud. I confess it made rather a droll picture to see the British soldier with all his warlike trapping about him, trouserless and kiltless, with these respectable belongings dangling round his neck, and very much bare-limbed, wading through the slough.

CHAPTER VII.

THE BATTLE OF EL TEB.

ON Thursday afternoon, accompanied by my Greek servant, Antone Mekali, we rode out with the troops to Fort Baker, marching in the lightest order—namely, a blanket, some biscuits, and a tin of meat, with a little *something* in my canteen or water-bottle. The troops were halted on the plain, close beside the north face of the fort, and the men were formed into a large square. The cavalry were halted, and picketed two or three hundred yards in rear of the infantry. One of a pile of bales of *tibbin*, or chopped straw, made an excellent bed for the night. Before lying down, however, I wandered about the ground, chatted with the officers about the morrow's work, saw to my horses, and, finally, about 11 p.m., pulled my blanket over me for the night, lying down booted and spurred. We knew the morrow would bring a battle, for no one had any faith that General Graham's warning, sent to the rebels by flag of truce, to disperse or take the consequences, would have the slightest effect upon them.

The formation of the square at El Teb is shown in the accompanying plan.

```
                    Gordon Highlanders (75th) in line.
┌─────────────────────────────────────────────────────────────┐
│  ↓ ↓ ↓                                         ↓ ↓ ↓        │
│  Naval Brigade.                                Naval Brigade.│
│  Two Gatlings.                                 Two Gardners. │
│  One Gardner.        Royal Engineers.          One Gatling.  │
│                                                              │
│                    Army Medical Department.                  │
│                                                              │
│                      Centre of Square                        │
│                   occupied by Camels,                        │
│                   Mules,   etc.,  with                       │
│         ||||      Water, Ammunition,       ||||              │
│         ||||      and Baggage.             ||||              │
│         Royal Marines                      King's Royal Rifles (60th)
│         in quarter column.                 in quarter column.│
│                                                              │
│                                                              │
│   Four Guns                                Royal Artillery   │
│   Camel Battery.                           Camel Battery.    │
│   T T T T                                  T T T T           │
└─────────────────────────────────────────────────────────────┘
                    Black Watch (42nd) in line.
```

(Left side: Royal Marines in line. York and Lancaster (65th) in line.)
(Right side: Royal Irish (89th) in line. 60th in line.)

The 65th and 89th, being short of their complement of men, the respective sides of the square were partly filled in with Royal Marines and 60th Rifles. The strength of the battalions were about as follows: 75th, 700 men; 42nd, 750 men; 65th, 470 men; Marines, 310 men; 89th, 400 men; 60th, 320 men; sailors, 150 men.

The account wired of the bivouâc and battle was substantially as follows:

THE BATTLE OF EL TEB.

Trinkitat, Feb. 29 (8 p.m.).

On Thursday night (28th February), the expedition encamped near Fort Baker. The infantry bivouac was on the right front and the cavalry one in the rear. The men were all on the ground before sundown, except the 65th, who did not arrive till eight o'clock. They had been intercepted on their way home from India, only arriving in Trinkitat in the afternoon. When they landed, ammunition and water-bottles were served to the men, and they trudged out to join us after nightfall. Their arrival was cheered by the rest of the troops. By that time all were quietly settled; fires had been kindled and coffee made.

Fort Baker was crammed with water and stores, and throughout the night transport camels and mules kept coming in.

The bivouac was unpleasant. The new moon was dim and feeble, and the sky was overcast. It showered at intervals, and towards morning we had a tropical drenching.

Reveille was sounded about five, and instantly all were on the alert. Fires were re-lit and breakfast got ready, and despite the wetting everybody seemed in capital spirits.

By eight o'clock the order was given to move forward, the men having fallen in some time previously.

The force was formed in an oblong, the front and rear being longer than the sides, owing to the strength of the regiments. The Gordon Highlanders in line formed the advance, with two Gatlings and a Gardner in the right corner, and two Gardners and a Gatling in the left corner. On the right side was the 89th in line, in the rear the Black Watch, with four camel-battery guns in each corner, manned by Royal Artillery. On the left side of the square was the 65th, and a company of the Royal Marines. Inside the square were General Graham's and Buller's Staffs and the officers of the Royal Engineers, with the company in line, and the Medical Department. The Marines were in quarter column on the left inside, and the 60th on the right inside of the square.

Our total strength was below 4,000, including 150 sailors under Captain Rolfe, of the *Euryalus*. We moved forward about half a mile, and then halted to get the men finally in thorough order; our front was about 350 yards long.

A squadron of the 10th Hussars, under Major Gough, went forward as scouts, and they covered our front and flanks, advancing in a semicircle 1,000 yards ahead.

When a mile beyond Fort Baker, on the road to Teb, the troops keeping well to the north, crossing low sand-knolls thick with scrub, the enemy opened fire with Remingtons. The range was too far, and no damage was done.

We could see a few hundreds swarming about the high ground on our front and flanks. They retired very slowly before us, keeping within 1,200 yards.

The main body of our cavalry kept following in the left rear 900 yards off. Colonel Herbert Stewart had formed them in three lines: Colonel Wood, with the

10th Hussars, leading, then Lieut.-Colonel Barrow with the 19th Hussars, and Colonel Webster. The 19th Hussars had English horses; all the others had Egyptian mounts.

About 9.30 Her Majesty's ship *Sphinx* fired four rounds from Trinkitat, but the range was too great, her shells bursting fully a mile short of the enemy's position, and she was signalled to cease firing, as the shells were getting dangerously near the cavalry.

The mounted infantry were now sent forward on the left under Captain Humphreys, to touch the enemy, who appeared obstinate about moving, although not disinclined to fight. The infantry force tramped steadily onward, halting but two or three times to rest, the Bluejackets and Artillery drawing the guns. The square was well kept all along. Where the ground was a little more difficult than common the men marched by fours right in column of companies. That was seldom, as, thanks to General Baker and Colonel Burnaby, of the Intelligence Department, who were in the square with General Graham, the route was so selected as to avoid, as far as possible, the broken and shrub-covered ground.

The way the infantry went lay along the lower and more barren sandy soil. At this time I was with the scouts, and passed directly along the track taken by the unfortunate fugitives from the disaster which befell Baker Pasha's forces.

The bodies studded the route to Teb, lying about in hundreds, polluting the air. Swarms of lazy carrion birds flew off on our approach.

By 10.30 we had marched three miles from Fort Baker, and here we could plainly see that the enemy had built some sort of earthworks, in which they had mounted guns and set up standards. Their fire had almost ceased, only a few shots were popping off on our extreme right and left, and these were aimed at the scouts.

It was a fine sight to see our fellows step out as if on holiday parade. It gave a grand idea of the power and pride of physical strength. The bagpipes played gaily, and the Highlanders, instinctively cocking their caps and swinging their shoulders, footed the way cheerily.

In this manner we marched to within 800 yards of the enemy's first position. An old sugar mill had once stood in the vicinity; a sun-dried brick building and a large-flued boiler marked the place. There were also a number of native huts. We could see what appeared to be a fort, with two guns. Here a halt was called.

Meanwhile the mounted infantry and the scouts had gone back to where the cavalry were, 900 yards off. The scouts, however, had done their work, and had run the enemy to earth. Many of the infantry sat down quite indifferent about the rebels' presence, but others showed more interest, watching the black faces that gleamed at us from behind every knoll of sand or vantage-point. Neither force seemed disposed to open fire. It was "Sir Richard Strachan and the Earl of Chatham" over again. (Sir Richard with his sword drawn, stood waiting for the Earl of Chatham. The Earl, longing to be at 'em, stood waiting for Sir Richard Strachan).

"Attention" was called, and as soon as the enemy saw us moving they opened the battle by sending a shell at us from one of the Krupps which they took from the Egyptians. It went wide over the square; but the next and the next were well aimed, bursting close to our men, and wounding several. For savages the fire was astonishingly accurate.

The ball having been set rolling, the rebels kept up a rattling fusillade from small arms, as well as by keeping the Krupps going. Bad as was the firing of the Remingtons, the Soudanese sent bullets by the hundred whistling about our ears.

A man of the Gordon Highlanders (75th) was the first to fall, dropping on my right badly wounded. The hits now became more numerous, and the Ambulance Corps and the doctors soon had their hands full.

Still steadily onward in square went our men, without replying to the enemy's fire. The object was to pass the north face of their works, and this was done.

Baker Pasha at this moment was hit by a piece of shell in the face, which made an ugly wound. Surgeon-General M'Dowell, who was in charge, not only attended him, but saw to all the other wounded whilst we pushed along.

About twenty men in all were hit; they belonged to different commands, and were borne along by the stretcher-carriers.

After going about 1,000 yards a halt was ordered, and the men were directed to lie down. It was now about noon. The day was clear, and a light wind carried the smoke of the firing quickly away, so that the enemy's movements were not hidden.

The guns were run out, and with these and the Martinis we now replied. The effect was speedily manifest, for the enemy's fire slackened and nearly ceased. The bugles sounded the "advance," and the troops rose, and wheeling slightly round on the centre of the square, advanced towards the enemy's works.

The Soudanese clung to their position with desperation. They were in no military order, but scattered about, taking advantage of the abundant cover which the ground afforded. There could not have been more than 2,000 on the front at the moment. We could, however, see hundreds of others hanging around two sides of the square.

As we moved, firing the while, numbers of the rebels—most of them armed with spears and others with huge cross-hilted swords—rose up boldly within 200 yards, and rushed for us at breakneck speed.

It was marvellous to see how they came on, heedless and fearless of death, shouting and brandishing their weapons. To the right and left they fell; but those who survived, even when wounded, rushed on. A few got within five or ten paces of the square, proving how many bullets it takes to kill a man. There was no running away yet on the enemy's part, only a sullen falling back.

At length our troops cleared the front with the Martinis, and then, with a cheer, rushed towards the fort.

It was a crescent-shaped open earthwork which we approached from the right corner. The 65th were the nearest to it, and their rapid advance was met by a rush of several hundreds of the enemy, before which the troops recoiled 30 or 40 yards, the distance they had outrun their comrades, thereby leaving a corner of the square open. On their falling back the Marines advanced to their support, the square was quickly closed, and in a minute all was well again, the troops being as steady as possible. The check was but momentary, and again they advanced, firing with great precision. Some of the 65th passed along the face of the work. An Arab running out, spear in hand, rushed for one of the soldiers. The man fired, and at eight yards' distance missed the savage; then the soldier appeared to be swayed by two instantaneous impulses —one to charge and give his foe the bayonet, the other to fall back to the line out of which he and other equally rash comrades had run to engage the Arabs. It ended by his furtively looking over his shoulder, a caving in of his chest, swaying to the rear for a step or two, and the Arab, who had not halted, bounded upon him, burying his lance deep in the wretched man's throat. Before the soldier had time to fall he was lanced again and again; but the savage was the same moment himself shot and bayoneted by two of the 65th—too late to rescue, but in time to avenge. Others of our men made equally wild, and, for themselves, dangerous misses as the poor fellow whose fate I have described. There were among the soldiers many who knew and trusted in their weapons. Cool, self-poised men, who fired at the closest quarters with deadliest aim; and did not hesitate to cross weapons with an Arab, parrying his thrust, and returning it with fatal interest with the bayonet.

Colonel Burnaby was the first to mount the parapet, firing with a double-barrelled shot gun into the rebels, many of whom still hung about the works.

As their hiding nooks were discovered, the Soudanese would rise and run at our men spear in hand. Several of our fellows got wounded in this way, and two or three were killed while standing in the ranks, and at times it was almost a *mêlée* of bayonets *versus* spears.

Captain Wilson, of Her Majesty's ship *Hecla*, who was a volunteer, entered the enemy's earthwork, and in protecting a soldier from the attack of a rebel, broke his sword over the Soudanese's head. Wounded as he was, the man fought with the fury of a wild beast, slashing here and there with his keen razor-edged blade. He cut Captain Wilson slightly on the head, but was finally bayoneted, and knocked down. This is but one instance out of hundreds which occurred of the fury with which the enemy fought.

When the fort was gained we found in it two Krupp guns, which the Marine Artillery at once turned with good effect upon the foe, Major Tucker directing their fire. The Arabs still contested the ground inch by inch. They seemed to swarm behind every bush, and could only be killed—not driven off.

The brick building and the iron boiler were next stormed, over 200 of the enemy having clustered about them. Here we had a repetition of our former experience, scores of the enemy waiting, sword or lance in hand, to charge us, but only to get shot or bayoneted. Several shells had been sent into the building by our artillery, and in bursting had killed many of the enemy but had failed to dislodge them, for they continued to cling to the spot with desperate tenacity.

The ground all around was full of shallow, grave-like trenches, dug evidently by the enemy to protect themselves, and Soudanese were in every hole, ready to jump out and charge.

It was one o'clock, and the enemy showed signs of bolting. As they ran the Gatlings and Martinis played havoc among them. Still pressing them, we advanced towards the wells of fresh water at Teb, and here they made a last stand; one or two of their sheikhs even rushed on us empty-handed to show that they bore charmed lives, but the Martinis shortened their career. The Gordon Highlanders Companies F and G, led by their own officers, carried the next earthwork where there was little or no resistance offered. Here we found two Krupps, a brass gun, a Gatling, and two rocket tubes. Their camp, huts, and wells were now in our possession, after from three to four hours of most arduous fighting.

All our men behaved splendidly, and as the square moved around on its centre nearly all present had a turn at the enemy. The 65th and Marines had the earliest serious brush when the first work was carried. Afterwards the firing was so general on three sides of the square that every man of the force had ample opportunity to reply to and repel the enemy's rush. There was no lack of ammunition, and the men were kept constantly supplied during the day.

The last work was rudely built of sand-bags and barrels. It was crescent-shaped, and facing south. As it was assaulted from the north they had turned their guns in that direction against us.

Baker Pasha had sent a message to the 10th to say he was anxious to see them at work. His wish was soon gratified. The enemy was now clearly on the move, and the cavalry, which had gone to our right, flanking them, charged. The Soudanese did not bolt, but struck at the troopers as they rode through them, wounding several soldiers. Back the gallant Hussars came at them again, and still the enemy struck blow for blow. Three Soudanese, part of the few mounted men seen by the troopers, actually stood their ground against the shock of these two fine regiments, to be cut down. A third time the cavalry went through them, and still they fought, starting up and thrusting with sword or spear as the Hussars galloped by. Lieutenant-Colonel Barrow was wounded by one of the spears, and two or three troopers were killed.

The enemy, though retiring, were doing so slowly, and firing was therefore kept up.

As we had gained Teb and the wells, General Graham decided to stay there for the night, strengthening the position, and go on to Tokar the next day. Arrangements for that purpose were therefore made, and the men were re-formed around the place, taking up strong ground.

At Teb were gathered many of the spoils of the enemy's victory over Baker Pasha, and these have fallen into our hands. Admiral Hewett and Staff also accompanied the expedition, remaining inside the square. We have been victorious, but there is likely to be a little more fighting in a few hours.

Suakim, Saturday, March 1 (4.30 P.M.)

In yesterday's fight there were many incidents which deserve mention. Whilst the 10th Hussars charged, Captain Slade and Lieutenant Probyn (attached from Bengal Cavalry) were killed. Lieutenant Probyn was a fellow-passenger of mine from England. He was full of hope and dash. He was the nephew of the Comptroller of the Household of the Prince of Wales.

Our loss was probably 30 killed.

The cavalry suffered more than was thought at first. Their riderless horses in many instances galloped back to Trinkitat. Many Soudanese were hidden in holes they dug about Teb; in fact, the ground was honeycombed with little trenches. They jumped out when the corners of the square passed and charged us savagely. One fellow actually got up and thrust his long, broad-bladed, bright, razor-keen lance into a Highlander's back. To keep them off one had to face in all directions.

The desperate bravery of these hidden foes was surprising. It was easy to see how a few bold men could stimulate mad devotion. The sheikhs and fanatics keep their followers' spirits well up, themselves fighting among them. Most of these swarthy savages wore a waistcloth only. As an illustration, among many incidents observed, of their desperate and universal valour, I may mention that a little lad of twelve tumbled dead into the shelter-trench where he was fighting, his teeth set and his hand grasping his baby spear. The ferocity and rapidity with which the Soudanese thrust their weapons were wonderful.

The officers commanding the regiments are worthy of all praise for the manner in which they handled their men. These officers were: Gordons, Colonel Hammill; Royal Irish, Colonel Robinson; Black Watch, Colonel Green; Rifles, Colonel Ashburnham; 65th, Colonel Byam; Marines, Colonel Tuson; Naval Contingent, Rolfe of *Euryalus*; Royal Artillery Battery, Major Lloyd.

As the square advanced against the first earthwork (it is called a gun-bank or mound in the official plan), the front became uneven through many of the soldiers, who were moving straight towards it, hanging back. The men to the east of it, the left of the face of the square then leading, pushed on, and some of them actually got to the south corner of the work, turning to their right to fire at the Arabs. It was in this position that the poor fellow of the 65th, whose fate has been described, had the encounter with the savage. Three or four more of our men were slain in the same way at this spot by the mad onrushes of rebels wielding spear or sword. It was from this same spot too that the Arabs made their only serious and threatening charge on the square at El Teb, when sallying forth from behind its shelter, several hundred strong, they sent the leading files of the 65th, or York and Lancaster, recoiling 30 or 40 yards, till the men fell back into their places, "felt the touch" of comrades, and again marched forward; the second time in solid, unbroken line. Here also did the Hadendowas, throwing themselves upon a British square, actually grasp the soldiers' bayonets in order to push them aside, and in some instances to try and unlock these weapons from the rifles.

The earthwork, or fort, with its two Krupp guns, was approached in the direction shown in the following plan:

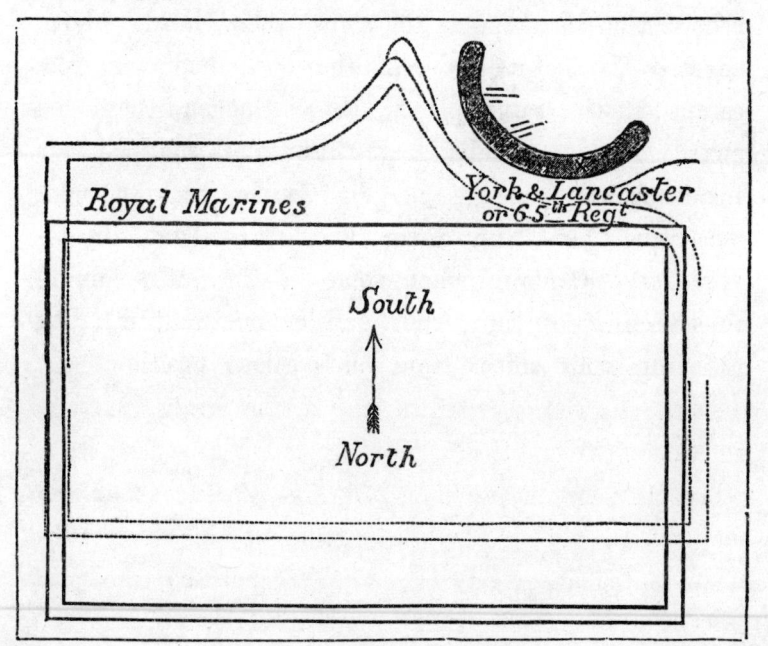

The dotted lines show the position the men were in when the troops captured the work. The parapet was between three and four feet high. The small mark X shows where Col. Burnaby advanced to and fired into the rebels hiding behind the two guns and at the south corner of the work. Col. Burnaby went to the top of the slope, and with his double-barrelled fowling-piece poured half-a-dozen rounds into the Arabs. Several of the savages rose from their hiding places, and ran at him, but the charge of shot at such close quarters blew them clean off their legs. Once or twice he was so closely pressed by their running at him that he had to retire down the slope to reload, the soldiers meanwhile giving the quietus to all the rebels who attempted to show their heads above cover. Capt. Littledale, of the 65th, had a narrow escape at the same place. He cut at and bent his sword over an Arab, then drew and snapped his pistol at the savage in the scuffle that ensued. The rebel bore him down, and was about to despatch the Captain, when some of the 65th, coming in the nick of time, shot and bayoneted the rebel, relieving their officer from his perilous position.

CHAPTER VIII.

AFTER THE BATTLE.

AFTER the last shot had been fired at El Teb, and the enemy had left us in quiet enjoyment of the wells—and thankful men and horses were to get at the ten mud-holes *called wells*—I had a hurried look, once more, over the ground. Having accompanied the infantry square from first to last, I knew all that had occurred there, but was not equally conversant with the cavalry's doings. I had seen their charges, and had helped in the cheer which greeted them as they first rode past the right face of the square to engage the Arabs; but looking on at a fight from a distance is like scanning a landscape painting; Nature may be reduplicated, but, all the same, you miss the bracing air of the scene, and the sense of reality. General Stewart gave me an outline of what had taken place under his command, so searching for Captain Scott, of the Headquarters Staff, I read over to him my notes of the battle, in compliance with the terms of a General Order, issued the day previous, that no reports of the fight would be allowed to be wired to

England that were not approved and signed by him and Colonel Clery, as press censors. The delay and worry necessitated by these small regulations were simply maddening, but there was no escape, especially for anyone in haste like myself. Submitting to his correction, and cutting down by over a half my first estimate of the killed and wounded (and even then the casualties were understated), I got his *visé* and galloped off to Trinkitat, getting in with the first news to that place. Several anxious hours were spent arranging the forwarding of the telegrams—a man I depended on having failed me. At last I hit upon another plan than the one first determined on, scribbled my message once more in long-hand, to reduplicate and ensure against every chance of its miscarriage. My Greek servant had got out of the way somehow before the fighting began, and it was not till Sunday I saw him, so every detail had to be attended to. Admiral Hewett was still at El Teb, and, by his orders, no steamer would go till he sailed with the official despatches. It would be too late for him to set out for Suakim that night, but it was said he would go at six o'clock next morning. By 8 p.m. my messages were all completed, and, giving them to a trusty Arab runner together with a solid *tip* and the promises of much "backsheesh" if he reached Suakim early next morning, I fortified him with passports and went out with him two miles on his way overland to that town. He reached Suakim about seven o'clock next morning, having passed several wounded and straggling Arabs on the way, was chased away from the forts by the Egyptians, and finally got within the lines between 9 and 10 a.m. Captain Hastings, the senior naval officer, saw the messenger, gave him an endorsement of receipt of the telegram, timed 10 a.m., which I now have, and having read it forwarded a brief excerpt to London. It was published as follows:

"ADMIRALTY DESPATCHES.—[FROM SENIOR OFFICER AT SUAKIM.]

"Dated March 1. Despatched 11 a.m.; "Received 9.29 a.m.

"No. 78.—Native messenger arrived with news of army from correspondent of *The Daily Telegraph*. Pith of his report is, hard day's fighting yesterday. Enemy fought courageously, but beaten on every point. Remained at wells for night, and advance [to] Tokar to-day. Our loss is 10 killed and 40 wounded. Enemy's loss about 1,000. Am expecting official confirmation by steamer.

"The Secretary of the Admiralty presents his compliments to the Editor of *The Daily Telegraph*, and begs to inform him that the above mentioned telegram has been received."

Perhaps one may be allowed to insert here what the Editor of *The Daily Telegraph* said in this connection.

"Our preceding despatches—which were the first to reach London on Saturday from Trinkitat—were received at Suakim from the special correspondent of *The Daily Telegraph* with General Graham's army, and were published in advance of any other accounts, in *second, third,* and *fourth* editions. They fully and clearly describe the concentration of the troops at Fort Baker, the tactical formation adopted on moving out towards El Teb, the incidents on the line of march, and the gradual preparations for battle. The changes which occurred in the array during the progress over rough ground are noted, and the turning movement, which brought the force on to the left flank and into the rear of Osman's selected and fortified position, is carefully explained. As General Graham states, the comparatively slight loss to the British must be referred to the unexpected and thoroughly successful manœuvre which directed the effective attack on the more exposed portions of the entrenchments. When the infantry fire and onset had put the enemy in motion, the cavalry were sent to the flank, and they charged thrice through the unyielding adversary. The resolution with which the Soudanese stood up against the rush of the Hussars is not the least remarkable characteristic of this vigorously contested fight. After resting one night at the wells, General Graham, it has been seen, marched on Tokar, which he occupied without resistance. He not only delivered the inhabitants from Arab oppression, but had the satisfaction of rescuing at least that portion of the garrison which had remained loyal."

Little has been said of the painful scenes witnessed on the way to El Teb, and which were again passed through on my way back to Fort Baker. I allude to the miserable Egyptians who perished when Baker Pasha's force was defeated, and that of Consul Moncrieff was destroyed. Surely army never marched to battle by sadder route than General Graham's force. About a mile outside Fort Baker we came upon the first of the bodies of the victims of these disasters. The polluted air warned us of their whereabouts long before we saw them lying, ghastly wrecks of humanity, on the sandy plain. Most of the victims appeared to have fallen on their faces, as if they were speared or cut down from behind by the pursuing Arabs. The bodies were all stripped, not a vestige of clothing remaining. Of some only the bare skeletons were left, but for the most part the remains were unattacked by the vultures and wild beasts. They were slowly desiccating and decomposing in the dry climate. Indignities of which one cannot write had been perpetrated on the dead by their ruthless slayers. The course the fugitives had taken was broadly marked from the fatal field. It was a belt not a hundred yards wide, and about three miles in length, along which the bodies were as thickly strewn as if an enemy were to murder the people passing down a street or road. Here and there a few of the runaways had apparently staggered from the line of flight, wounded and maimed, to crawl under a bush to die. Man had been cruel, but already Nature was at work in many places, covering the poor remains with soil washed down by the tropical rains from the little mounds and slopes dotting the plains. At the spot where Baker Pasha's troops had been first surprised, the dead lay in irregular heaps over an area of 300 yards. Just beyond these heaps, in the direction of El Teb, there was a low mound, crowned with hundreds of little sticks, from which small strips of calico of various colours waved. It was thought at first they were the enemy's flags, marking their position; so they were, but it was the position where 100 Arabs who had fallen in that engagement were buried. The practice of raising a cairn over their dead, which they frequently make rude attempts to embellish by surrounding it with white quartz pebbles, or rare stones of odd shapes, surmounting all by a stick and flag, is a common one in the Soudan. We found similar graves at Tamaai, Tamanieb, Otao, and elsewhere. Those who have been in the highlands of Scotland have seen cairns of exactly the same description. What can the Ancient Britons have had to do with the Arabs? The world is a small place, after all.

CHAPTER IX.

EL TEB TO TOKAR.

HAVING sent my despatches off, I set out early the following morning (Saturday) to return to El Teb. My servant had not yet returned. The night at Trinkitat had been passed in the Ordnance tent, where, thanks to the hospitality of Major Mills and Captain Houghton, I had been well entertained. My horse was fresh enough, and in three hours from the time of starting he had carried me to the wells of El Teb. The country appeared perfectly safe, for unprotected convoys were moving backwards and forwards, and I rode alone, as on my way down, through the mimosa-covered plain. Clad in a dark blue suit, burdened with as few articles as were necessary—a water-bottle, a pair of field-glasses, a serviceable army revolver with a moderate supply of cartridges. Such is the correspondent's usual field kit. Pockets crammed with biscuits, a tooth-brush, a piece of carbolic soap, and a towel jammed into the holster attached to the saddle invariably completed the outfit. With these one felt equal to any bivouac. In the morning the tub or bath whenever procurable. At Tamanieb, or rather on the way there, we used to scoop a hole in the loose soil, put a waterproof sheet therein, pour the water from the skins the servants carried, and have a refresher. Note, we wasted nothing, for, using no soap, when we had finished (a major and a distinguished chaplain have been glad to utilise the same water after rising from the night's bivouac) the horses were led up, and they drank every drop out of the improvised bath-tub. When men were compelled to manage on two quarts a day, and each horse on one gallon, one had to see to it closely that the nags were equal to going about from daylight to long after dark; so that is how we came to give extra measure to the horses out of the bath.

The following telegrams tell what was wired home after my second ride to El Teb:

Trinkitat, March 4 (11.30 a.m.) (*viâ* Suakim).

The incidents in Friday's fighting would fill columns. The camp-fire stories repeat the tale of the enemy's frenzy and the pluck of our men. The under-censor reduced my estimates of killed and wounded; the total is now known to be over 140 wounded and 36 killed, the cavalry faring worse than the other troops. It was not at first believed that missing men should be counted dead.

The casualties in every branch of the service show the nature of the contest; and it is to be regretted that our dead, whom the enemy could get at, were mutilated.

It was almost impossible to save wounded Arabs, or take prisoners, as the dying savages, in their last throes, strove to thrust or cut with the keenest knives, lances or swords. The troops had to shoot or bayonet all as they advanced, for the wounded often started up, killing or maiming soldiers, and a grim pleasure lit their faces whenever they could bury their weapons in a man's body. Even unwounded Arabs hid themselves among their slain to await our approach to rush out and kill. Luckily nearly all had their careers cut short by bullets before being able to run amuck among us; some, however, got up to the line; and one, after being hit with a bullet, charged the 65th, then swerved towards a gun, when a gunner snatched a rammer and knocked him down by a blow on the head, and before he was able to spring up he was bayoneted.

Colonel Herbert Stewart had narrow escapes during the charges. Two squadrons of the 19th Hussars and Mounted Infantry, after charging, became ragged for a moment, and Colonel Stewart and two Staff officers galloped to assist, the officer commanding, Colonel Barrow, having been wounded in riding through the enemy scattered to the south-east of Teb. The cavalry charged twice in squadron into 4,000 Arabs, and once with squadrons in échelon. The ground prevented the troopers from keeping knee to knee.

The enemy showed the greatest indifference to the cavalry, waiting their approach, throwing themselves prone at the proper moment alongside bush or knoll, dodging around like lightning to hamstring with swords or knives the troopers' horses, despatching riders checked or thrown by such dexterous manœuvre. The Hussars' swords were too short to reach the crouching foe, and our weapons were badly-tempered compared with the Arabs' lances, which would have been more effective in a cavalry pursuit. Even the enemy's horsemen—total estimate, 130—when attacked, rode forward to meet our regiments, the Arabs jumping off, sheltering under horses, and cutting at the troopers in passing in the same way as their footmen did.

So much for the enemy's daring. Now to relate our soldiers' deeds. Private Hayes, 10th Hussars, was attacked by a native footman after his squadron had passed. Hayes tried to cut the man down, but his horse being restive, he dismounted, parried a furious lance thrust and killed his assailant. Colonel Wood yesterday spoke to the regiment on parade, praised Hayes and also the whole regiment for its steadiness, Colonel Stewart having desired him to express his admiration of the men's conduct. Captain Littledale, 65th, bent his sword, then closed in a tussle with a native, was thrown undermost and cut on the shoulder before the Arab could be killed by timely assistance.

The tribes fighting on Friday were Hassanab, Artega, Gemilab, Hendawa, Hadendowa, Ashrab, and Demilab.

General Graham throughout displayed high qualities; he was cool, firm, and kept the troops well in hand. General Buller was active in watching and strengthening threatened points during the fight.

The force bivouacked at Teb, supplies being brought forward from Fort Baker. The night was quiet, and on Saturday, at nine in the morning, the troops moved out of the enemy's works at Teb for Tokar, which was taken the same day. A garrison was left at Teb, consisting of the Black Watch and a squadron of the 10th Hussars. They used the enemy's guns, and two of ours were left behind to strengthen the position. They also improved the earthworks.

The Tokar force marched in quarter-column of companies, cavalry scouring in advance from Teb. We could see mountain ranges thirty miles eastward of the route. The first eight miles of march was towards the north-east, to avoid bush and stunted trees. Tokar was not visible; indeed, the mirage and flatness prevented us from seeing objects of low elevation over a mile. The force, going guardedly, then turned south-east, marching several miles through a sort of cedar-bush, the country being broken by knolls and shallow gullies formed by rains. At length the infantry halted, formed square, and the cavalry searched for Tokar.

About 3 p.m. a building was seen, and Tokar was found. When the cavalry had got within a mile the Arabs opened fire, and shortly afterwards 400 of the enemy streamed out, going north—Suakim way. Colonel Stewart sent a galloper to General Graham with the news, and, thinking the enemy meant to attack the infantry, tried to check their rush with three squadrons, who dismounted, and fired 100 rounds. The enemy did not attack the infantry, but kept on going seemingly to join Osman Digna. They passed between me and the infantry, and quickened an undesired return on my part to Teb. I resumed my journey about sunset, getting into Tokar after dark—distance about ten miles from Teb. Colonel Stewart, after the enemy had passed, moved on to within 800 yards of Tokar Fort; eight troopers went forward to within 200 yards, and these were met by a man with a flag of truce. Learning it was the English, he expressed delight, and returning in a few minutes with men, women and children, they all came screaming out to meet the troops, exhibiting intense joy, shouting, dancing, and kissing one another with Oriental fervour. They kissed the soldiers' hands and garments, vowing we had saved their lives, as the rebels meant to massacre them before leaving, but our sudden arrival had averted that calamity. Scarcely any one among the troops credited them with truth-telling; indeed, many officers held that some of these 300 heterogeneous Egyptian soldiers fired on us, and served the Krupps well.

The story told by the garrison is strange. Twelve days ago, some say fourteen, they agreed to surrender to Kader Ali, who commands under Osman, on condition that their lives were spared. They accepted the Mahdi as Prophet, but still they went in perpetual fear, as the rebels were exceedingly fanatical. On Friday, after the defeat, the Arabs plundered Tokar (so the people said; but there were few signs of their having been looted; indeed, it looked the other way), swearing they would ensure the converts' salvation by killing them. The population is about 4,000, chiefly negroes and Arabs.

There were no signs of looting by rebels, but abundance of provision and animals. Tokar stands on a plain of sandy clay, has several sun-dried brick, low, flat-roofed buildings, which look well afar off, but approach destroys the effect. They are all tumble-down, dirty, mud structures; and there are also many squalid Arab huts built of reeds and matting. The fort, an enclosed village, rather than an earthwork, extends 300 by 200 yards. For a considerable portion of the exterior there is a 6-ft. trench, and interior parapet or wall from 4ft. to 7ft.—the wall being often merely the side of some house. In places there is no ditch, but only the wall of mud houses forming the defence. As there is high ground, many houses, and plenty of cover outside, and as the ditch or parapet is easily passable, it is hardly credible that the place could for a moment have withstood an Arab assault. The whole surrender story looks like a sham, even taking into account the rebels' dread of earthworks. An old Greek dealer and his wife remained in Tokar all the time. They had little to tell of the siege. They were forced to forswear their religion, and accept the Mahdi. The man's name was changed to Ahmed, the woman's to Sclim. The woman—tall and strong—told the story laughing. She kept much indoors, being protected by townsmen.

The troops captured a standard belonging to the rebels in the fort, dedicated to Sheikh Ahmed Deris.

During the night, the Chief Sheikh Sayd Abou Bekr, an Ashrab, entered our camp. The infantry formed square just outside the town, near the wells, built a new zereba in which the cavalry were placed in the centre. Sayd, a liberal-minded person, who had stood between the rebels and townsmen, protecting the latter, stated that the rebels owned to having 1,500 killed in fighting us. Kadir had written to Osman for help, but got no reply. Sayd said our trying to make peace with the rebels would be useless on account of their fanaticism. He wanted peace himself, but the fanatics were too strong. A company of infantry and signalmen having been placed in the fort for the night, the troops bivouacked undisturbed. Camels, with water, ammunition, and a convoy of provisions, escorted by two squadrons, came from Teb late. The men kindled fires, and soon had a comfortable meal.

On my way to El Teb I passed two small detachments of our men who were out looking for the bodies of those who fell in the former conflicts. With the assistance of several who were present in Baker's affair, the remains of nearly all the officers were discovered. I rode up to the little party engaged in performing the last offices to poor Morice Bey, Dr. A. Leslie, and Capt. Walker, all of whom I had known personally. Beyond the positions in which they lay there was little to identify them by. Culpable neglect and indifference to consequences on the part of those responsible for the administration of Egyptian affairs, alone permitted, led, and hastened their unnecessary butchery. Having waited whilst they were being interred on the lonely plain, I saluted the dead and rode forward. At El Teb, I found that General Graham had gone on to Tokar with most of the troops, having set out at 9 a.m. Our cavalry had become transformed into Lancers, each trooper carrying a Soudan spear picked from the field, as they preferred these weapons to their short unhandy swords. Captain Piggott carried a nine-foot Indian pig-sticker, which he wielded to advantage at El Teb. A small garrison had been left to guard the wells, keep the position and the spoils which had fallen into our hands, and bury the dead. For this purpose, there had been told off six companies of the Black Watch (42nd), a troop of the 10th Hussars, and 20 men of the Royal Marine Artillery under Major Tucker. This small force was commanded by Lieut.-Colonel Green, of the Black Watch. The Marines had possession of the enemy's guns, and the second earthwork which we carried had been strengthened, and was now held by our men as the key of the whole position. Whereas it was open to the west and south when captured, our men had thrown up a parapet and dug a shelter trench completely around the high ridge where the work was, and had further strengthened the position by enclosing it with mimosa bush. This improved fort dominated the wells and the battle-ground of the day before. Once more I wandered over the battle-field. The Arabs lay about in every direction where they fell, many of them still grasping, with dead men's clutch, their weapons. Their features generally wore an eager look, rather that of enthusiasts than of blood-hunters and ferocious savages. Some of them were "greybeards," and among them were a half-score of lads, whose ages ranged from ten to fourteen years. Already our soldiers were at work, warm as the day was, burying their own as well as the Arab dead. The rifle pits and trenches the savages had dug to seek shelter in were their ready-made graves. These holes were filled, and the loose earth in front of them was shovelled over the bodies. Our slain, officers and men, were borne to a spot near the fort, where two deep, wide, and long pits were dug. Dressed as they had fallen, but with their overcoats covering them from too curious gaze, the dead were laid in rows; comrades in death as in life, and with religious rites buried for ever from mortal eyes.

I wended my way to the boiler and the old mill where the ground had been so stubbornly contested. The ground there was still saturated with pools of blood. Stepping inside the sun-dried brick mill-building, it was found crammed with dead Arabs, the only living thing beside myself being a cobra, which glided from under a body near the doorway as I entered. Seeing them lying there so thickly one could not help marvelling what the fighting and killing of such brave people was all for.

Our wounded were all gathered under canvas, two or three tents having been erected; some of the injured were being sent back to the base at Trinkitat, to be looked after there. Surgeon-Major Greene and his assistants were busy alleviating suffering. There were about six Hadendowas who had been made prisoners, squatting close to the field hospital. Three of these were wounded, and their wounds had been dressed by the doctors. With the exception of a lad, who was among the lot, they all were silent, morose, and discontented-looking; there was a sort of "meet me by moonlight alone" expression on their faces that showed it would have fared ill with any of us, had we encountered them at an unguarded moment in the desert.

As there was no time for moralising, I betook myself to hastening after the troops who had now two hours' start of me on their march to Tokar, and had disappeared behind mimosa and mirage. Mr. Macdonald, of the *Daily News*, agreed to accompany me on the trip. When, and in what direction were the troops seen last from the fort? we inquired; but no one appeared to have any clear idea. With one it was to the west, with another to the south-west, and so on. Which direction was Tokar in? provoked even more diversity of reply, and it was clear nobody at El Teb knew where it was except that it was somewhere further inland. Before us stretched the plains with the background of the black Soudan mountains as we two set out to overtake Graham's force.

There were no correspondents with them, and— happy thought!—suppose a battle, or, better still, a *catastrophe!* Why, we would have it—the news—

all to ourselves. The fancy of such a thing happening lured us on.

No escorts or convoys were to start until the General sent word back; so ahead we went, following the clearly-defined tracks of the infantry and cavalry. Major Cholmondeley Turner, of the Egyptian service, who had charge of the Egyptian Carrier Corps, and a negro sergeant, were on the outskirts of the battle-ground waiting orders to join the troops with a camel convoy of water and ammunition. Turner and the sergeant each had a rifle, and were mounted on trotting dromedaries.

The Major decided to go forward for his orders, and our party was now made up to four. The sun's rays were strong, so we pushed along gently, following the trail through the bush. The mimosa was higher and thicker set together than we had yet seen it. There were few barren places on the plain, and the bush was ten feet high in favoured patches. It was ground that would afford splendid cover for an enemy. Riding abreast and warily scanning the ground to avert surprise by any lurking Arab, we journeyed through the dreary waste for over two hours. I had called my companions' attention to the fact that the trail was circuitous. We voted it was the longest ten miles on record, and still neither Tokar nor our troops were visible anywhere within the range of our glasses.

Suddenly the desert stillness was broken by the far distant sound of rifle firing upon our left. We instantly concluded a fight was in progress, and, turning our animals' heads in the direction of the sound, moved rapidly towards it. A cry from the black sergeant that there were Arabs in front of us, whom his keen eyes observed lòng ére we did, and that they were coming our way, soon halted our party. Turner assured himself such was really the case, and shouting to us that we must run for it, we all turned tail. As we sped along the back track—it was useless going by the roundabout trail—we made for the fort at El Teb, the direction of which I was sure I knew perfectly. We therefore changed our course slightly to the right. Slackening up for a minute or two we saw several mounted Arabs and others on foot about 1,000 yards distant, going furiously, as if attempting to cut our retreat off. Turner again cried that we must hasten or we would be overtaken. He bade Macdonald and I ride ahead, as his dromedaries would outlast and overrun our horses; but knowing my nag was a fairly good one, I preferred to keep by him, well aware that fast as the rate was at which we were going, it left me with something in hand for a rush if necessary. We naturally swerved once more to the left, as the enemy came on riding and running in an almost parallel line. The firing, which we had only heard for about ten minutes, had ceased, and fearing all sorts of mischances had befallen, for we could see no signs of our soldiers, we galloped back, grasping our weapons, expectant that some at least of our pursuers would close up. The chase lasted nearly an hour, when, sighting El Teb and the Arabs having fallen back, Macdonald, who rode five or six stone lighter than I, rode ahead to tell them there what had occurred. Pulling rein we came in slowly—Turner, the sergeant, and myself. It was a near "go," for the Arabs were no respecters of persons or non-combatants.

We found out later on that we had been cut off from joining the troops by the Arabs streaming out of Tokar on the advance of General Graham's force. They made off out of the place, the soldiers said, as if they were going back to El Teb.

CHAPTER X.

TOKAR, DUBBA, AND AFAFEET.

BY no means content at having been compelled to ride back so hastily to El Teb, I was more than ever anxious to know what General Graham and the troops were about. Standing upon one of the ridges I looked through my glasses to see if there were any sign of our men, but there was not even the far-off cloud of dust on the horizon which invariably accompanies and always forewarns, that a force of some sort, mounted or afoot, is moving in the distance. Major Turner had his men and camels all ready to start. Colonel Green said he would probably send a scouting party out about 4 p.m. Just as they were getting ready to set out, two troops of cavalry came riding in from Tokar and told us the news about the capture of that place, and how the Arabs had fired a few shots and then trotted off as the infantry square moved up. The rebels ran out between the troops and El Teb, going, as was stated in the telegram, towards Suakim, no doubt to join their forces with those of Osman Digna, who was then practically investing that town. At length the convoy began to move, escorted by the cavalry, towards Tokar. Once more I set out for that place, but as the pace at which the loaded camels travelled was terribly slow, I proposed to Mr. Scudamore of *The Times*, Lieutenant Ruffee, and another subaltern of the Egyptian service, who were attached to the Intelligence Department, that we should ride in advance and get into camp at a reasonable tea and coffee hour. Off we went, making the most of the daylight that was left, and taking the inside curve of the trail to Tokar. We were soon out of sight and hearing of the convoy, adrift on the wide, desolate plain. Fast as we cantered the road appeared quite as long as it had to me a few hours previously, and as unmarked and leading-to-nowhere-or-anywhere appearance. The sun set and darkness stole quickly in. It looked uncommonly like as if we would have to make up our minds to dismount and stand by our horses till daybreak. The situation was discomforting. The Arabs would perhaps be creeping about the bush, or mayhap some wild animal might feel tempted to prowl around and stampede our nags. To keep on was to run the risk of bringing up goodness knew where. Bad as were the chances we resolved to keep right on. I went to the front and "picked up" a wheel track. It was the "run" of one of the machine gun limbers no doubt. The others followed me in Indian file. Telling them to keep a sharp look-out for anyone moving about, leaning forward in my saddle and with my eyes set on the wheel ruts, I spurred my horse along at a rapid gait. The track led out and in; among the thick bushes, now curving to the right and then to the left. Over barren patches, across narrow dry water-courses, up and down little nullahs it took us, but we never lost sight of it, though the night had fairly come and it was only the first quarter of the moon that lit the deep blue vault of the clear Soudan sky and showed us the way. Once or twice we pulled up to rest the horses. Ruffee and his brother officer said if we got into camp safely that night we would all drink to our ride. Time pressed as the moon was getting low down and casting long shadows from the mimosa, so, putting our horses to their mettle, we rattled on. In a short time we caught sight of a light, then of another, then of scores of them. They were our soldiers' camp fires; we were safe enough now, so we rode straight for the genial lights, arriving about a quarter past eight o'clock. We found that a new zereba had been constructed, within which the infantry and cavalry were encamped. It was close to the wells, and half a mile from the collection of mud huts and sun-dried brick buildings, by euphuism termed the town of Tokar.

Riding up to the zereba we were directed to the face opposite the wells, where the opening was left in this rampart of thorny bush for ingress and egress Our arrival, so long after dark, was a surprise to our friends, and we were congratulated on our little adventure having terminated so fortunately. An abundant supply of piping hot tea and cocoa were tendered us. Mr. Scudamore and myself, who were the only correspondents with the force there, were kindly taken care of by our good friends the Blue-jackets, who made us heartily welcome, sharing their provisions with us. Our horses were also looked after, for sailors naturally take to, pet, and spoil, every animal, so they were carefully watered and fed. We went to the wells, and then started to walk into Tokar to see the town. A sentinel, however, halted me, and said that, by orders, no one was allowed to enter the place. There were only a company of men in the Governor's house, which they were using as a block-house and signal-station, trying to flash by lamps back to El Teb. We returned to the zereba, to bivouac for the night. The convoy which left El Teb came in an hour or two later, and was unloaded and encamped outside on the east of the zereba. Scudamore and I lay down to sleep on the ground, a short distance from a Gatling gun, having each our saddle for a pillow. I had nothing, not even an overcoat, for covering, to keep me warm; for although the days were hot, the nights were still very cold. Huddling together for warmth, and with a small square of waterproof sheeting, we turned in for the night. Both of us were tired and soon were fast asleep. I awoke about two o'clock in the morning, feeling quite chilly on one side; I turned over and tried half-an-hour more of it, but as it was almost freezing I got up, and began walking and stamping about to keep myself warm. There were lots of others in my predicament, so some of us hunted about for pieces of brush and old ammunition and provision boxes, and made a bonfire to warm ourselves. Having toasted myself, I went back and lay down for another hour, but the cold was more biting than ever, and both of us rose and went over to the fire, where we basked in the smoking warmth, listening to the yarns of the men, or drowsily nodding the hours away. At length morning broke, and with the daylight came the pleasant warmth. An early breakfast of cocoa, biscuit, and tinned corned meat, put us in a good frame of mind. We two thereafter saddled and mounted our horses, and accompanied the three squadrons of cavalry which fell in at an early hour to ride towards the Arab villages of Dubba and Afafeet, up the Tokar valley, to where the tribesmen we had been fighting at El Teb for the most part lived. What occurred the telegrams sent home will give a general idea of. We ransacked hundreds of huts, some mere shelters of brush and cane, far less comfortable, one would think, than a wild beast's lair. Others were big, circular, and oblong structures, the framework of bamboo or boughs of trees, covered with straw matting, or thatched with Indian corn and dhurra leaves and stalks, with the sides protected by the same material. Within, on the ground, were spread mats, cloths of camels' hair, and skins of goats, gazelles, leopards, and other animals. About were strewn the domestic utensils, mortars, nodules of hard, grey granite and black trap rock for grinding their grain, water-bottles, earthenware, jars, etc. There were also rude musical instruments in many of the huts, Pandean reeds, pipes, and a hybrid-looking thing with four strings—third banjo and rest harp. In every hut we found traces of loot taken from Baker Pasha's force. I longed to see the stores of grain and ammunition destroyed, and the General give the word to fire the huts. I became impatient, and tried to borrow a match and start a conflagration on my own account, but could not procure one. Then the order was passed around that we were not to destroy the Arab stores. The Remingtons were struck upon the ground and their stocks broken and barrels bent, and so left lying. The ammunition was buried in shallow pits, and, doubtless duly and safely disinterred by the rebels the moment we left. The grain and stores were untouched. The natives had driven their camels and the most of their cattle into the hills, three miles to the south. I took a deer-skin bag out of a hut, filled it with a variety of "curios," some of them evidently taken from Europeans, together with specimens of Arab manufacture, caps, slippers, horse-trapping, musical instruments, etc., and tied it to my saddle. I also picked up two kids after a smart chase, in which they were knocked over with the butt-end of a spear, to take back to camp to improve our cuisine. This done, I outrode the cavalry on the return journey, clinging tightly to my goats. The thong, fastening my bag of loot, broke on the way with the jolting, and I lost all my spoil, but saved my dinner, turning over the kids to the sailors.

The following are the telegrams already referred to:

Sunday (8 A.M.)

One squadron of the 19th, two of the 10th, with the Mounted Infantry, started at a sharp gallop to go to the Arab villages, Dubba and Afafeet, six miles southeast. Spies and townsmen reported that the rebels had stored plunder and arms there, guarded by a force. A squadron, with Colonel Colville, also went to scout five miles to the eastward. General Graham, General Buller, and Colonel Stewart accompanied the expedition to the villages named, and I went with them. The country was more open. We saw no armed men; we had Arab guides who ran alongside the troopers, keeping the horses going at a sharp canter. At Dubba found many things taken from Baker's force; at Afafeet discovered everything plundered stored in natives' huts—valises, books, papers, clothing, even the cap of a soldier killed on Friday—also a stand of 800 Remingtons stacked in a kraal, with a brass gun, a Gatling, and a lot of ammunition. I found visiting cards and papers of Dr. Leslie and others with Baker, also personal belongings. The villages had been hastily deserted, the people having gone towards the mountains. We destroyed the Remingtons, and brought several cattle, fowls, and goats, the brass gun and Gatling, back to camp. The enemy appeared to have abundant provisions. We went a mile further to another village, which was full of women and children only—the men had fled—not a shot was fired. Leslie's instruments, several valises, and other things were taken away. We returned about two.

The General intends remaining with the force two days at Tokar to rest. The Black Watch and the 60th were sent back to Teb on Sunday afternoon. Saturday and Sunday were spent in burying the dead. A party went to the scene of Baker's defeat, a mile and a half east of Teb, and found the bodies of Morice Bey and all the others, and buried them decently. Our dead at Teb were likewise interred, the officers being placed in a separate trench; while those who perished in the cavalry charges were brought in and laid with the others. Some more wounded were borne into Trinkitat on stretchers and sent aboard the *Orontes* and *Jumna*, told off as hospitals. The vessels here are ordered to coal and make ready to return to Suakim, and I expect we shall go there in a few days.

On my return from the Arab villages of Dubba and Afafeet, I explored Tokar, and tried to learn the truth about its siege and surrender. It may as well be stated that no one credited the story that it ever was besieged in any true meaning of the term. My information all went to show that the people in that convict settlement, had little to fear from the rage of the Arabs; on the contrary, the country people would have done wisely to have stood in awe—as no doubt they did—of the terrible prices the miserable citizens exacted for their wretched stores of oil, calicoes, and paltry stores. Heliographic signalling was organised on Sunday from the roof of the Governor's house to the Fort at El Teb. Starting about 2 p.m., with Mr. Scudamore, we rode together straight through the bush, making direct for El Teb, which we reached in about an hour and a quarter. My servant was there, with a long story to tell about his searches after me since Friday. He had been outside the infantry square, behind with the cavalry, at the battle of El Teb. From there he had got further and further behind as we advanced, till he found himself back at Fort Baker. He had remained there till next day, followed me to Trinkitat, and then back to El Teb. Changing horses with him, after a quarter of an hour's rest for dinner—coffee, canned pears, and biscuit—I set out for Trinkitat, telling Antoine to follow at his leisure. My horse was in capital condition, and I reached the sea-shore long before nightfall, without a halt by the way. As the steamer carrying the mail had left, I sent the following message by a native runner on Monday afternoon to the telegraph station at Suakim :

Trinkitat, Monday.

On Saturday, a Marine, moving about the enemy's dead behind the boiler at Teb, was killed by a wounded Arab hidden among the slain. The Arab managed, with a sharp, thin-bladed, pruning-shaped knife to disembowel the Marine. The Arab was bayoneted dead.

Since the fight Colonel Stewart has procured about 700 of the enemy's spears, with which he has armed the cavalry. Major Turner sent to Trinkitat from Tokar, on Sunday afternoon, 100 men, women, and children, some of them slaves. Others are coming to-morrow. One portion is going in the morning to Suakim ; the rest will follow. One-half the population will remain.

Troops and stores are coming to the base. The cavalry, the 42nd, the 60th, and the Marines are expected to-morrow; the forces at Tokar will also return. Ships have been ordered to prepare to leave, it is believed for Suez, many hope Suakim. The Kasala expedition is practically ended. Much credit is due to the Medical Department and those remaining at the base for the way they have worked night and day. Special Ordnance Commissary-General Mills and Assistant Houghton kept the troops well supplied with ammunition, water-cans, and so on.

No mail to-day, Admiral Hewett remaining at Suakim. I send this by runner. The natives say that Osman Digna said our force were Egyptians, led by Ismail Pasha. Had they known we were Feringhees they would never have fought us. General Buller has returned to Trinkitat.

There was no more to be done at Trinkitat, El Teb, or Tokar, except to withdraw our men and stores. It was impossible to follow, except with cavalry, the Arabs, who had betaken themselves up the valleys or gone among the hills. We could have starved them into surrender, had we so minded, by burning their grain and killing all their cattle; but the Home authorities had forbidden any resort to violent measures, and we were killing people and making what the Americans used to call a "white kid glove war," or a war with gloves on our hands.

Trinkitat, Tuesday, 5.35 p.m. (*viâ* Suakim).

The Marines and Naval Brigade, who arrived at Trinkitat to-day, were received with great cheering from the fleet and camp, and embarked for Suakim. The military are awaiting orders from England. It is to be hoped that the force will go to Suakim to fight Osman, who has sworn on the Koran to give us battle. My runner passed through the enemy, and heard them bewailing their children and brothers who were killed. Some of them were wounded; they reproached the Mahdi for telling them that bullets would not hurt them. Major Harty and Mr. Bewley found Moncrieff's remains through soldiers who were standing beside him when killed. The body has been interred. Osman's defeat, it is hoped, would end the whole sad business.

Lieutenant Lloyd, R.A., the brother of Mr. Clifford Lloyd, attached to the 19th Hussars, takes the standard captured at Tokar to present it to the Queen.

Whilst these events were happening, we heard occasionally from the outer world as to what was doing at Suakim, Cairo, and Khartoum. It was all over, rumour said, with Tewfik Bey and the brave garrison at Sinkat who had fallen in trying to cut their way out. The rebels were stated to be hanging near to Suakim, and an assault might be feared at any moment. Their presence there exercised and engaged a great deal of the time and attention of Admiral Hewett. That place, however, we thought safe, as the Marines and Blue-jackets would hold it against all the Mahdi's power. For Gordon we feared much; remote, unsupported, opposed by a victorious horde of Arabs, what could one man do against their fanaticism? His vigour and his proclamations but indicated the desperate straits he was in. All of us hoped once Osman Digna was disposed of, that a hurried march on Berber by the cavalry would be effected, whilst at the same time boats would be sent to meet us there; and when Khartoum's garrison and Gordon were withdrawn down the Nile, the campaign would be closed for the season. The garrisons south of that place, it was held, could be much easier removed by way of Abyssinia with the assistance of King John, who was reported as very friendly to the British.

Before passing on to other matters herewith are submitted to the reader the official despatches which were sent to England recounting the events described. They will be found in the next chapter.

CHAPTER XI.

OFFICIAL DESPATCHES—TEB AND TOKAR.

HER MAJESTY wired the following acknowledgment of the services rendered by the troops, sending it necessarily through the proper official channel.

"Cairo, March 2 (6.40 p.m.)

"To GENERAL STEPHENSON,

"Pray convey my congratulations, and deep sense of his service and of those under him, to Sir Gerald Graham, as well as my sorrow for the loss of distinguished officers and men, and my anxiety for the wounded."

Appended are the first brief official reports describing the action :

From Major-General Sir G. Graham, Teb, to the Secretary of State for War.

(Despatched Suakim, 1st March, 4.30 p.m. Received 4.20 p.m.)

No reply received to message sent to rebel chiefs.

Advanced this morning from Fort Baker, with entire available force of 3,000 infantry, 750 mounted troops, and 115 of Naval Brigade, six machine guns, and eight Royal Artillery seven-pounders.

Found rebels entrenched at Teb with Krupp guns.

Moved to right, so as to turn their entrenchments, which were stormed and carried in rear, two successive positions being taken.

Captured four Krupp guns, two brass howitzers, and a Gatling, besides a quantity of arms and ammunition.

Loss of rebels very heavy, nearly 900 bodies being already counted in positions captured, irrespective of cavalry operations.

Action lasted three hours, enemy showing desperate resolution and tenacity; their force is reported as about 10,000.

Our loss amounted to 28 killed, 2 missing, 142 wounded.

The infantry moved, at first in a hollow square, with transport animals carrying reserve ammunition, gun ammunition, and hospital equipment only inside, but found some difficulty in attacking in that formation, which was accordingly altered.

Our loss would have been far heavier had the entrenchments been attacked in front.

The cavalry were very ably handled and made some dashing charges; but I regret their heavy loss.

Tents and every necessary appliance for the wounded have been supplied from base.

I leave this post entrenched to-morrow, and push on to Tokar.

Moderate water supply here. Have sent, through prisoners, a summons to the Chief at Tokar to make submission to-morrow, and have repeated the terms offered yesterday.

List of casualties as follows:

OFFICERS KILLED.

Lieutenant Freeman, 19th Hussars.
Major Slade, 10th Hussars.
Lieutenant Probyn, 9th Bengal Cavalry.
Quartermaster Wilkins, 3rd Battalion King's Royal Rifles.

OFFICERS WOUNDED.

General Baker Pasha, severely.
Lieut.-Colonel Burnaby, severely.
Lieut. Barrow, 19th Hussars, dangerously.
Lieutenant Royds, R.N., dangerously.
Brevet-Major Brabazon, 10th Hussars, slightly.
Captain Kellie, Royal Artillery, slightly.
Veterinary-Surgeon Beech, slightly.
Quartermaster Watkins, Irish Fusiliers, slightly.
Surgeon Turner, slightly.
Major Dalgetty, York and Lancaster Regiment, slightly.

Captain Littledale, York and Lancaster Regiment, severely.

Lieutenant Gordon (? Wolrige Gordon), Royal Highlanders, slightly.

Lieutenant Macleod, Royal Highlanders, slightly.

Captain Green, Royal Engineers, slightly.

Captain Wauchope, Royal Highlanders, Staff, slightly.

Captain and Adjutant Poe, slightly.

Major Allen, Royal Marines, slightly.

Staff-Surgeon Martin, R.N., slightly.

The garrison left at this place have orders to search Baker's battle-field and bury European dead.

The following additional information regarding the casualties at El Teb has been received from Major-General Sir G. Graham:

The following should be added to the list of officers wounded—Captain Kelly, Staff, slightly, and Captain Wilson, Royal Navy, slightly.

The two men reported missing are—1800, Private Frederick Stride; and 1754, Private James Douglas, 10th Hussars. They have since been brought in dead.

The wounded are doing fairly well.

The following are the non-commissioned officers and men reported killed at El Teb, Feb. 29:

Royal Artillery—6th Battalion 1st Brigade Scottish Division: 25356, Gunner Angus.

Royal Engineers—26th Company: 16310, Second Corporal Ough.

10th Hussars — Sergeant Cox; 1742, Private Brindley.

19th Hussars—1342, Sergeant Gray; 1979, Corporal Ibbott; 1313, Private Cottle; 2342, Private Garside; 1666, Private Hughes.

1st Battalion Royal Highlanders—923, Private Boycott; 2000, Private Henderson; 1056, Private Rowe.

1st Battalion York and Lancaster Regiment—505, Lance-Sergeant John Connor; 2216, Lance-Corporal Callanan; 1354, Private Edwards; 1742, Private Kemsley; 748, Private Hickey; 1848, Private Kirby; 1809, Private Burke.

Royal Marine Artillery—12th Company: Gunner Jenkins.

Royal Marine Light Infantry—47th Company: Private Holder. 5th Company: Private Anderson.

Royal Navy—A.B. Beard; A.B. Marston.

The following telegram has been received at the War Office from Sir G. Graham, K.C.B., dated Suakim, 2nd March (1.20 p.m.):

"Tokar garrison relieved. Arabs, under Khaden, have been in possession since 16th, and have been oppressing the garrison and inhabitants, who rejoice greatly at their deliverance. No opposition from Arabs, who have retired into the mountains."

From Admiral Hewett:

"Suakim, March 1, 1884 (4.30 p.m.)

"General Graham fought battle at Teb yesterday, driving enemy from entrenched position, capturing four Krupp, two howitzer guns, and one machine gun.

"Enemy's loss very severe; ours 4 officers and 24 men, 142 wounded, Lieutenant Royds, of Carysfort, very dangerously.

"Serapis left this morning for Suez with all women and children.

"Everything has been arranged for conveying the wounded across the lagoon, and boats to take them on board the *Orontes*.

"Naval Brigade lost two men killed—J. Beard, of *Briton*, and T. Marston, of *Dryad*—and seven wounded.

"I intend returning to Trinkitat to-morrow morning."

The subjoined message to the Admiralty was despatched at 3.20 p.m. from Suakim, and received at 2.56 p.m.:

"Sunday.—Tokar garrison relieved. Had been in possession of Arabs since 16th. Much rejoiced at their deliverance. Particulars later by *Sphinx*. Lieutenant Royds dead.—Admiral. Trinkitat."

1. From Sir G. Graham, Tokar, dated Suakim, March 4, 6.0 p.m. (received 8.20 p.m.): "Remains of Consul Moncrieff have been identified and received interment."

2. From Sir G. Graham, Tokar, dated Suakim, March 4, 6.0. p.m. (received 8.20 p.m.): "March 3,

1884.—Garrison and Egyptian inhabitants of Tokar are being sent in to Trinkitat; transport being provided for my camels. Marines and Naval Brigade march to base to-day, also 10th Hussars. Shall withdraw remainder of force to-morrow to Teb and concentrate at Trinkitat on 5th. Wounded doing well. No sick."

3. From Principal Medical Officer, Tokar Forces, dated Suakim, March 4, 5.35 p.m. (received 7.50 p.m.): "Wounded are on board *Jumna* and *Orontes*. Colonel Barrow, 19th Hussars, spear wound of left arm and abdomen; not out of danger. Captain Littledale, York and Lancaster, and all other wounded officers doing well."

4. From Sir E. Graham, Tokar, dated Suakim, March 4, 6.0 p.m. (received 9.30 p.m.): "Bodies of following identified near Teb, and received proper burial: Morice Bey, Abdul Russi Bey, Dr. Leslie, Captains Forestier, Walker, and Rucca; Lieutenants Wilkins, Morice, Demarchi, and Smith; Adjutant-Major Palioka, Messrs. Donebaun, Masconas, and Wells, and many Italian police. Those of Consul Moncrieff, Major Yusef Bey, Lieutenant Bertin, Carrol, and Cavalier not found. Further search will be ordered for them, and report sent if successful. Proceeded this morning to group of Arab villages south of Tokar; found abandoned guns and Gatlings, quantities of ammunition, and nearly 1,000 stand of Remingtons. Latter have been destroyed, and guns brought in. Rebels all retired to mountains.

"To-morrow, 10th Hussars, Naval Brigade, and Marines will return to Trinkitat for re-embarkation, leaving Royal Artillery, York and Lancaster, Irish Fusiliers, 19th Hussars, Mounted Infantry, and Gordon Highlanders only before Tokar; Royal Highlanders at Teb, and Rifles at Fort Baker and Trinkitat. Buller will proceed to Trinkitat, and command at base. All but two wounded sent to base yesterday. All well. Remainder will follow to-day if bearers arrive."

From Major-General Sir G. Graham to the Secretary of State for War.

(Telegram despatched Suakim, March 5, 5.20 p.m., received 5.15 p.m.)

"Trinkitat, March 6.

"Sick and wounded, 130, leave Trinkitat in *Jumna* to-morrow for hospital at Suez."

The following have died of wounds:

Royal Navy.—Lieutenant Royds, H.M.S. *Carysfort*; A.B. Seaman John Beard, H.M.S. *Briton*.

Royal Marines.—16th Company: Private William McCann.

1st Battalion Royal Highlanders.—810, Private R. Humphries.

3rd Battalion King's Royal Rifle Corps.—2512, Private G. Cannon.

The following are serious cases:

Royal Artillery.—6th Battery 1st Brigade, Scottish Division; 20578, Gunner W. McDonald.

Royal Engineers.—26th Company: 16343 Sapper White; 14232, Sapper Henry Shrives.

OFFICIAL LIST OF KILLED AND WOUNDED.

10th Hussars.—1508 (1583 ?) Corporal John Cramp.

19th Hussars.—1150, Sergeant W. D. Brown; 2320, Private J. Sankey; 1921, Private Fitzpatrick.

1st Battalion Royal Highlanders.—2238, Colour-Sergeant H. White; 175, Sergeant J. Ewen; 2603, Private J. Smith.

3rd Battalion King's Royal Rifle Corps.—436, Corporal J. Grainger.

1st Battalion York and Lancaster Regiment.—1833, Private Thomas Ward; 1741, Private J. Smith.

The wounded generally are doing well.

A telegram has been received from Rear-Admiral Sir Wm. Hewett, dated Suakim, March 4, 6.55 p.m., forwarding following return of casualties among Naval Brigade:

Dead.—Lieutenant Frank M. Royds, H.M.S. *Carysfort*; Samuel Marston, H.M.S. *Dryad*; John Beard, H.M.S. *Briton*. (Note.—According to office returns, Joseph Beard, A.B., was serving on board *Briton*.)

Wounded.—James Murray, seaman (seriously), Jeremiah Sullivan (seriously), William Bethell (slightly), Frank Glanville (slightly), Alexander Grieve (slightly), H.M.S. *Euryalus*; Alfred H. Rewell (seriously), H.M.S. *Carysfort*; Thomas Tolman (seriously), H.M.S. *Hecla*. (Note.—Probably intended for John Toleman, boatswain's mate); James C. Tickell (seriously), H.M.S. *Briton*; Thomas Maddox (slightly), H.M.S. *Dryad*. (Note.—Probably intended for Thomas M. Maddocks, A.B.).

FURTHER OFFICIAL DESPATCHES.

"War Office, March 27.

"Despatches, of which the following are copies, have been received by the Secretary for War.

"From Major-General Sir G. Graham, Commanding Tokar Expeditionary Force.

"Camp, Tokar, March 2.

"My Lord,

"I have the honour to submit the following report on the operations of the Tokar Expeditionary Force since the 28th ult.

"In the despatch then sent I informed the Chief of the Staff in Egypt that on the evening of that day I sent an officer to the front of Fort Baker, carrying a white flag on a staff, to which a letter was attached, calling upon the sheikhs of the tribes to disperse their forces now in arms before Suakim, informing them that the English were not at war with the Arabs, and recommending them to send delegates to Khartoum to meet General Gordon.

"Captain Harvey, who is on General Baker's Staff, and now attached to my Intelligence Department, advanced about two miles, the latter part of which was under an ill-directed fire of musketry, and after planting his staff he retired according to my instructions. The following morning at daybreak the same officer went out to see if any answer had arrived, but the staff with all attached had been taken away.

"At about 8 o'clock a.m. I gave the order to advance in the formation of a rectangle, having an interior space of about 500 by 150 yards.

"In front were the 1st Gordon Highlanders, in rear the 1st Royal Highlanders, on the right the 2nd Royal Irish Fusiliers (supported by four companies of the 3rd King's Royal Rifles), on the left the 1st York and Lancaster, supported by 380 of the Royal Marine Artillery and Light Infantry.

"On the march the front and rear faces moved in company columns of fours at company intervals, and the flank battalions in open columns of companies.

"Intervals were left at the angles for the guns and Gatlings, the Naval Brigade occupying the front and the Royal Artillery the rear angles.

"The men marched off with their water-bottles filled and one day's rations.

"The only transport animals were those carrying ammunition and surgical appliances, all being kept together in the centre of the square.

"To secure my base I had left a company of the 3rd King's Royal Rifles, all sick and weakly men and all departmental details armed, under Lieutenant-Colonel Ogilvy, and three companies of the same corps at Fort Baker, with a Krupp gun and two bronze guns at each place manned by the Royal Marine Artillery

"About an hour before daybreak, on Feb. 29, there was a short, but heavy fall of rain, which caused the ground for the first two miles of the march to be very heavy; the Naval Brigade and Royal Artillery dragged their guns by hand, so that frequent halts had to be made to rest the men.

"The front and left of the square were covered by a squadron of the 10th Hussars, the right by a troop of the 19th Hussars, the cavalry being in rear under Brigadier-General Stewart. About 10 a.m. reports came in from the front that the enemy were entrenched on our left, on which I inclined the square to the right; but about 11.20 a.m. I found that we were immediately opposite to a work armed with two Krupp guns, whose position had not been reported to me by the reconnoitring party, so I moved the column still more to the right, on which the guns of the enemy opened fire with case and shell. Fortunately aim was bad, so that few casualties occurred, and I succeeded in getting on the left flank of the work, which was on the proper left rear of the enemy's line.

"The square was now halted, men ordered to lie down, and four guns of the Royal Artillery and machine guns were brought into action at a range of about 900 yards; the practice from the guns was carried on with remarkable accuracy and great deliberation, and with the help of the machine guns of the Naval Brigade, which poured in a stream of bullets, the two Krupp guns were completely silenced, as they were taken slightly in reverse, and the gunners were driven from the guns.

"The infantry now advanced, the square moving by its left face, which, by the flank movement, was opposite to the work attacked. The fighting line was, therefore, composed of the 1st York and Lancaster, supported by the Royal Marines. The 1st Gordon Highlanders and 1st Royal Highlanders moving in column of fours on either flank, the rear of the square being formed of the 3rd King's Royal Rifles and the 2nd Royal Irish Fusiliers. The York and Lancaster advanced steadily till within a short distance of the works, when, with a cheer, a rush was made to the front; and, assisted by the Blue-jackets on the right, who managed to bring their guns into the fighting line, the work was carried and the guns captured. The enemy made several desperate counter attacks, sometimes singly and sometimes in groups, on the advancing line, many hand-to-hand fights taking place with the York and Lancaster and men of the Naval Brigade.

"About 12.20 p.m., the battery which is marked "A" on the accompanying plan was taken, with two Krupp guns and a brass howitzer.

"At this period the cavalry, under Brigadier-General Stewart, moved round the present right flank of the square, and charged in three lines across the plain to its right front where the enemy were in large numbers, who attacked the flanks of the lines, so that they had to change front in order to shake them off. Colonel Barrow, of the 19th Hussars, was severely wounded in executing one of these charges, when, I regret to say, many other casualties occurred.

"The enemy, as reported by Brigadier-General

Stewart, fought simply with fanaticism, and spared no wounded or dismounted men, although, in most cases, instantly paying the penalty with their own lives; and it is to the desperate character of the struggle that the large proportion of deaths in the Cavalry Brigade is to be attributed.

"The enemy were still in possession of the village and wells of Teb, but by the capture of the work on his left flank, my infantry had got in rear of his position, and the captured guns were turned on another work also armed with two Krupp guns, which they took in reverse. These captured guns were admirably worked by Major Tucker, of the Royal Marine Artillery, and with the aid of the guns of the Royal Artillery the enemy's remaining battery was soon silenced. The enemy's infantry, however, still clung with desperate tenacity to numerous rifle pits and entrenchments they had constructed, and large numbers occupied some buildings in the village, which were afterwards found filled with dead bodies; they seemed not to dream of asking for quarter, and when they found their retreat cut off would charge out singly or in scattered groups to hurl their spears in defiance at the advancing lines of infantry, falling dead, fairly riddled with bullets.

"About 2 p.m. the battery marked 'G' on plan, now abandoned, was occupied, and the whole position taken.

"The enemy had now given up all ideas of further fighting, and the last work on the right of their line, shown as a mound on plan, was occupied by the

Gordon Highlanders without opposition, as they streamed away in the directions of Tokar and Suakim.

"Nothing could be better than the dash with which the charges of the cavalry were executed, in the midst of a horde of desperate fanatics, who displayed extraordinary activity and courage; nor could anything exceed the cool deliberation and efficiency with which the Royal Artillery served their guns under fire, or the skill and gallantry displayed by the Naval Brigade in keeping up with the front line of Infantry, and protecting their own guns by hand-to-hand encounters with the enemy, when at least one deed of gallantry was executed, of which I shall make a special report.

"The first time the square came under fire was a very trying one for young troops, as we were then moving to a flank—an operation at all times difficult, and especially so when in such a cramped formation. A slight disorder occurred, which was, however, speedily rectified, and nothing could have been better than the steady advance of the first battery.

"In advancing on the scattered entrenchments and houses, the formation became somewhat disordered, owing to the desire of the men on the flank faces of the square to fire to their front.

"The Gordon Highlanders speedily rectified this, moving one half battalion into the fighting line, the other half being thrown back to guard against flank attacks.

"The Royal Highlanders were somewhat out of hand. I would, however, beg to observe that the ground was a most difficult one to move over, and that the desperate tenacity with which the enemy held a house on the right of the Royal Highlanders caused the men to form in an irregular manner so as to pour a converging fire on it.

"The other battalions, especially the York and Lancaster, which had several hand-to-hand encounters with the enemy, and the Royal Marines, behaved with great steadiness and gallantry.

"The 1st Gordon Highlanders, 3rd King's Royal Rifles, and 1st York and Lancaster, also showed steadiness and good discipline under fire; the latter formed the left flank of the fighting line in the attack on the second position, when they advanced with great gallantry.

"I append a list of killed and wounded, and deeply regret the numerous fatal casualties in the Cavalry Brigade of which I have already made mention.

"The force of the enemy was difficult to estimate, and in my first telegram I put it at 10,000. Subsequent native testimony obtained makes me estimate it at 6,000 fighting men, and I am informed that they admit a loss of 1,500 killed.

"In the immediate neighbourhood of Teb 825 dead bodies were counted, and I am informed that it is the custom of these people to carry off their dead when practicable. I am also informed that the women of the tribes were present with hatchets to despatch our wounded.

"I must now beg to express my sense of the services

of the officers holding responsible positions in the force I had the honour to command on this occasion, without whose loyal co-operation and self-devotion the expedition could not have been carried out successfully.

"Brigadier-General Sir Redvers Buller, V.C., K.C.M.G., C.B., who was specially appointed second in command, showed himself worthy of his high reputation as a thorough soldier and most valuable officer.

"Major-General Davis was most indefatigable in his exertions, and afforded me all possible assistance in preserving formation and discipline during the action, as he has done in expediting the disembarkation of troops since his arrival at Trinkitat.

"Brigadier-General Stewart, C.B., showed himself, as he is known to be, a most able and daring leader of cavalry. My instructions to him were to avoid engaging the enemy until their formation was broken, and until they were in full retreat. The time of making the charge I left entirely to Brigadier-General Stewart, as I wished to keep him well away from my square, not knowing on which side it might be attacked.

"We did not anticipate having to attack the enemy in an entrenched position, but thought he would come out and attack my square in large numbers, be repulsed, and then be cut up by the cavalry.

"The charges actually made were upon masses of the enemy not yet engaged with my infantry, and although most gallantly and skilfully executed, the loss of officers and men is deeply to be regretted. As I have already had the honour to observe, the scouting and reconnoitring duties of the cavalry brigade were admirably performed, and I cannot too highly praise the ready efficiency of the mounted infantry, under Captain Humphreys.

"Among the many valuable staff officers attached to this force I would especially bring to your notice Lieutenant-Colonel Clery, my Assistant-Adjutant-General, who is an invaluable Staff officer, ready in resource, indefatigable in work, combined with coolness, excellent in temper, and a thorough knowledge of his duties. I beg also to observe that Lieutenant-Colonel Clery is mentioned by both the officers commanding infantry brigades for his distinguished gallantry in the action of Feb. 29, when I also observed his extreme coolness and presence of mind.

"My thanks are also due to Deputy-Surgeon-General M'Dowell, who has conducted the duties of the Medical Department to my entire satisfaction, and has shown great judgment and forethought in providing for the wants of the wounded, who have been well and promptly attended to.

"Assistant-Commissary-General Nugent has been indefatigable in arranging for getting up supplies. Although water transport is a most difficult thing to arrange for a force of this size, including so many horses and transport animals, the supply has never failed, although sometimes unavoidably late.

"The supply of ordnance stores, under Assistant-Commissary-General Mills, was also satisfactorily conducted.

"Lieutenant-Colonel Ardagh, Commanding Royal Engineers, was chief of the Intelligence Department. In both of these important positions he has given me great satisfaction, and I beg to recommend this and the above-named officers' valuable services for your lordship's favourable consideration.

"I propose forwarding the names of other officers who have distinguished themselves, in a supplementary despatch, and to recommend them for favourable consideration.

"I cannot, however, close this despatch without recording my sense of the great services rendered to the Expeditionary Force by Rear-Admiral Sir William Hewett. I cannot sufficiently express my admiration of the high sense of duty displayed by this officer under the most trying circumstances.

"Had Admiral Hewett himself been in command of the Expedition for the relief of Tokar he could not have done more to further its success.

"Suakim was threatened with attack by an overpowering force, and a portion of the garrison were in actual mutiny; notwithstanding which, Admiral Hewett insisted on almost denuding his ships of sailors in order to give me the magnificent Naval Brigade, whose services I have in a previous part of this despatch endeavoured to depict.

"Not satisfied with this, Admiral Hewett also gave me nearly 400 of the Marines and Marine Artillery—troops of the first quality. He also gave me the 1st Battalion of the York and Lancaster from Aden, although empowered to employ them for the defence of Suakim. Considering all these important services and his constant readiness to give every assistance in furthering disembarkations, water supply, etc., I think I am justified in stating that it is impossible to over-estimate the services rendered by Rear-Admiral Sir William Hewett towards the Tokar Expedition.—I have, etc.,

"GERALD GRAHAM,
"Major-General Commanding Tokar Expeditionary Force.

"P.S.—My thanks are also due to Lieutenant-General Baker Pasha for the valuable information and assistance rendered by him throughout the operations. General Baker was, I regret to say, severely wounded in the early part of the action on February 29th. His wound was in the face, and must have been very painful, notwithstanding which, after getting it dressed, he returned to the field, and only at the end of the action could I persuade him to retire to the base."

[ENCLOSURE.]

" To Sheikh Khadr and Sheikhs of Tribes around Tokar.

" I summon you for the last time to make submission to me to-morrow morning, or the consequences will be on your own heads.

"I have already told you that the English Government is not at war with the Arab tribes, but it is determined not to allow warriors to collect near Tokar and Suakim. You should send delegates to treat with

Gordon Pasha at Khartoum as to the settlement of your affairs.

"You have seen to-day the beginning of what results from your opposing the English, who did not fire upon you until you commenced. To-morrow is your last opportunity for submitting."

"From Major-General Sir Gerald Graham, V.C., K.C.B., Commanding Tokar Expeditionary Force, to Rear-Admiral Sir William Hewett, V.C., K.C.B., K.C.S.I., Commanding East Indian Station.

"Tokar, March 3, 1884.

"Sir,

"I have the honour to inform you that the Naval Brigade, with Gatlings and Gardner guns, under Commander Rolfe, R.N., and the force of the Royal Marine Artillery and Light Infantry, under Colonel Tuson, C.B., M.R.A., marched off this morning for Fort Baker, which place they will reach this evening, and report to you at Trinkitat to-morrow.

"In parting with this force, which you so generously placed at my disposal, at a time when you were weak-handed and threatened with an attack on Suakim, I feel bound to report to you on the admirable conduct of the officers and men composing it, and to endeavour to express my high sense of the services it has rendered and the important part it has taken in contributing to the success of the expedition.

"The Naval Brigade showed all the traditional qualities of the British sailor, and I cannot fully express my admiration at the hearty cheery way in which they went through the tremendous toil of dragging their guns through the rough and heavy ground, and at their gallantry in action when they kept up with the front line of infantry and defended their own guns, repulsing the enemy's desperate charges in hand-to-hand combat.

"Brigadier-General Buller has brought to my notice an act of gallantry witnessed by him in one of these encounters with the enemy, and I beg to enclose his report and endorse his recommendation that the name of Captain Wilson, R.N., Her Majesty's ship *Hecla*, should, with your approval, be submitted to the Lords of the Admiralty for the distinction of the Victoria Cross.

"Commander Rolfe, R.N., commanding the Naval Brigade, gave me great satisfaction by the perfect coolness and ready promptitude with which he worked his guns.

"Sharing their toilsome march on foot, Commander Rolfe showed great consideration for them on the march, and when in action directed their movements, so that with abundance of dash there was no flurry or confusion, every man showing perfect confidence in his commander, his officers, and his comrades.

"Commander Rolfe has brought to my notice the names of Lieutenant Graham, second in command ; of Lieutenant Montresor, who acted as adjutant ; and of Mr. E. M. Hewett, midshipman, his aide-de-camp.

"Mr. Thomas Gimlette, surgeon, is also mentioned by Captain Rolfe as having been most assiduous in his attendance on the wounded, and as having shown great energy throughout.

"The guns were admirably worked under the immediate orders of Lieutenants Almack, Conybeare, and Houston Stewart. Brigadier-General Buller also specially noticed Mr. R. A. Cathie, gunner of Her Majesty's ship *Sphinx*.

"I beg that you will bring to the notice of the Lords of the Admiralty the admirable manner in which the Royal Marine Artillery and Light Infantoy were handled by Colonel Tuson, R.M.A., and the steadiness and gallantry of the officers and men under fire.

"I have as yet received no report from Colonel Tuson, but I beg to bring under your notice the readiness and gallantry of Major Tucker, R.M.A., who, on the first Krupp guns being captured, immediately turned them on the enemy and worked them with great effect.

"I have, &c.,

"G. GRAHAM,
" Major-General.

"P.S.—Major Tucker, R.M.A., was left in charge of the captured guns at Teb, and has been directed to bring them in to Trinkitat.

"I enclose a copy of a General Order I issued to the troops before withdrawal from Tokar."

"From Brigadier-General Sir Redvers Buller, V.C., &c., Commanding 1st Infantry Brigade, to the Assistant Adjutant-General, Headquarters, Tokar Expeditionary Force.

"Camp, Teb, March 1, 1884.

"Sir,

"I have the honour to bring to the notice of the Major-General commanding the following distinguished act of bravery which came under my observation yesterday, which I would recommend as worthy of being submitted to the Lords of the Admiralty for the distinction of the Victoria Cross.

"Captain Wilson, R.N., H.M.S. *Hecla*, on the staff of Rear-Admiral Sir W. Hewett, V.C., K.C.B., attached himself during the advance on the Krupp Battery yesterday to the right half-battery, Naval Brigade, in the place of Lieutenant Royds, R.N., dangerously wounded.

"As we closed on the battery, the enemy moved out on the corner of the square, and upon the gun detachment who were dragging the Gardner gun. Captain Wilson sprang to the front and joined for a second or two in single combat with some of the enemy, protecting his detachment till some men of the York and Lancaster Regiment assisted him with their bayonets.

"But for the action of Captain Wilson I think one or more of his detachment must have been speared.

"Captain Wilson was wounded, but remained with the half-battery during the day.

"I have, &c.,

"Redvers Buller,

"Brigadier-General Commanding 1st Infantry Brigade."

CHAPTER XII.

CHANGE OF BASE TO SUAKIM.

THERE being nothing further left to be done at Trinkitat, and it being outside the scope of Major-General Graham's orders to proceed to Sinkat to ascertain the exact condition of matters there, the troops were directed to embark as quickly as possible for Suakim. It was known Osman Digna was in that neighbourhood threatening the town, and it was thought the presence of English soldiers there would induce that leader, in view of the defeat of his followers at El Teb, to come to terms, and end the war in the Eastern Soudan. Herewith follows the brief telegraphed chronicle of events immediately preceding and following the change of the base of operations from Trinkitat to Suakim.

Trinkitat (*viâ* Suakim), March 5 (4.30 P.M.)

There is only one half battalion of the 60th here; the Mounted Infantry are out at Fort Baker. The rest of the expedition is rapidly embarking; the 42nd and 10th Hussars are aboard. Generals Graham, Buller, and Staff have gone in the Admiral's boat, the *Sphinx*, to Suakim to-day.

Fort Baker will be evacuated to-day, to-morrow, and Friday, and on Saturday Trinkitat will be deserted.

Among the thousand Tokar people shipped to Suakim, where all disembark, are 129 regular soldiers, 101 criminal exiles, 3 Arabists, 305 women, children, and servants, 14 Egyptians, 2 Government employés, 14 merchants, and 60 villagers.

Altogether there are fourteen transports, four of which are still expected, with the *Carysfort* and *Briton* to assist. The treasure taken has not been used, being brought back. Everybody is glad to get away. The crew of the flagship *Euryalus* manned yards at Suakim, and cheered General Graham on his arrival there to-day.

Suakim, March 5 (9.0 P.M.)

Sir General Graham and Staff have inspected the outposts at Suakim. It is understood that whenever the troubles here are settled Admiral Hewett will proceed to Massowah, thence visit King John, and arrange for a cession of territory.

The naval and military officers are strongly pressing on the Home Government the necessity of giving Osman a lesson.

Putting Antoine and my two horses once more on board the *Northumbria* transport, bound like the rest of the steamers for Suakim, I embarked later on in the day—the 5th March—on the *Sphinx*, for Suakim. The *Sphinx* is a paddle steamer, and can really make 14 knots an hour, so that in about four hours from the time we got under way we entered the harbour of Suakim. The channel leading in is rather tortuous, but the harbour itself is large enough to hold a fleet, and has good anchorage, and is quite land-locked. There were a dozen large vessels there when we arrived in the afternoon, including two or three foreign war-ships, namely, a French, a Russian, and an Italian vessel. On the left were the tents of the military camp, which had been located on the mainland to the south-east of the town, bordering as they did the harbour and sea-shore. In front was the islet of Suakim, almost round, and not more than 500 to 600 yards in diameter. The flat-roofed, sun-dried brick houses, were dazzling with whitewash. Above them rose the little domes and minarets of three small mosques, with their tinting of blue paint, and quaint wooden balconies and brackets. Truly we were back from the wilds, and again on the fringe, at least, of civilisation. I jumped into the first gig going ashore, and was soon landed near the telegraph office. Hastily scrawling a brief despatch, I handed it across the counter, when in came, in a terrible plight, Admiral Hewett's gentlemanly and good-natured private secretary, Mr. Livingstone. He had come ashore in a steam-launch, and he said he had got himself into a row for permitting me to land and get to the telegraph office first. Admiral Hewett had openly reprimanded him, for that gallant officer was fired, like the military, with a laudable zeal always to wire the first news. Any correspondent would have taken the chances with him, or them, in a race, had they only left the wires open to any first-come, first-served rule; but it was driving us too hard to hold the wires and allow nothing to go forward until their despatches were prepared, sent, got to the telegraph office, and went on before a single line of a correspondent's could be wired home. I expressed my sincere sorrow for getting him into trouble, and my regret that so small a matter—as the news that day was unimportant—should have put the Admiral out of humour.

My message, of course, was stopped, and the Admiral's took precedence. Early and prompt news of any event, it might be thought, would have been of more value to the English people and Government, than gratification of official sense of dignity. Independent information is always of the utmost usefulness, wherever it is desirable the truth should be known and the public sympathies knit closer to any event, than mere official records can ever bind them.

Having got my telegram off, and got the material for another by a trip to the camp, my attention was turned to "house-hunting," or rather, finding quarters for the night. I had gone on board the *Sphinx* without any baggage, except a haversack; and the prospect of spending a night in the narrow, dirty lanes of Suakim was not inviting. The place was as full of uncleanliness as a pigsty; and for the porcine species there were legions of mangy, wolfish dogs howling and prowling —far more objectionable to anyone wanting quiet sleep, Suakim boasts a native bazaar that counts for nothing beyond myriads of flies, fruit, dates, Arab sweetmeats, greasily-cooked lentils, beans, and fish. It also had one European *café* and two shops, the latter part hardware, part provision, part drapery stores.

I wandered about searching for quarters. Mussulmen don't take in "single gentlemen lodgers," and, with two or three exceptions, even if they did, rather than become the inmate of some of their reeking hovels, I should have preferred to have passed the night in the streets, or migrated to the mainland. There were half-a-dozen Europeans in Suakim who had hired houses, and had set up establishments. A few years ago there was not one living in the place, and until quite recently not an Englishman had ever been domiciled in the town. Meeting the British Consul, Mr. Baker, he kindly asked me, if I did not succeed in finding quarters, to come to his abode, and sleep for the night on a divan. A few minutes later a fellow-correspondent came up and asked me, not having found quarters, whether I would share in his mess, and that of two or three others who were putting up at the residence of an Austrian subject, named Guido Levi. Would I? Delighted at the chance, I followed him to a three-storey, square-built house on the north side of the island, and quite close to the causeway that connects Suakim with the mainland. The causeway is about 100 yards long by 40 feet in width, and at the island side there is a huge arched stone gateway, with a strong double door, which is kept closed at night, and guarded by Egyptian soldiers. The door, however, is opened at any hour during the night, if you wish to pass in or out. Mr. Levi's mansion, like that of every house in Suakim, had no glass windows, but, instead of these usually considered indispensable adjuncts, had wooden shutters fitted with Venetian screens. These shutters themselves were an innovation and a novelty, for most of the houses were without even such a luxury as that. The builders had left openings enough, that served to let in "sweetness" and light; and the natives, to impede the ingress of a too plentiful supply of these blessings, were accustomed to hang mats over these openings. But in a climate like the Soudan, where cold and rainy weather are phenomenal, if you have a roof over your head to keep the heavy dews off which come down at certain seasons, you really require nothing more. With a good rug or blanket, the open air need not be feared for a bivouac by even delicate persons, except among the hills and in winter.

Our landlord, Mr. Levi, was quite a celebrity. He had visited the camp of Osman Digna, with whom he had a bygone acquaintance when that vigorous Arab dwelt, traded, and speculated in Suakim. Osman rather feared his wily, whilom friend, and Mr. Levi was not favoured with much of his society during the visit he paid to him and his warriors at Tamaai camp. The visit was made in the interest of the Egyptian Government, and was undertaken at the time Baker Pasha went to that neighbourhood for the purpose of obtaining information about the enemy's numbers and position. Osman, a tall, thin man, with a short, brownish beard, pretended to be exceedingly devout, and frequently retired by himself to engage in prayer. He seemed perpetually afraid of assassination, and even suspected him, Mr. Levi said. That gentleman wanted Osman to stop the war and come in and discuss the situation with the English officers, but the Arab would not entertain the proposal. His followers used Mr. Levi rather roughly, hustling him about and threatening his life repeatedly. Levi, for the time, became a Mussulman, donned the approved costume—a sort of night shirt and a bath towel wrapped round your head—accepted the Mahdi, and recommended himself highly to the more fanatical by his apparent devoutness. A good opportunity occurring one night after he had been about a week in the rebels' camp, living on coarse Arab fare, he gave them the slip, and ran back to Suakim arriving in a truly pitiable, broken-down condition.

We agreed to board with Mr. Levi, he finding the food and cooking our meals for us. The room to which I was assigned was on the upper storey, and you step out of a doorway on to the flat roof of one of the wings of the house. This roof was used as my bath and dressing room. At first I had no bed, but speedily an iron bedstead was erected and a cotton mattress put thereon. Blankets and sheets were too great luxuries to expect. A deal table was subsequently added, and it was thus I lived, slept, and was "at home".

to all callers. There were six of us Europeans boarded at Mr. Levi's. We usually had breakfast about 7.30 a.m., lunch any time, and dinner any hour between 7 and 9 p.m. Our army friends were wont to drop in whenever they passed, and as we stood on the highway between the town and the mainland, and the troops were all quartered outside, we saw a great many of them. Sometimes our acquaintances from the Government House or the fleet would drop in to dine, and after the day's news-hunting and writing, we would entertain our friends and have jolly sing-song evenings. Suakim, perhaps, never saw or heard so much campaign merriment, so much discussing of battles, anecdote telling, capering, fencing, dancing, and singing from the day the first mud brick was laid in the place. Major Mills and many of the officers of the Highland regiments sang finely, and "our boarding house" party helped to swell the quota of fun and good-fellowship.

Our landlord enjoyed it like the rest, and used to go into convulsions of laughter at some of the antics the "youngsters" occasionally played. The amusement kept us all in good spirits, and there was perhaps more of an eye to business in it than a casual observer would dream of. My servant and horses arrived a few days after I reached Suakim, and I had them safely landed and stabled at the water's edge alongside of Mr. Levi's house. They were faithfully groomed, and what with a regular sea-bath they were soon in the pink of condition. Every day I took them out for a little canter, riding around to the camp on the mainland to inquire at General Graham's headquarters, and see the different officials there, who kept us informed as to all intended movements of the troops. A ride to the wells and Forts Carysfort and Euryalus—which were a mile to the westward—and a run outside also formed part of my ordinary day's routine. The forts named are two of a series of detached earthworks, which bar any attack upon the harbour and town from the westward. They are connected together by an extended earthwork parapet and trench which in semicircular form encloses a considerable portion of the mainland. The huge barrier of earth thus thrown up should make any land attack from that side difficult to an enemy with artillery, and impossible of success to a force without guns. The weak points in the chain of defensive works are at the north and south ends, where the trench runs down towards the sea, but is not carried quite across the low ground, terminating before it reaches the water. A detached work at either extremity would close the gaps thus left, but no doubt it was contemplated that the shipping in the harbour could be left to do that if occasion demanded. A flat, dry water-course runs from the hills and approaches the parapet near Forts Carysfort and Euryalus. A breach has been left for the water in the rainy season to flow through down to the sea. Just outside this point there are a number of wells of good water which contain a plentiful supply the whole year. Three large sycamore trees afford ample shade close to the water, and there are a number of date trees growing about nourished by the moisture drawn from the damp soil. Their strength and greenness are a pleasant relief to the otherwise treeless and withal barren landscape. The Marines and Blue-jackets held the two forts already named.

CHAPTER XIII.

EVENTS AT SUAKIM.

EVENTS were moving on apace at Suakim, and we were increasing the area of the excursions outside the forts into the country. One day the Marines in a small fort called my attention to two armed "Johnnies"— the name by which we dubbed all the Arabs—hanging about, 800 or 900 yards away. I rode out to where the men were, circled around one, "coaxed" him to lay down his spear and shield, and marched him in triumph our first prisoner into Fort Carysfort. An inquiry was instituted. The savage turned out to be friendly, and next day, with thanks, his spear and shield, which I had secured as trophies, were returned him. It was hard on me; but if Arabs will go about undressed, looking exactly like enemies, when, as they state, they are hunting after their strayed goats and camels grazing outside our lines, what other fate can one expect?

I must now let the reader resume the perusal of some more of my telegrams, sent home at this period:

Suakim, March 16 (7.5 p.m.)

According to one of the Sinkat survivors, Osman Digna, learning we had spared stores and grain at Dubba and Afafeet, sent to bring them to his camp at Tamanieb, seventeen miles out from Suakim.

Captain Parr has organised Mounted Infantry from the Marines; twenty joined from the *Carysfort*.

The *Humber*, *Teddington*, and *Osiris* have arrived from Trinkitat; and the Black Watch, 10th Hussars, 65th Engineers, and camels are being disembarked therefrom.

Suakim, March 7 (12.50 p.m.)

More transports have arrived from Trinkitat. Mahmoud Ali, the chief of Fadlab, sent his son to-day to announce that he was coming in. Colonel Tuson, Deputy-Governor, and a few officials went out about a mile on the north side of the bay, and met Mahmoud, who was still dressed in the red coat Baker Pasha had presented to him. He had with him about a hundred of his warriors. There came in also Mahomed Hassab, chief of the Nourabs, who, with the Fadlabs, dwell in the Amarar country. The warriors had the usual weapons. Sixty camels came into the Custom House, escorted by a company of Abyssinians.

Scouts state that Osman Digna is still at Tamanieb. Whether he will fight or not is uncertain. Mahmoud has 3,000 warriors.

Suakim, March 7 (Friday) (1.30 p.m.)

The Sheikhs Mahmoud and Mahomed state that 1,000 of Osman Digna's men, sent to Teb, were slain in the fight.

The first deputation from the tribes who fought against us at Teb, and other hostile tribesmen, will come in this afternoon. A few days must intervene before the tribes with Osman decide upon their future course. Many are now wavering as the news of our victory spreads. It is not yet time, however, to treat for peace.

As at El Teb so at Suakim, attempts were made by means of messengers, peace proclamations, and correspondence, to get the rebels to disperse or come in, before we actually sallied forth to give battle. Our overtures, as then, were doomed to come to naught; for Osman encouraged his followers with the tale, that, though defeated at first—as the Mahdi himself in his conflicts with the unbelievers—he had always prevailed in the end, and would again. Besides, he added, a mistake had been made in dealing out the wrong talismanic bullet-proof shirts and robes. Osman and the Mahdi had followed historic precedent, and gone into the old clothes line of giving to their adherents blessed garments that would turn aside evil, sickness, and death.

Here is the correspondence that passed between the Arabs and our commanders:

"PROCLAMATION.

"We, the English Admiral and General, ask the sheikhs to come and meet us at Suakim.

"We warned you that England had come to relieve Tokar, and that your wrongs, under which you had so long suffered, should be redressed.

"You trusted in the notorious scoundrel Osman Digna, who is well known to you as a bad man; his former life at Suakim has shown it. He has led you away with the foolish idea that the Mahdi had come on earth.

"We tell you that the Great God that rules the universe does not allow such scoundrels as Osman Digna to rule over men.

"Your people are weak, and England always spares such people.

"Awake, then, out of your delusions. Chase Osman Digna from your country, and we promise that you shall be protected, and pardon granted to all.

"Come in at once, or the fate of those who fell at El Teb will surely overtake you.

"W. HEWETT, Rear-Admiral.
"G. GRAHAM, Major-General.
"March 5, 1884."

"[ENCLOSURE No. 2.]

"To the Sheikhs of the Tribes in Arms at Tamanieb.

"We, the Admiral of the English Fleet and the General of the English Army assembled at Suakim, hereby summon you to disperse peaceably and return to your homes.

"The English army will march to your camp, in the valley of Tamanieb, and will treat any who may be found there in arms as rebels, in the same way as those at Teb were treated.

"Be warned in time, and listen no more to the evil counsels of Osman Digna. If you have wrongs to be redressed send delegates to Khartoum to meet Gordon Pasha, who, as you all know, is a good and just man.

"If you desire to send your delegates to us we promise to keep them from harm, and to send their statements by telegraph to Gordon Pasha, from whom we can have an answer for you in a day.

"We desire you to send a reply by the bearer; or the consequences will be on your own heads."

"[ENCLOSURE No. 3.]

"(Translation.)

"In the name of the most merciful God, the Lord be praised, the gracious God, pray to the prophet our lord Mohamed and his people.

"From the whole of the tribes and the sheikhs who received your writings, and those who did not receive them, to the Commandant of the English soldiers. God help them to Islam. Amen.

"Then your letters have arrived with us, and what you have informed us in them to come over (or deliver), then know that the most gracious God has sent his Mahdi suddenly, who was expected, the looked-for messenger for the religious, and against the infidel, so as to show the religion of God through him, which has happened. You may have seen who have gone to him from the people and soldiers, who are countless, God killed them, so look at the multitudes. (Verses of the Koran.)

"You hate God from the beginning who never know religion until after death. Then we are sure that God, and God only, sent the Mahdi, so as to take away your property, and you know this since the time of our lord Mohamed's coming. (Pray to him to be converted.) There is nothing between us but the sword, especially as the Mahdi has come to kill you unless God wishes you to Islam.

"The Mahdi's sword be on your necks wherever you may escape, and God's iron be on your necks wherever you may go.

"Do not think that you are enough for us, and the Turks are only a little better than you.

"We will not have your heads unless you become Mussulmans and listen to the Prophet and the laws of God. And God said in his dear book, those who believe him fight for him, and those who do not believe him shall be killed. (Here follow verses from the Koran referring to it being permitted to kill infidels.)

"Therefore, God has waited for you for a long time, and you have thought that he would always go on waiting for you. God said he would wait for you as you were bad people; but, know that during the time of the Mahdi, he will not accept bribes from you, and also will not leave you in your infidelity, so there is nothing for you but the sword, so that there will not remain one of you on the face of the earth. Therefore, Islam.

"Sealed by the Sheikhs of the following tribes:— Hahalab, Samelab, Humdab, Omrah, Abdel Rahnamab, Bischariab, Shebidinab, Sherab, Meshab, Samarab, Gidab, Mohamed el Amim, Ahmed el Kulhabi, Sheikh of Khorahad, and eight other Sheikhs.

"ALF. B. BREWSTER, Sub-Governor, &c.

"The original is returned herewith.—A. B. B."

CHAPTER XIV.

ADVANCING TO ATTACK OSMAN DIGNA.

THE troops having nearly all been got together at Suakim, and everything having been prepared as rapidly as possible for another advance against the enemy, not a moment was wasted in setting the little army in motion. The Transport, Naval and Military, the Ordnance, the Medical, and the other Departments worked without stopping to bring the campaign to a speedy and successful close. The enemy were not allowed long to recover from their defeat at El Teb, as may readily be gathered from the date of this new movement, as well as from what followed:

Suakim, March 9 (8.0 p.m.)

The force is now all at Suakim except a wing of the 60th Rifles, which, with the rest of the stores, embarked to-day in the transports *Abydos* and *Rinaldo* at Trinkitat, and will sail early to-morrow for Suakim, finally abandoning Trinkitat. On Saturday and Sunday we were busily occupied in disembarking camels and mules on the islet of Suakim, and stores on the mainland, south harbour, where the camp is formed. The tents are numerous, and present an imposing appearance, many, however, being pitched on an old Arab graveyard. The men are fairly comfortable, though several cases of mild diarrhœa have occurred among the troops. The weather is warm, and the heat is telling.

At eight o'clock this morning a squadron of the 10th Hussars, under Major Gough, Colonel Stuart and others going with them, scouted to the south-west as far as Baker's zereba, eight miles out, but saw no signs of the enemy. They went a mile and a half beyond, towards the mountain range, without entering the defiles, and selected the zereba for an advanced camp. It is square, has 100 yards of front, and is enclosed by two feet of earthen mound and brush.

Osman's camp is in the valley, nine miles to the westward of the zereba. The cavalry found the country tolerably open, though there is some mimosa nearer to the hills, yet clear ground suitable for mounted troops. The party returned to camp this afternoon. A squadron of the 19th afterwards picketed the ground in front of the outposts at Suakim until dark. Whenever General Graham is able to get three days' supplies and water stored in the zereba, the whole force will move to attack Osman's command, which the best estimate at present attainable puts at 1,900 warriors. The Arabs show a disposition to desert him, and a few keep coming in. It is expected that the force will actually advance on Tuesday night or Wednesday morning.

Suakim, Sunday (8 p.m.)

Baker Pasha and Colonel Burnaby are improving. They will sail on Tuesday for Suez.

Official inquiries respecting the instances of especial bravery amongst the cavalry in the charges made at Teb have resulted in the discovery of numerous cases of men, themselves dismounted, having saved their comrades. Colonel Barrow was rescued by Quartermaster Marshall, of the 19th, and a trumpeter by one of his comrades. These and other cases will be mentioned for recognition.

The zereba referred to got its name from the fact that it had been constructed by General Baker's force, when they advanced on reconnaissance from Suakim. It is far more substantially built than most of the British soldiers' work of the same kind, and the addition of the low mound of earth all round affords perfect security against rifle fire, as the country is quite flat there.

Suakim, March 10 (8 p.m.)

The 42nd have occupied Baker's zereba, having arrived there at eleven forenoon. They were detained at starting, going finally without two cannon, which followed in the afternoon. The battalion, unluckily, did not go on the evening of the 9th, as at first decided, but fell in again and marched out next morning (the 10th), when owing to absence of a breeze and the intense heat, the men were unable to proceed except at the slowest rate, and with frequent halts. Even then there were hundreds of stragglers from the ranks. The officers did all in their power to keep the men together, but it was nearly 1 p.m. before they were all got into the zereba. The Highlanders suffered on the march, as the morning was close and hot, and five men who fell from sunstroke were invalided back to Suakim. Many others were temporarily disabled from heat and exhaustion. Each soldier carried 100 rounds of cartridges, besides his rifle, and the water-bottles were filled at starting, that quantity having to suffice on the journey. As soon as they arrived the bottles were refilled.

The zereba enclosure is too small to hold the entire force; and when the army marches thither the majority will have to camp outside, reserving the zereba for the stores and transport animals. It is unlikely that we shall enlarge the enclosure.

I visited the zereba this morning: light as are its defences, accurately described yesterday, they are sufficient to enable infantry to withstand any attack, except shell fire.

Some one, smoking, set fire to-day to the sparse grass and bush covering the plain. The flames crackled and spread in every direction, and the horizon was soon covered with smoke. It was like a prairie fire—the birds and animals scampering from the flames—but without its volume or intensity, as bald spaces of sand divided the fire. The wind carried it south of the zereba, and the soldiers easily prevented it from burning the surrounding brushwood. The ammunition was protected, meantime, by the men's blankets, Colonel Green directing everything.

Camels and mules, conveying water and stores, have been passing out all day, and already there are 10,000 gallons of water and a large quantity of ammunition and food in store. Nine convoys went out, and to-morrow the number will be doubled.

The orders which were issued directing the troops to advance to the zereba on Tuesday were countermanded to-night. This was owing to the experience gained in getting the 42nd out, and was for the purpose of having the others brought out in the cool of the morning or evening.

It is probable that the rest of the force will go to the zereba on Wednesday, and march thence for Osman's mountain camp.

Should the rebels retire inland without fighting, the force will return. Our army will be the same as that which fought at Teb, with one exception—the Marine battalion will be increased to 600. The total number of the troops will be 4,200 rifles.

The Naval Brigade will be commanded by Commander Rolfe, of the flagship.

Small parties of the 'friendly tribes' continue to come in.

Suakim, March 11 (8.15 p.m.)

The infantry composing the expedition against Osman Digna's force left the camp at six to-night to march to Baker's zereba. A bright moonlight favours the men, who thus escape the noonday heat. The cavalry remain here to water their horses. They will set out at six o'clock to-morrow morning, thus saving the supply stored at the front.

Our troops will be the same that fought at El Teb, the only additions being an increase of 200 in the strength of the Marine battalion and a mule battery from the navy of four 9-pounders, Major Holley, of the Artillery, commanding this detachment.

The 1-6 Scottish Division Royal Artillery, with 7-pounders, paraded at the wells, close to the Marines' camp at El Kaff. The men were in fine spirits, and all looked fit and ready, the weak and sickly having been weeded out during the last two days by the doctors, and ordered to remain in camp. General Buller took command of the force, which trudged off in column, each man carrying 100 cartridges, and full water bottles. General Graham and his Staff went forward two hours later.

The present order is that, when the cavalry arrives at the zereba to-morrow, after the horses have rested, they will make a reconnaissance towards the hills at Tamaai, not Tamanieb Khor, on the river, which is some miles to the south. According to the latest information from spies and 'friendlies,' Osman is encamped there. The natural defences of the valley are further said to have been strengthened by the advice of Sayd Khameesa, and the Egyptians from Tokar and elsewhere, who are with the rebels. The enemy, it is said, have both rifles and cannon. To-morrow afternoon the whole force will march from the zereba, going about six miles to the south, and within four miles of the enemy's camp. Unless we are attacked or a fight is brought on, we shall bivouac there, and on Thursday morning probably push on to Osman's headquarters.

To-day convoys have been going constantly to the zereba. Last night half-a-dozen Egyptian camel-drivers thought they saw the rebels in their path, and of course the Egyptians bolted, leaving the stores and camels to their fate. The animals came in unloaded during the night.

About eleven o'clock this forenoon Colonel Green, commanding the 42nd, heliographed into camp that between 200 and 300 rebels were on foot, and that camels were sweeping around on the left, as if to cut off the convoys. The Mounted Infantry trotted to meet them, and two miles south of the line of communications the enemy opened fire at long range. Our men got close and returned it, and the rebels at once ran off. There were no casualties.

The sunstroke patients are improving, several having returned to duty. Suakim is full of natives, who may prove a source of trouble. To-day a party of them engaged in loading camels struck work for no assignable cause. The garrison here will be composed of Marines and invalids.

Baker's Zereba, (viâ Suakim),
March 12 (3.20 P.M.)

It was midnight before the Infantry Brigades and Artillery arrived here, and bivouacked just in rear, the regiments lying down in the square formation.

Even the night march was fatiguing.

This morning at six the cavalry paraded, and came on at a walk, arriving about ten.

After early dinner the whole force fell in, and moved out from the zereba towards Tamaai (formerly called Tamanieb), starting about 1 p.m. Cavalry scouts covered the advance, extending two miles on the front and flanks, the main body walking in rear of the infantry.

A grey haze obscured everything, so that it was impossible to see distant objects clearly.

The order of the advance from Baker's zereba is illustrated by the following. The character of the ground at times necessitated the throwing out or drawing in of portions of the force, distorting the straight lines shown.

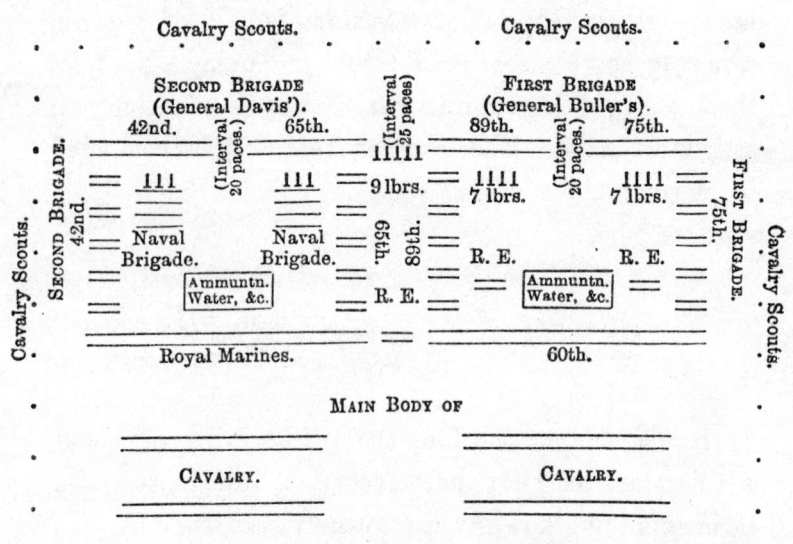

```
                    Cavalry Scouts.              Cavalry Scouts.
   •           •                         •                          •           •
                SECOND BRIGADE                    FIRST BRIGADE
                (General Davis').                 (General Buller's).
                42nd.    (Interval   65th.        89th.   (Interval   75th.
                         20 paces.)                       20 paces.)
   •     ≡ ≡    ≡ 111  ≡  ≡ 111  ≡ 11111 ≡ 1111  ≡   ≡ 1111 ≡    ≡   •
Cavalry  SECOND                    9 lbrs. 7 lbrs.     7 lbrs.   FIRST   Cavalry
Scouts.  BRIGADE  Naval    Naval  (Interval               R. E.  BRIGADE Scouts.
         42nd.   Brigade. Brigade. 25 paces.) R. E.              75th.
                 ┌──────┐         65th.  ┌──────┐
                 │Ammuntn│ ≡ ≡  89th. ≡  │Ammuntn│
                 │Water,&c│              │Water,&c│
                 └──────┘  ═ ═  R. E.    └──────┘
                Royal Marines.            60th.
   •           •      MAIN BODY OF        •                         •
                ─────────────────   ─────────────────
                     CAVALRY.             CAVALRY.
                ─────────────────   ─────────────────
   •       •         •    Cavalry Scouts and Mounted Infantry.    •       •
```

The oblongs also were at times thrown out of alignment by the nature of the ground the troops had to pass over. The sailors dragged the machine guns with ropes.

The infantry, it will be seen, moved in an oblong, or rather two squares going side by side, making an oblong, front and rear being longest. One half-battalion of the 42nd were in line, behind the left rear, the other half of the battalion was in column. After an interval of twenty paces, came in similar formation, the York and Lancaster; and in rear of both regiments the Marines. The ammunition and water were in the centre of the square; while the Naval Brigade was on the right and left corners front, all forming the 2nd Brigade.

On the 2nd Brigade's right, after an interval of twenty-five paces, came the 89th; then, after an interval of twenty paces, the 75th, in the same formation as the two leading regiments of the 2nd Brigade. In rear of the 89th and 75th were the 60th. In the centre of the 1st Brigade square were also ammunition and water. On their left was the 9-pounder battery, lent from the navy, of M 1, R.A.; on the right the 7-pounder battery; and behind each battery the Royal Engineers.

The Mounted Infantry and Abyssinian scouts started out at seven in the morning to "drum up" the enemy.

Osman's forces were found in the place already stated, and smaller bodies of rebels were seen extended right and left of his position for several miles.

I was accompanied by two natives, who were hired as runners, in addition to my servant, for special express. The natives were Fadlabs, and to distinguish them as "friendlies" they carried a piece of white rag in their hands. This enabled them to safely traverse the route back to Suakim. With an enterprise that did them credit, they soon became possessed of sundry strayed mules and donkeys, and even a camel or two, mounted on which, they ambled on their errands, whether to carry despatches or bring up water, forage, and provisions. One of them captured a wandering camel as we went to the front, and we thought at the time the way he set about it was exceedingly clever. The animal was without saddle, bridle, strap, rope or trapping of any kind upon it, and was nibbling and munching the tangled and stringy grass of the barren plain. The Arab longingly eyed the brute and nodding our assent, the fellow trotted towards it, moving as if he were going to pass it. Suddenly he darted at the scrubby bobtail of the camel, clutching it like a vice. The animal tried to shake him off, twist him off, and outrun him. It was useless, for the Fadlab clung to the stumpy tail, pulling always to one side, as if he were trying to steer it in a circle. The struggle was laughable. Without a word, on seeing his tribesman had fast hold, the other Fadlab slipped off his mule, and, with a piece of rope in his hand, ran like a deer for the now frightened camel.

Coming up with the brute, he managed to throw the rope over its long neck, and pulling on it they soon brought the camel down on his knees. The two natives made a halter of the rope, and, both mounting in triumph, rejoined our party a camel richer.

Suakim, March 12 (9.20 P.M.)

Our line of march from the zereba was south-west, and we started at eight minutes past one o'clock. The Mounted Infantry having reported that the low hills were clear of the enemy, it was deemed advisable to gain and occupy that vicinity before dark, and, if practicable, attack the enemy, and drive them out of their camp at the wells.

From the zereba, the dim outline of low black hills

of red granite and syenite could be seen looming up six miles away. Everybody went off in the lightest possible marching order.

The racecourse has its dog always in the way, and an army its runaway mule. Our mule, like his species, got in front of everybody, gaily leading the advance through knee-deep grass, scrub, and underbrush.

In some places the mimosa and cactus were seven feet high. There were very few halts, the infantry, cavalry, and artillery going slowly and steadily. It was said that the rebels would not fight, as they had sent their women and children into the hills. At Teb they kept them, and supplied them with spears and hatchets to kill our wounded. They had not even deigned to reply to General Graham's proclamation, and this, too, was construed into meaning peace.

To facilitate the march in squares, the men moved by fours in companies. Our total front, reckoning the two brigades, was 400 yards, the rear the same and the sides half that length. By a quarter to three we were within a mile and a half of the nearest outlying low hills, the squadrons of the cavalry scouts, extended two miles along our front, were composed of men from the 10th and 19th Hussars, Lieutenant Fanshawe and Major Gough leading them. Riding here and there about the bush they searched it closely without finding any traces of an enemy. They pushed on so fast that they were frequently over a mile in front of the square. I accompanied the scouts the greater part of the time, being desirous of seeing how the Arabs would fare in a skirmish with our men, and what tactics they would adopt.

Generals Graham and Stewart, with their Staffs, rode forward just behind the scouts. By three o'clock the scouts had left the square a mile and a half behind, the guns, which were mostly dragged by men, keeping the infantry back. Half an hour later the cavalry scouts had "circled," and then mounted the outlying low hills.

Going to the top of the highest, about 120 feet, with the Staff, we saw spread out in panoramic view the broad intervening valley of Tamaai. The haze had partly lifted, and opposite to us were low ranges, two miles away, of the same height as those we looked from, the last one being close to the foot of the chain of the Soudan mountains. On these hills we could plainly see the line of our black foes; on more prominent points they clustered thickly, some on foot, and others on camel and horseback.

The infantry square, having arrived about four o'clock at the base of the hill whence we had our outlook, halted for a few minutes. The cavalry scouts were then pushed forward to unmask the enemy's position, and at the same time the square faced south, left flank leading, and marched about 1,000 yards in order to reach rather open and sandy ground, on which were very few bushes, but clear of the rocks and stones, which abounded round the base of the hills. At a quarter-past four the rattle of skirmish fire told us that the cavalry scouts were feeling the enemy in our front. As the scouts pushed up to within 500 yards the Arabs showed in great numbers, and we were able to estimate their force at 5,000 men. Meanwhile the square refaced the enemy, the men quickly dressing up. The firing lasted about ten minutes, finishing as suddenly as it began.

General Graham afterwards issued orders for the men to bivouac where they stood, and for bushes to be cut and a new zereba made. A troop of the 19th, under Lieutenant Walker, afterwards passed along the enemy's front to note the position of the wells. The enemy opened a well-directed fire at short range, wounding Walker slightly. Our men saw a large body of Arabs on the left, whilst small groups stood at intervals along the entire front of their position. The troop did not reply to the fire, but fell back as the enemy came forward.

The operations for the day thus closed, and everything being made snug in the square, the men were directed to take advantage of the semi-circular crest of the sand-ridge. This step, though strengthening the position slightly, altered the lines of the square, which at places were bent outwards. The cavalry were sent back to Baker's zereba to water their horses, and remain there for the night.

We advance to attack the enemy after daybreak to-morrow, as it is too late to push on with success to-night.

That night I slept in the square. When the cavalry went off we all felt how much alone we were and that our lives depended on the courage, cohesion, and discipline of our men encamped there on the open plain within rifle-shot of the huts of a numerous and fierce enemy. While the daylight lingered, we could see hundreds of the black woolly heads of the savage foe, bobbing about among the bushes on the low ridges, scarcely 1,000 yards away.

CHAPTER XV.

THE NIGHT BEFORE THE BATTLE.

In war, more than in anything else affecting human affairs, the improbable often happens. Who could have guessed before the event that a British infantry force would march some seven or eight miles from its advance base into an enemy's country, and halt for the night on a waterless plain within a mile and a half of a running stream from which the soldiers were only barred by a horde of undisciplined savages? Doubtless under all the circumstances General Graham decided wisely in not risking a battle in the waning afternoon, preferring the lesser evil of bivouacking for the night near the foot-hills, putting the force on short commons and a scant supply of water, drawn from the stores carried with the force. With any civilised, or even half civilised, foe on our front the position would have been untenable for an hour, unless we had strengthened it in some other way than by merely placing all around the square a hedge of prickly mimosa bushes. Had the low outlying hill already spoken of as affording an excellent view been taken possession of, and a redoubt or wall of loose stones built thereon we could have held such a position against all comers, moving the bulk of the force out of the range of rifle fire behind the shelter of the hillside. The men were marched from 800 to 1,000 yards to the south, as elsewhere stated, to get quite clear of the rocks. Upon the open plain the newest zereba was quickly made by "details" told off for that purpose from the different regiments. As there was barely enough water to supply the actual wants of the men the cavalry were sent back in the gloaming to Baker's zereba to water the animals there, so that they might return refreshed and full of work next morning. It was like parting with one's best friends to see them ride off leaving us alone in that wilderness. It was a relief to know the troops were to be favoured by a full moon and a cloudless sky, as these would enable the sentries to give timely warning of any attempted night assault on the zereba by the Arabs. Strangely enough all those professing to know anything of the Arab character assured us, that the race disliked darkness and would never assail any position except during daylight, a prediction we lived to see falsified before morning. My servant had been sent back, late on the afternoon of the 12th (Wednesday), to Suakim telegraph station, with the news of the advance and the day's skirmishing, taking at the same time with him the messages of two of my confrères, for we campaigned as friends, the only stipulation being if my servant carried my messages mine should be wired first to London. We managed to make shift to have a fairly good meal of biscuits and canned meat, and, having secured some water, washed it all down with very substantial tea. The horses were not neglected, but were watered, cleaned, fed, and tethered to a small bush for the night, near which we had decided to plant ourselves till morning. The currying of the poor brutes was on a liberal scale, but the feeding and watering were meagre. Little as they had, it was sufficient to keep them in spirits and mettle beyond many others less fortunately situated. Major Cholmondeley Turner, of the Egyptian Service, who had charge of the Egyptian Carrier Corps, did what he had often done before: after the cavalry returned to Baker's zereba. He marched out with a number of camels carrying water and forage, getting into camp between nine and ten o'clock. Their arrival was a most welcome event, as it ensured a good supply for the morning of that genuine necessity—water. Tired with their day's exertion the infantry lay down about twelve feet within the line of the irregularly shaped square formed by the mimosa bushes. The men were two deep, officers in rear, and they slept with their great-coats on and their arms in their hands. Between the mimosa hedge and the sleeping soldiers, walked the vigilant sentinels, keenly on the alert, as each man knew the peril of the situation. The hedge having been made by cutting bushes on the immediate front of the faces of the square, this left a clear open belt of 50 to 100 yards, across which any enemy would have to charge in full view of our troops. After walking about the camp, I lay down in as soft a place as could be got on the stony ground, and drawing my blanket over me, was soon fast asleep. About one o'clock in the morning we were awakened by one of those terrible weird rushes of sound, half cry, half roar, that mark all night alarms. There was á crash and whizzing as a hundred rifle bullets flew overhead, a babel of voices, the snort and neigh of horses, and a chorus of echoes from neighbouring rocks, that startled all into wakefulness in a moment. I rushed to saddle my horse, calling to my colleagues to do the same, and as the bullets went pinging past, clapped on bridle and saddle as quickly as possible. Before getting half through with the work, we realised that we were not about to endure an assault, but were only in for a night's skirmish fire. I visited the battalions, walking around the square, and afterwards went to the ambulance waggons, seeing the doctors and others, and learning who were injured. Going back to my bush near the General's headquarters, I wrote out by the bright moonlight the following paragraphs, briefly descriptive of that night's bivouac, and then lay down and went to sleep, resting soundly till 5 a.m. After adding a few words at reveille the following messages were sent :

Tamaai (*viâ* Suakim), March 13 (12.15 p.m.)

Shortly after sunset last night, the infantry were formed into a single large square, the intervals all being closed. General Graham ordered five shots from our 9-pounders to be fired into the enemy's central position. The range was 2,000 yards. The shells burst over the enemies' heads, and apparently did execution; thereafter all was quiet for a time.

About eleven o'clock Commander Rolfe, having got permission, stole out of the camp alone to observe the enemy. He returned about midnight, and reported having seen Arab pickets a mile and a half in front. He passed two of their dead killed by our shells, and saw six men asleep. Creeping among the bushes to the top of the ridge, he was able to see the enemy's numerous camp fires in the hollow close beside the wells.

At a quarter to one in the morning several parties of Arabs who had approached to within 1,000 yards of our camp on the S.W. and S.E. sides opened a sharp rifle fire upon the square. Their shots mostly were too high, but one or two animals were hit, and an Egyptian driver received a slight wound.

On the first alarm our men were speedily on the alert, waiting with their Martinis grasped in their hands, ready to receive the Arabs.

The bright moonlight was favourable to us, as objects were visible for a considerable distance, and any sudden rush could have been quickly checked.

At this moment an Egyptian camel-driver jumped over the prickly mimosa bushes, which had been cut and piled two to three feet high, just outside the square. As he bolted past the lines, some of our men thinking he was one of the enemy, shot at him, and he fell dead, pierced with half-a-dozen bullets.

Three of our own fellows received accidental bayonet wounds from their comrades, whilst rushing to the front, but within the square there was no commotion, even the Egyptian drivers and carriers recognising that 1,000 British bayonets interposed on every side between them and the enemy.

A Gardner gun was placed in position on our left front for use if needed, but the General's orders were for the men to lie quiet till the foe came close, and not a shot of any kind was fired from our ranks.

The Arabs kept up a persistent fusillade till just before daybreak, killing one man, Private Sheldon, of the 65th (who was shot in the head while lying down), and inflicting a few slight casualties.

About four in the morning Mr. Wyld and the Abyssinian scouts crept out towards enemy's firing party on our left. They state it was composed of 150 men, supported by others, and that the enemy appeared in force.

The scouts were seen by the Arabs, pursued and fired at, but they got back without sustaining any loss.

The night's bivouac was not altogether a pleasant one. On first settling down in camp the men kindled fires and made coffee, but all lights were ordered out at nine, and those who were without blankets suffered from cold before the morning.

Many passed a sleepless night, the rifle fire disturbing their repose. The enemy made a point of aiming at the two hospital waggons, the high-rounded tops of which stood out conspicuous in the moonlight. As a consequence, the doctors and General Graham's Staff had many narrow escapes, Colonel Clery just escaping a bullet which struck the ground at his feet.

At six o'clock in the morning (sunrise), the Gardner and one of the 9-pounders were turned upon the enemy, who were then within 1,300 yards. The guns made excellent practice, speedily dispersing the Arabs, who retired to their main position near the wells of Tamaai.

General Stewart arrived from Baker's zereba with his cavalry about half-past six, and at seven a few squadrons trotted off to our left to turn the right of the enemy's position.

Our present camp is two miles south-west of the old battle-field where Kassim Effendi and his 600 black troops were annihilated several months ago.

CHAPTER XVI.

THE BATTLE OF TAMAAI.

THE first news of the victory of Tamaai was wired from Suakim to England in the following despatch of General Graham, of which I had the honour to be the bearer. By official order, all messages were to be held till its arrival and despatch, and, although I offered my brief message first, under the instruction, it had to be kept back till the General's was sent off.

"Official telegram from Sir G. Graham to the Secretary of State for War, dated Osman Digna's Camp, March 13, 11.40 a.m.:

'Camp taken, after hard fighting since eight o'clock.

'Killed, over 70, among whom Montresor, Almack, H. Stewart, Naval Brigade; Aitken, Royal Highlanders; Ford, York and Lancaster. About 100 wounded.'"

The following is the narrative of the battle. The story is told in a somewhat disjointed way, having been broken into sections to secure promptness in wiring and delivery in London.

BATTLE OF TAMAAI
13th March 1884.

From a sketch by Lt Colonel H E Colvile Gr Gds

Reference

1st position of Brigades shown thus ☐
2nd position .... ☒
The Cavalry are shown in position taken to cover 2nd Brigade ....
Mounted Infantry are shown in position taken up to cover first advance. ....
Huts of Osman's encampment. .... ▲▲ ▲▲▲
The huts and tents were hidden in flat sandy depressions.
Heaps of enemy's dead .... ∴∴∴
Zeriba Nº 2 was the bivouac on nights of 12th & 13th

Plain with scattered mimosa bushes.

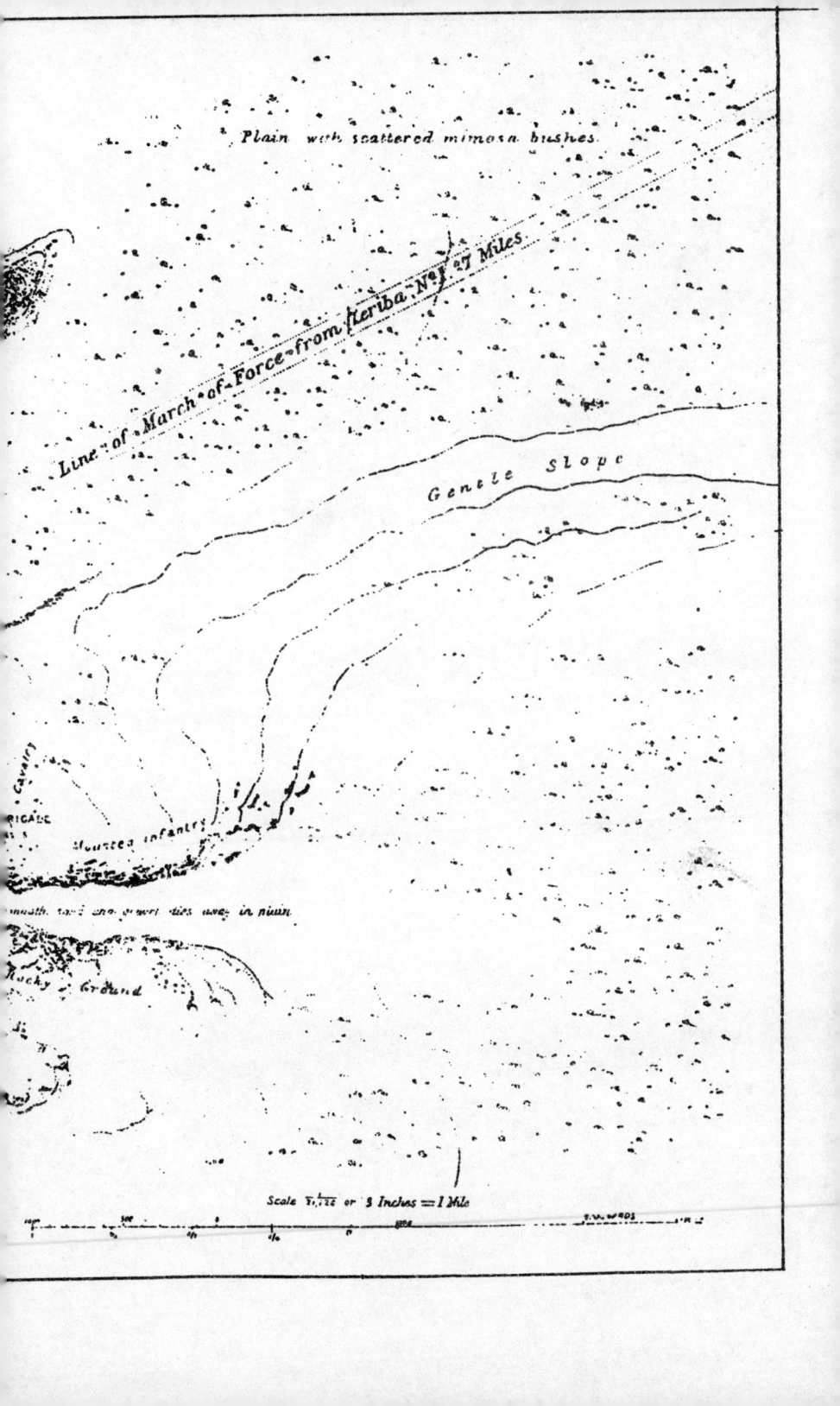

Line of March of Force from Heriba. N°1 27 Miles

Gentle Slope

Cavalry
RIGADE
Mounted Infantry

mouth and one power dies away in plain

Rocky Ground

Scale 1/21120 or 3 Inches = 1 Mile

THE BATTLE OF TAMAAI.

Osman Digna's Camp (*viâ* Suakim),
March 13 (1.45 p.m.)

We advanced from bivouac at eight this morning in two brigades, formed precisely as yesterday, but separated by a wider interval, and in échelon. Artillery and Royal Engineers were placed with oblong of 1st Brigade. A series of fights shortly after followed. General Graham, who was with the 2nd Brigade, became first engaged. The Brigade received a check. The enemy making a rush, confusion ensued, particularly among the 65th, and then the same fate befell the Marines. We fell back several hundred yards, losing all our Gatlings and Gardners. The 1st Brigade checked the enemy's onrush, and the 2nd Brigade re-formed, and, after half-an-hour's fighting, recaptured the lost guns. The 1st Brigade then advanced, clearing the nullahs and hills, and finally captured Osman Digna's camp.

I was with both brigades successively in both actions. The camp contains several hundred tents, and has an abundant supply of running water. Fighting is over for the day.

I have brought in General Graham's despatch announcing the victory.

I regret to say our loss is about 100 killed, including a good many officers. The enemy's loss is about 2,400.

Suakim, March 13 (2.30.)

I have just galloped in from Osman Digna's camp, which our troops have taken after four hours' hard fighting.

There have been a series of contests, in which on at least one occasion we had for a short time the worst of it.

In the end, however, discipline, pluck, and superior weapons enabled us to defeat the enemy, who fell back among the rough red granite ranges of the Soudan, to where it was impossible to follow them.

Our force will encamp to-night at Digna's camp, otherwise Tamaai, where there is plenty of good water. There are also hundreds of Arab tents in the khor, most of which are filled with loot of various kinds.

General Graham will probably send some of the cavalry a short way up the valleys, to drive the enemy further off; but unfortunately the country is much broken up, and very difficult for man or beast.

To resume my connected narrative of to-day's movements and fighting.

Our troops left the scene of the bivouac at eight o'clock, marching in the same formation as yesterday, by brigades. To-day, however, the brigades were separated by an interval of 1,000 yards.

They moved in échelon, the 2nd Brigade leading. This Brigade was composed of the 42nd, 65th, Royal Marines, and Naval Brigade, with Gardners and Gatlings.

The 1st Brigade comprised the 89th, Gordon Highlanders, 60th Rifles, with Royal Artillery, nine and seven pounder batteries, and Royal Marines.

As the 2nd Brigade moved off to the left or

southerly direction, led by General Davis, it was joined by General Graham and Staff.

We could plainly see the enemy ranged all along the hills on our front and right. Their black forms stood out boldly against the glare of day. Some were within 1,200 yards. The main body, however, appeared to be about a mile away.

Our route lay across dry water-courses towards a deep nullah full of boulders and huge detached rocks.

Meanwhile the cavalry, which had taken up a position on our left rear, sent forward two squadrons, together with the Abyssinians, to skirmish.

These were quickly engaged, and a hot fire was soon raging.

The enemy coming on, the skirmishers fell back, and the 2nd Brigade went forward 700 yards, firing as they went.

The troops had opened out nearly into line, their rear to a great extent being covered by the 1st Brigade, which was half-mile away on our right.

As we gained the edge of the nullah the fire became very hot on our front, the enemy mostly contenting themselves by attempting to rush at us with their spears and swords. The gaps in the square were meanwhile closed.

Our men could not easily be got, despite trumpet calls and officers' shouts, to reserve their fire and aim carefully. In a few minutes our line was obscured by dense smoke from our own rifles, and under cover of this the enemy crept up the sides of the nullah, and a succession of rushes by our brave and resolute foes was made at the troops.

The 65th, who were on the right, and 42nd on extreme left, were nearest the brink of the nullah, which, on 65th's front, made a bend inwards towards them. Marines were in the rear.

The enemy appear to have gathered there 1,000 strong. Creeping up under cover of the smoke and sloping ground they dashed at the Marines and 65th. A hundred swarthy Arabs came bounding over the rocks up the plain, spear and sword in hand. Half were instantly shot down, but thirty or forty were able to throw themselves upon our bayonets, giving and receiving fearful wounds.

Quick as lightning the rush increased, and in less time than it takes to tell the 65th gave way, falling back upon the Marines. To their credit be it ever said many men disdained to run, but went back with their faces to the foe, firing and striking with the bayonet. The bulk of the regiment crowded in upon the Marines, throwing them into disorder, and back everybody was borne in a confused mass, men and regiments being inextricably mixed up.

General Graham and his Staff tried their best to hold and rally the troops, and General Davis and all the officers laboured to get the men to stand their ground in an orderly way. Even the 42nd were thrown into disorder by the general confusion; but here and there the Marines and Highlanders retired slowly, firing steadily at the rushing Arabs, whom they bowled over like ninepins, though, truth to tell, these were instantly replaced by others.

The Naval Brigade, who had been sent to the front with their machine guns, during the rush lost three of their officers and many of their men. The machine guns had to be abandoned, partly owing to the hurried retreat, and partly because of the nature of the ground. The Blue-jackets, despite the misadventure, managed to remove the sights and otherwise temporarily disable the weapons, which all fell into the hands of the rebels.

We came back about 800 yards, moving in a more easterly direction than the line of advance. By this time the fire from the 1st Brigade on our right as well as our front, and the cavalry on our left, held the Arabs; and the officers succeeded in checking the retreat, the Black Watch, who were fairly in hand, and a portion of the Marines largely assisting in stopping what might have been a much more serious disaster to the Brigade.

The Brigade was re-formed, and the men who had got out of their regiments were sent into their own lines again.

I must revert to the way in which several hundreds of Marines and Highlanders fought back to back, firing and retiring in excellent order. They were over 200 yards to the Brigade front when it was halted and re-formed, and to their great coolness and steadiness is largely due the final success of the day. Ten minutes after the rally was effected four Marines brought in a wounded comrade on a stretcher, and a private of the

Black Watch came limping up to the square out of the jaws of death.

In that single struggle we lost over 70 men killed. I counted the bodies of 30 of the 65th and about an equal number of the 42nd within a radius of 50 yards, all shockingly mangled and hewn with sword-cuts and spear-wounds. The Arabs lay dead in hundreds.

I rode over to the 65th corner as they were driven in, and had an ample opportunity of seeing how the enemy did their work. Fearless and daring, they ran amuck, so to speak, at our men, hitting right and left even when themselves badly wounded. It was this very recklessness of death on their part which made them so dreaded. Still, all the same, many of our fellows soon realised that with the bayonet and Martini and coolness they had nothing to fear from the rudely armed and nearly naked savages.

It was nine o'clock by the time when the 2nd Brigade was re-formed and once more re-advanced in lines, going 100 paces, when a quarter of an hour's halt was called. The enemy, meantime, kept up a dropping rifle fire, which, fortunately, did little damage.

The 1st Brigade came up on our right, and a portion of the cavalry moved to our right also, near the bivouac, and with the 100 Abyssinian scouts, began skirmishing with the Arabs, who were trying to creep to our right rear. This time the 2nd Brigade was formed in line—the Royal Marines on the right, the 65th on their left or in centre, and the Black Watch on the extreme left of the

Brigade, and 160 of the Naval Brigade were in their rear. Every man had got a fresh supply of ammunition, about thirty rounds per man having been wasted in the first attack.

The troops were strictly forbidden to fire till the enemy should come well within range, and on this occasion they obeyed orders more faithfully. The Marines were thrown forward to gain the nearest edge of the nullah, and the whole of the men returned to the work most willingly, cheering and pushing along. The soldiers now fired deliberately, and in ten minutes we had regained the lost ground and recaptured the lost machine guns. Thanks to the position taken by the 1st Brigade they were able to pour a raking fire into the enemy, and prevent any attempt to again rush our flanks. We soon cleared the nullah, killing every rebel found behind rock or under bush.

Short as was the time, the Arabs had run one of the Gatlings down into the nullah, and set fire to an ammunition limber belonging to one of the guns. The gun was recovered, but the limber blazed, hissed, and fired shots for half an hour afterwards.

It was now the turn of the 1st Brigade, which was under General Redvers Buller's immediate command. The 2nd was halted on the north of the nullah, and forward, down, and across it went the 1st Brigade. The men were formed in square, the Gordon Highlanders on the right and the 89th on the left being leading regiments, with the 60th in the rear, and the nine and seven pounders, under Major Gough, in the centre.

The objective point was the second intervening ridge, 800 yards off. The red granite boulders and rocks were rugged and sharp and hot, and the march was a most trying one. With a cheer the men took the first ridge, firing, as they went along, occasional shots at the enemy's main body, whom we could see gathered on our right on the second ridge.

The Arab fire in reply to ours was feeble and wild, and they soon began trotting off towards the mountain, as we advanced. General Graham, with a portion of his Staff, directed the advance, and, with a ringing cheer, we carried the second ridge, the defence of which was insignificant.

Gaining the top we saw in the valley Tamaai, 180 feet below, the tents and huts composing the camp of Osman Digna. There were very few Arabs about, and of these the troops soon made short work. A poor wounded negress stood behind a hut bleeding from a wound in the shoulder. Need I say that she was at once attended to. She was the only person visible among the hundreds of deserted tents and huts.

The enemy had evidently beaten a disorderly retreat, for all around lay ammunition and stores. There were also their loot and trophies gained in former victories.

It was eleven o'clock when the 1st Brigade advanced, and by noon all the enemy's positions, as well as his wells, were in our hands. General Graham decided to rest for the day, as the troops had had a fatiguing time, and they formed their bivouac at Osman Digna's camp.

I regret to say our total killed in the day's fighting

THE BATTLE OF TAMAAI. 161

is about 100 ; the wounded probably just slightly over that number. Among the killed are Lieutenants Montresor, Almack, and Houston Stewart, of the Naval Brigade ; Captain Ford, of the 65th. Major Dalgetty and Dr. Prendergast, of the 65th, wounded slightly. Among the 42nd killed are Major Aitken ; and of the slightly wounded, Major Macdonald. In the Marines 5 men were killed, and about 10 wounded. Of the Gordon Highlanders 3 were killed and 8 wounded. The Mounted Infantry had several wounded.

Of course this list is incomplete and hurriedly got together, but I have inquired at every regiment. Though not troubling you with details, I regret to say that, owing to the embargo and censorship instituted by the naval and military authorities, my messages, although handed in first on wires, must follow Government telegrams.

Suakim, March 13 (5.30 p.m.)

The nullahs were about 60 feet deep and 200 feet to 300 feet wide, with steep sides, almost impassable for cavalry.

At Osman's camp two standards were captured.

Convoys of supplies and 40 Blue-jackets have gone up to Tamaai this afternoon, to bring down the wounded.

The machine guns, as well as the nine and seven pounders, were fired by the troops before and during advance of the 2nd Brigade. The artillery made splendid practice from their position with the

1st Brigade, sending shell after shell bursting among the enemy, who were gathered on the ridges. When the Arabs got very close to the 1st Brigade square, the shells were reversed in the guns, and bursting just in front of the enemy carried death and havoc among them. When the Gatlings were recaptured the sailors had several chances of turning their fire on the Arabs, which they did with telling effect. I again noticed the poor quality of the steel wrought into cutlasses and bayonets for the soldiers. If these weapons touched a bone, they bent like hoop iron without piercing the body of the Arabs. Their spears and swords, sharp as razors, cut, as I saw scores of them do, through bone, sinew, and every obstacle without turning the edge of the weapon. Another matter worth notice was that the savages made better use of their weapons than the troops. When they made a thrust it was invariably for a vital part, about the head, throat, or chest.

Tommy Atkins (the name the British soldier is always known by), after missing his man at short ranges, too often struck in such a way as to make grazing or slight flesh wounds. Two officers of the Black Watch, on the other hand, killed several of the enemy with their claymores, running the blades up to the hilt every time.

Nearly every man present during the fight had narrow escapes occasionally. Colonel Green, of the 42nd, had a spear glance off his holster and his ear cut by a pebble dislodged by a rifle bullet. General Buller had his horse shot through the ear, whilst many officers had their steeds killed.

During the fight a small water convoy coming from the bivouac zereba to the rear of one of the squares was attacked and thrown into panic by a single Arab. The black sergeant of the convoy, a plucky fellow, whose valour was well known, seized his rifle and dropped the rebel.

All sorts of rumours were circulated about Suakim before my arrival, of the troops having sustained a disaster. The news was, it seems, in part heliographed from the zerebas, where, judging as well as the mirage would admit from the manner of the 2nd Brigade's retreat, it was magnified into a rout.

Admiral Hewett found it necessary to stop messages for England based on these rumours, and it was not till my arrival with General Graham's despatch that the news of the result of the day's fighting became known, and press messages were permitted to go on.

CHAPTER XVII.

INCIDENTS AT TAMAAI.

AFTER the description of the chief events in a contest like that of Tamaai, having as it were in the earliest messages given the fullest possible outline, one naturally turns to fill in the details. Everybody was full of them, and for weeks after all who bore part or played witness in that day's work could speak of little else but the fight. It was the King Charles' head in all conversations whether in tent, field, parade, or that most solemn of all events to Englishmen, at dinner. Here is one point from my notes respecting the advance of the 2nd Brigade at Tamaai from the zereba: it was too rapid and the ground in front was not thoroughly cleared of the enemy before we were pushed on to attack the khor. The next few pages also narrate the advance towards and capture of the enemy's camp.

Suakim, Friday (6.30 a.m.).

Although the enemy fell back to the hills, they made off slowly and sullenly. Doubtless the nature of the ground rendered a rapid movement on their part difficult and needless, yet it was plain that they acted like men defeated but not routed.

As our troops carried their ground some of the retiring Arabs would walk away as if sauntering down the Bazaar, with their arms folded or swinging them by their side. Often they were shot down as they thus withdrew, but that did not deter others following their example nor did it hasten their speed.

Judges of native character here, however, say that the Arabs are so allied by family ties to one another that the great loss of life experienced in yesterday's defeat will appal them on reflection, and break their faith in the Mahdi and the representative sheikhs.

Our men who fell, even for a few minutes, into the enemy's hands, were, as at the battle of Teb, dreadfully cut and gashed by sword and spear, but not otherwise disfigured.

We took no prisoners during the fight. Indeed it was impossible to do so, for whilst life lasted the wounded Arabs would lie still rarely uttering a cry or a moan, but watching a chance to strike at our fellows with knife or spear as they advanced. For the victors it was like walking among wounded vipers.

Many of the Arabs got away in spite of their hurts, but it could be but to suffer and die, as the natives are without surgical skill.

During the fight their skirmishers crept among the bushes and behind the rocks and nullahs, all across our front flanks and rear, firing into and threatening the troops on every side.

The cavalry, mounted infantry, and Abyssinian scouts deserved great praise for the way they engaged these parties—checking and repelling them by their fire.

Suakim, Friday (8.10 a.m.)

At Osman Digna's camp three wounded Arabs killed a Marine last night, and another wounded man, whilst General Stewart's aide-de-camp was giving him water, drew a knife and attempted to stab the general.

Two hundred sailors went out last night to bring in the wounded.

Suakim, March 14 (6.50 p.m.)

I have just returned for the second time from Tamaai.

The cavalry last night returned to Baker's zereba, and General Graham, thinking it safer to leave the ravine of Tamaai, burned most of the huts and tents there, and marched the infantry back to the new zereba, about a mile to the north of Tamaai. In both zerebas the troops were undisturbed during the night, not a shot having been fired.

This morning, General Stewart's cavalry having returned to the new zereba, the troops set out about nine o'clock to drive any lurking rebels out of the nullahs and destroy their villages. The infantry advanced in two brigades, each in square and composed of the same regiments as yesterday.

After marching beyond the battle-ground a mile and a half in a south-westerly direction, the infantry squares were halted on the crest of a ridge overlooking a considerable portion of the country.

There were a few rebels to be seen among the higher hills, two miles to the west; so the mounted infantry and some skirmishers were sent forward to fire at long ranges with a view to keep them off. The cavalry then advanced about three-quarters of a mile further, General Graham and his Staff accompanying them.

A large number of Arab huts and tents were found in the last nullah. These dwellings were said to be the town of Tamaai. They were numerous enough to accommodate 6,000 or 7,000 natives. The troops burned them, together with much ammunition found in them. About one o'clock they were all in flames, the smoke rising in immense black volumes, broken here and there by the white vapour of exploding gunpowder.

The effect of this spectacle must have been more telling upon Osman Digna and his followers than any number of proclamations.

The wounded native woman found in the village says that the rebel chief, just before the battle, went off twenty miles into the hills to some holy spot, in order to pray for the success of his men.

After the destruction of the village, the infantry marched back to the new zereba, which later on was altogether evacuated for Baker's zereba, where the infantry and more severely wounded remain for the night, returning to Suakim to-morrow.

The cavalry have already all come into Suakim.

What our next move may be none know here. We await instructions from England. It is, however, expected that after a few days' much-needed rest, to recruit the men and horses, the cavalry will push on to Sinkat, or even beyond that place, to open the Berber road and clear the line of retreat for the garrisons of Berber and Khartoum.

Suakim, March 14 (8.15 p.m.)

I regret to say our loss is 91 killed and 19 missing. The latter may be put down as killed; making a total of 110.

The Regimental returns give 111 as wounded, but only 99 have been received by the Army Medical Department, over which Deputy-Surgeon-General M'Dowell presides.

The Black Watch this morning had the sad duty of interring 60 of their comrades, 40 of whom were laid in one trench. Need one say anything of the mournful scene more than that the dead were carried from the field where they lay, mangled with wounds, to the new zereba, and there accorded Christian burial.

The 65th, who were nearest the bend in the ravine or nullah, in which the enemy gathered for their rush, lost 30 killed.

The great loss of the 42nd should be put down to the stubborn hand-to-hand defence made by the men, and by the enemy getting into their rear through the breaks in the ranks of the other battalions. The smoke from the Martinis, as well as the nature of the ground, enabled the Arabs to gather about 1,500 strong for their charge.

The Naval Brigade was completely disorganised for a time, through the temporary loss of the machine guns and so many of their officers.

The Highlanders tried to protect the guns with their battalion, but the enemy came crowding on so thick and fast, despite bullets, swords, and bayonet-thrusts, that they fairly forced the position the 2nd Brigade had taken, close to the edge of the nullah.

The practice of the Arabs, both at El Teb and Tamaai, was to rush down upon us with a thick round cow or rhinoceros-hide shield in their left hands, grasping in the same hand a sword or spear. In their right hands they generally carried a short bent stick like what is used in the Scotch game of "shinty" or Irish "hurly." When within ten paces of the soldiers, without pausing, they would throw the piece of wood violently in our men's faces; then, seizing the weapon from their left hand, charge full at us. Upon their feet they wore a kind of sandal. It was merely a leather sole, tied round the great toe and ankle with a piece of thong.

As to the wounded, there are 24 cases classed as severely, 50 as less severely, and the remainder as not dangerously hurt.

Many men received slight wounds and contusions, of which no report was made. The latter were caused chiefly by the thick bent sticks which the Arabs threw into the soldiers' ranks as they charged, and by pieces of stone.

This afternoon 200 sailors and 200 of the Black Watch were detailed to carry the more severely wounded on stretchers from the front down to Baker's zereba. The Medical Department had a busy time, but all of the sufferers were attended to before starting.

The convoys back to the base formed a most mournful procession. The less dangerous cases were brought straight through to Suakim, either in ambulances, waggons, cacolets, or on horseback.

Among the slightly wounded who are doing well are Captain St. Leger Herbert, attached to General Stewart's Staff, and Surgeon Cross, of the *Téméraire*.

As my pen-and-ink rough sketch of the position of the two squares at the critical moment differs materially from the official plan regarding the exact location of the troops and the point to which they fell back, it is submitted on the next page.

PLAN OF THE BATTLE.

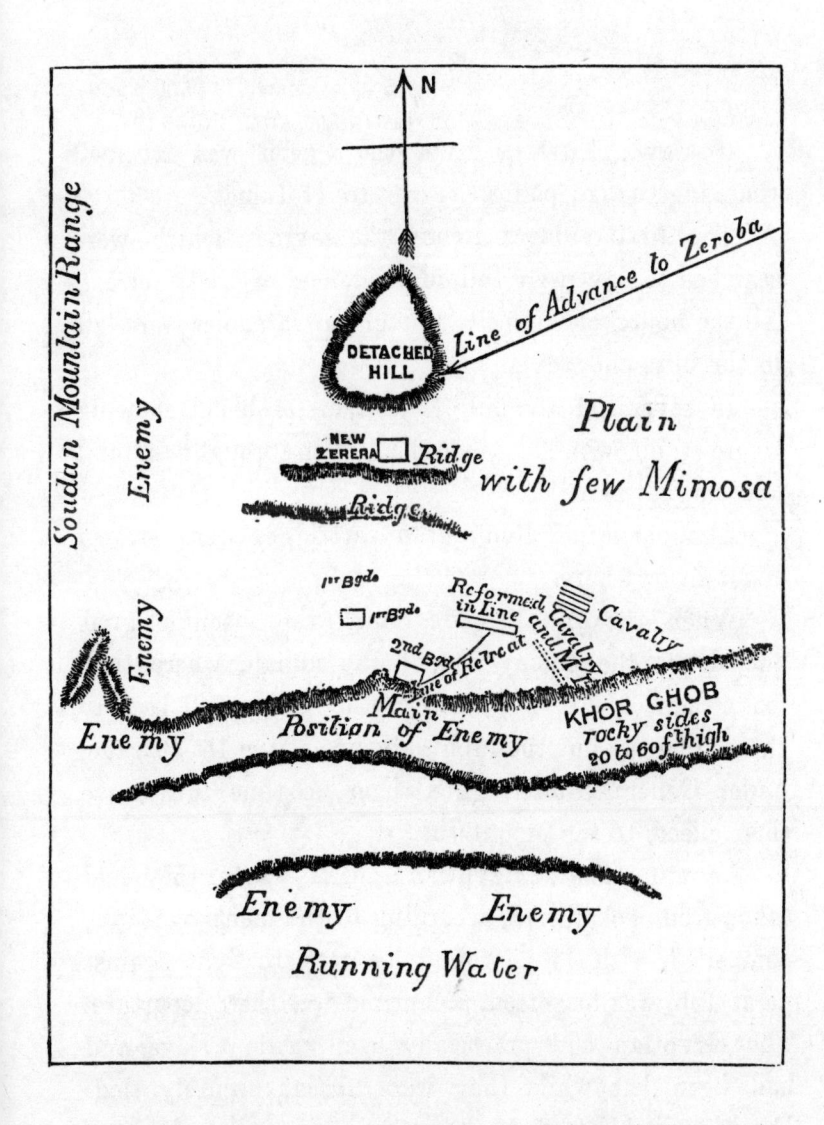

M. I. means Mounted Infantry. The enemy's dead lay to the south of the zereba all about the 1st Brigade square, and very thickly near the indent in khor, where the 2nd Brigade square advanced to and from there, fully half way to where they halted and re-formed, not in square but in line.

Suakim, March 14 (9.50 p.m.)

To-day a message from the Queen was received thanking the troops for the capture of Tamaai.

The Arab villages among the ravines, which were searched to-day, were full of evidences of hasty retreat. All the household utensils and cheap valuables were left in the huts and tents.

In several of the huts were traces of blood, showing where their wounded men had been brought in and laid on goat-skins.

Abundance of Remington cartridges were strewn about everywhere.

When the 2nd Brigade retook the machine guns and drove the enemy out of the nullah, where they made their chief stand, many of the Arabs went back to their villages; but the rapid advance of the 1st Brigade, under General Buller, gave them no time to remove their effects to the mountains.

An unfortunate Egyptian soldier whom they had taken from Tokar, and, according to the man's own tale, compelled, with a rope round his neck, to fight against us at Teb, was forgotten, so hurried was their departure. The Egyptian had practically been made a slave, and had been left while they were absent securely tied. Freeing himself from his bonds he crept up to the new zereba about eleven last night, and was admitted.

He gave the General Commanding valuable information about the enemy's strength and whereabouts, telling him that the backbone of the rebellion in this neighbourhood was broken.

When the cavalry went to Tamaai to-day he accompanied the force, and pointed out Osman Digna's hut and the tents of other sheikhs.

The silver watch of Digna was found, and a large quantity of shells for brass rifled cannon and Remington cartridges.

On this occasion General Graham did not spare their stores, the mounted infantry setting fire to every hut in the nullahs. The flames leapt up to a great height, with accompanying masses of dense black smoke. In a few minutes the ammunition caught, and for nearly an hour there was a discharge of shells and a rattle of cartridges as if a great battle were raging.

Hundreds of the enemy watched the conflagration from the mountain ranges, keeping well beyond the Martini fire. In Suakim the white gunpowder smoke made nervous people think another battle was raging.

The Arabs had hidden the rifled cannon taken from Kassim's force, but the limber and wheels were discovered and burned.

The returning men and horses went to the running stream in the adjacent nullah. As the day was very hot, it was a pleasant sight to see the trickling stream, three inches deep and three feet wide, running under the rocks, in this desert land!

The cavalry got back to Suakim about sunset, and about the same time all the infantry had marched back to zereba. By to-morrow the severely wounded will be sent down from there, and put on board the *Jumna* and sent to Suez.

General Graham to-day and yesterday was heartily cheered by his men as he passed the lines, and to-day the Marines and sailors cheered each other. Everybody is glad to get back to the base, as all have been on the shortest commons, with not too much water to drink, let alone to wash with.

I was eye-witness to scores of instances of heroism on the part of our troops, being present with the 2nd Brigade from first to last during the fighting, and afterwards galloping after and joining the 1st Brigade, entering Tamaai with them.

Whilst the Black Watch were retiring, hard pressed by the Arabs, a private rushed at one of the enemy who was slashing right and left and ran him through with the bayonet, doing it so violently that he thrust the point of his rifle into the savage's body, and had to drag the wounded man with him for some distance before he could extract the weapon.

What occurred to Section 1, Company B, of the 42nd, will illustrate the terrible nature of the contest where the fight raged fiercest. Of 20 men who went into the first charge of our troops up to the edge of the nullah—the regiment was obeying orders—it might have been wiser and better had they felt their ground advancing steadily—but 3 escaped alive, and they were badly wounded.

One of the finest and strongest men in the Black Watch was with Section 1, namely, big Jamie Adams, and he was pluckily backed by Colour-Sergeant Donald Fraser. Both men faced the rushing horde of nearly naked Arabs, charging partly over the brink and down into the nullah. The battle was too fierce to permit of time to withdraw empty cartridges, let alone load rifles. These men and their comrades opposed steel with steel, fighting with all the physical power they possessed, which was vastly greater than the sinewy strength of the swarthy savages. The two Highlanders made over a dozen of their foemen bite the dust before they fell from loss of blood sustained by cuts from thrown spears. While they fought they used not only their rifles, the butts as well as the bayonets, but when the Arabs closed in they hit out with their fists in the scramble.

Another man of the same section, Private George Drummond, who came out alive with three wounds, whilst bayoneting an Arab was cut over the head by a horseman on a gray charger with one of those huge cross-hilted swords. Drummond's helmet and the swerving of the savage's horse saved him. Though stunned, he rallied in a moment, and drove his bayonet through the Arab's body. Whilst tugging to get it out, another Arab rushed at him, spear in hand, but his fighting chum, Kelly, shot the savage. Poor Kelly was killed almost instantly afterwards, and Drummond had his work cut out to get away. It has since transpired that the man on the gray charger was Osman Digna's cousin, Sheikh Mahomed, and that the follower who rushed to his rescue was his steward or wakil.

During last night the Arabs appeared to have stolen

in and carried the sheikh's body away. They also searched for other sheikhs who were among the dead, and buried them before the morning, for to-day we found these new graves.

This time we have not buried their dead, but left them stiff and stark all over the ridges and nullahs of Tamaai. Over 1,500 lie within an area of 200 yards. Others are scattered about in all directions.

To-day I saw many bodies of men who had crept behind rocks or under bushes to die of bullet wounds. The flocks of vultures and jackals and hyænas will for some time feast to satiety on the remains.

There were very few of the rebels on horseback, and those who came on in that way appeared to be leaders. One of them, seated on a brown horse, tried to induce his men to charge the second square, but he was bowled over long before he reached it, and his men fell back.

This afternoon the first and only prisoner taken, excepting the wounded woman, whom I don't include, was brought into the new zereba. He was found lying within 400 yards of the enclosure, with a shot through his leg and a bullet in his shoulder. The doctors dressed his wounds, an operation which he bore without a murmur, subsequently drinking some milk. It was he that told who the man on the white charger was.

Suakim, March 15 (11.0 a.m.)

During last night there was a slight alarm at Baker's zereba. How it originated has not been cleared up, but it is believed to have been through panic-stricken Egyptians.

Some of the latter ran off to Suakim, whilst the men of the Transport Corps outside came into the zereba.

There were a few rifle shots fired, and two men were bayoneted while jumping into the zereba. Quiet was soon restored, and it was found that none of the enemy were near.

To-day Baker's zereba is being abandoned—if, indeed, it has not been abandoned by this time. Only one company of the 42nd and some wounded men were there an hour ago.

The soldiers, as they arrived from the front this morning, were loudly cheered.

CHAPTER XVIII.

GENERAL COMMENT ON TEB AND TAMAAI.

WRITING after the smoke of battle has rolled away, much of deep interest yet remains to be said about the military operations of the 12th and 13th of March. The total strength of the force under Major-General Graham's command when he set out from Suakim to engage Osman Digna, was just under 4,000 combatants, cavalry included. The Staff and the Intelligence Department Officials, as well as many others, were amply provided with a variety of maps which were supposed to depict with much accuracy, the positions of hills, valleys, water-courses, wells, and villages. From this it might properly be inferred there could be no difficulty in shaping our course for Tamaai so as to find the enemy by the shortest, best, and most direct road. Nothing of the kind. The location of Osman Digna and his hordes of almost nude savages must be searched for over rough ground, and across nullahs two or three miles to the north of where Tamaai lay hid in its khor. Bear in mind too, the khor in question widened out, and sloped gradually towards the plain, which in turn shelved at a flat grade down to the sea. On my way back to Suakim with the news of the battle, I rode down this khor to the plain. Our search for Tamaai was, in a small degree, a repetition of our search for Tokar, after the battle at El Teb. It may be recollected that in that instance, the expeditionary force, after camping for the night at the captured wells, set out next morning (March 1st) for Tokar. Nobody seemed to have any clear idea of where the town was. As it was a place set in a hollow, not on a hill, and surrounded by pretty thick mimosa bush, much marching and time were consumed in finding it. The distance from El Teb to Tokar was only eight miles. The cavalry scouts scoured the country in front and on both flanks, till at last as a happy thought they were allowed to look in another direction to that at first indicated, and they thereupon soon succeeded in finding Tokar, Major Giles of the Egyptian service who was attached, being the first, I believe, to make out the place through the mirage. This was done only after we had wandered five or six miles out of our way. It is perhaps as well to state plainly and once for all, that there were many Europeans available as guides—men who had lived at Suakim—passed through Tokar, and several who had gone back and forward between the sea-coast, Berber, and Khartoum. There were also Egyptians and Arabs who knew the country perfectly, but none of these people were either systematically sought out or called upon to assist as guides. No doubt the always prevailing mirage, the nature of the ground, and the character of the enemy, had much to do with preventing the General in command from gleaning accurate information about the number and exact whereabouts of Osman Digna's forces. It cannot but be difficult for anyone who has never been out of Europe to understand how effectually the mirage screens, at moderate distances, objects of low elevation. The bright glare of the tropical sun, the intense blue of the cloudless sky, instead of assisting vision, but blur the sight, and at 1,000 yards' distance a moving figure appears to float along the horizon. Then comes the puzzle to determine what the moving object is: a man? a horse? a camel? or only some buzzard sailing about; not 1,000 yards off, but 300 or 400 yards away. The ground near Tamaai was broken up by dry water-courses, running parallel with which were numerous narrow valleys—here they are called khors. These are nothing more than water-courses during the period of heavy rain in June and July. Their level is a few feet above that of the true water-courses which convey the mountain floods to the sea. The foot-hills leading to the rugged mountain ranges of the Soudan rose abruptly from the head of the khors, affording complete shelter to the enemy. Under such circumstances effective scouting by cavalry totally unacquainted with the country was out of the question. How much more so must it have been the case when there were no guides who knew the routes across the plains or among the hills, and no natives to be caught and interrogated? It was not permitted that small parties of our cavalry should scour the country in all directions miles in front of the main body of troops. The risk was too great to allow venturesome horsemen to attempt such work, for most surely the quick-moving Arabs would have swooped down on these isolated scouts and cut them off to a man. In this dilemma it was resolved to trust to native spies for information. Their general untrustworthiness was well known, as also their incapacity to master figures. Yet a good many of these useful creatures were sent out to the camp of Osman Digna by the Deputy-Governor of Suakim (Mr. Brewster) and by the Intelligence Department attached to General Graham's force, presided over by Lieutenant-Colonel Ardagh, C.B., It was about the best that could be done, but whether the best use was made of the information so gained is another affair. The spies certainly, or at least two of them, returned with the story that the Arabs were at the waters of Tamaai and meant fighting; furthermore, that Osman Digna intended making a stand in one of the khors to the north-east of Tamaai, hiding his men in a nullah until we should get close up, and then rushing upon us, hoping to bear all before him. The story was discredited, and few, if any, steps were taken to test its accuracy until we proved its truthfulness by stubborn battle. This, however, is anticipating. In a campaign like the one just closed there is always a good deal of talk and criticism flying about. Sharp remarks have been exchanged among all ranks as to the conduct more particularly of those whose position entailed serious duties. From such comment no one escaped who occupied a responsible post. Criticism, like envy, loves a shining mark, and, in justice to the critics, it can be said that they peppered their targets almost beyond recognition. Why the General moved so tardily—so hastily; why he failed to do this, and took the trouble to do that; disposed of his forces in the way he did, etc., enumerates not a hundredth part of the queries which, for want of desired answers, the questioners answered to their own satisfaction. Nor were the assumed sins of omission and commission of lesser officials handled in much gentler spirit for a time. Luckily the close of the campaign brought about a better state of feeling and induced fairer comment all round, the prospect of leaving the Soudan leading everybody to quietly drop further discussion of their unpleasant experiences. To summarise the chief grounds of the fault-finders, they were: "Too little consideration was shown in selecting the hour of marching, especially for the infantry, who were frequently ordered to set out during the hottest part of the day, and the routes taken were not always the best or most direct." Loaded as the infantry were—each man with 100 rounds of ammunition, and burdened with heavy clothes and equipment—his total allowance of water *per diem* for all purposes was frequently but two to four pints, far too little when the sweltering heat is considered. Now Major E. Gunter, in his excellent note-book and "Field and Reconnaissance Aide

Memoire," lays down that, in marching camps, men should be allowed four gallons of water a day. Another fruitful scource of fault-finding was the absence of complete information as to the enemy's numbers, location, and disposition by the Intelligence Department. Possibly that which affected the men keenest of all, giving rise to no end of acrimonious comment, was the repetition of orders at El Teb and Tamaai for the infantry squares to charge the enemy's positions, and that when our force was not suffering from anything like a galling fire or even an annoying one. With respect to the Commissariat, Transport, Ordnance, and Medical Departments, their work from first to last was splendidly done. So far as these Departments are concerned, their organisation and efficiency left nothing to be desired, and should serve as models for any future campaign. The Transport Department was, to a certain extent, crippled for want of animals; but energy and skill prevented the insufficient number of camels and mules and the lack of necessary equipments from being severely felt. Much, perhaps, of the success the Supplies Department met with was due to the men and officers of the fleet, who, as usual, worked with untiring heartiness to help the military along. Still, too high a meed of praise cannot be given Deputy-Commissary-General Nugent.

On the forenoon of Wednesday, March 12th, the expeditionary force under General Graham had collected at Baker's zereba, a point on the mimosa-covered plain, nearly nine miles in a south-westerly direction from

Suakim. The infantry had bivouacked in the zereba the night previous, but the cavalry had ridden out that morning from Suakim, which they left at 6 a.m. After an early dinner, or at 1 p.m. to be exact, the force fell in to move forward towards Tamaai, supposed to be from eight to ten miles further south-west, and among the foot-hills, which, with the mountains rising behind them, we could clearly see stretching across our front, and as far as eye could scan away to right and left. After going two or three miles in this order, small parties of the enemy opened fire on our front; and to get the benefit of their long rifles, the mounted infantry went forward and exchanged shots. The firing had no effect upon our onward movement, as the cavalry were well in advance of the infantry, and pressed the enemy's skirmishers so closely that they fell back rapidly, and there was not even a slackening of the pace maintained by the infantry. By 3 p.m. the cavalry were leading the squares by nearly two miles. Mounting one of the isolated granite foot-hills which was about 130 feet high, I got a fine view of the surrounding country. General Stewart and his Staff were among the first to ascend, and half an hour later General Graham and his Staff came to the top. The elevation was sufficient to take us out of the line of the mirage which hung in the rarefied air near the surface of the plain or desert, so that we could see the enemy. The Arabs were in considerable numbers, and were occupying the crest of a low ridge a mile and a half to two miles south. Their black bodies stood out in bold relief against the horizon as they looked at us invading their native fastnesses. By 4 p.m. the infantry squares had got to the foot of the hill, but General Graham decided it was too late to attack that day. Only two hours of daylight were then left, and as we could not have hoped to engage the enemy for another hour, it was determined that the force should bivouac for the night. The troops were marched off towards the south, the square swinging to the left. The enemy began once more firing rapidly at us, but the Abyssinian scouts under Mr. Wylde, as well as the mounted infantry, pushed onward engaging them hotly, and very soon their fire slackened. The infantry proceeded 800 yards across the plain, and were halted on the swelling crest of a low ridge. Men were detailed to cut bushes of the prickly mimosa and make a new zereba enclosing the infantry squares with a bristling hedge 4 feet high, and 6 to 8 feet thick. The ground was sandy, with patches of small angular stones and gravel. It was covered with scant vegetation, mimosa bush and bunch grass. It would have yielded readily enough to pick or shovel, but not a spadeful of earth was thrown up by us. The men had been ordered to lie down for a short time until the bushes were cut and piled around the infantry squares, but as the work of making the zereba approached completion, other details went off to light fires, so as to prepare coffee or tea, and cook the evening meal. Instructions were sent back to Baker's zereba for the camels to be brought forward with water for the men. To prevent undue scarcity of that necessary of life, the cavalry were ordered to go back to the other zereba for the night. General Graham's headquarters were in the centre of the new zereba, being marked as usual with a small square red flag attached to a short light pole. This red flag was always borne on horseback by a sergeant-major behind the General whenever we were on the march or in action. Like General Stewart's red jacket, or Chief of Staff Colonel Clery's ditto, these blood-red articles invariably drew the enemy's attention and fire, and enabled us to tell the situation of these officers. Perhaps it was to the fact that they were so much aimed at that these officers owed their immunity from bullet wounds. The garbs of everybody else, rank and file, were grey, dun, or blue. Close to the spot General Graham had selected for his bivouac, were standing two round-top waggons of the Army Hospital Corps, of which and their inmates more anon.

With two others I had chosen a spot on the sand ten paces to the south of the General's bivouac. A number of transport camels with water and ammunition came in long after sunset, entering the zereba through a small opening left for that purpose on the north-east side. The infantry lay down with their rifles three or four yards from the inside line of the bushes. Sentinels were placed within short distances of each other all around the zereba, but also within the line of bushes. There was a full moon, and it shone brightly the whole of the night. The soldiers were good-humoured and cheerful, in anticipation that on the morrow Osman

Digna would get a "settler," and the Soudan or Eastern Soudan War would be terminated. In this belief the men dropped off to sleep, and as all lights had been extinguished at 9 p.m., and not a sound was audible, save the sentries' muffled tread, one might have passed within a yard or two of the place without knowing an army was slumbering near.

At 12.45, midnight, we had a startling awakening. A rattle of rifles, whizzing of bullets, accompanied by a roar of halloas which, starting on our right front, swelled round the square in vast chorus, caused everybody to spring to attention. The officers were on the alert in an instant, the men were directed to lie still and not fire until the Arabs got within ten yards. Knowing what it meant, to prepare for eventualities, I speedily put bridle and saddle upon my horse, which was tethered near. The bullets rained by meanwhile, for the white round-topped hospital waggons pointed the enemy's fire. A horse was killed near me. Deputy Surgeon-General McDowell and the Rev. Father Brindle, who were inside the hospital waggons, had a warm time of it, but they manfully held their ground—or beds rather—only turning out when duty called in order to attend to the two or three wounded men who were brought in from the lines. When the alarm arose three or four men were more or less injured in the scurry by the careless handling of bayonets in the hands of comrades.

Two chaplains—Father Brindle and the Rev. Mr. McTaggart, Presbyterian minister, of the Black Watch—deserve more than even ordinary commendation for the untiring and unshrinking way in which from first to last in this campaign they not only discharged their own duties, but assisted others. They marched on foot with their men amid the heat and dust; shared their bivouacs and dangers in the fights; mounted guard over water or food when necessary; and ministered to the sick. The wounded men never lacked for anything that either of these clergymen could get, borrow, or beg to alleviate suffering. I am glad to be able to tell that Father Brindle and Mr. McTaggart were staunch friends, sharing whatever they had, and helping one another on all occasions.

The enemy kept firing away at us till about 5 a.m., when their fire ceased as suddenly as it had begun. It appears, from what we subsequently learned, that a body of between two and three hundreds of them crept up to 900 yards from the zereba on the south-west corner, and potted away for a short time from behind a low ridge. A few more crept round to the south-west face, so that their line of fire extended about one mile across our front. Fortunately they hit upon the sides of the square covered by the ridge on which the leading regiments were halted. Had they opened fire from the west, or, better still for them, taken up a position on the conical hill on the north, 800 yards distant from the zereba, our casualties must have been considerably greater. As it was, they only succeeded in killing one man of the 65th, a few horses, a camel or two, and disturbing the sleep of many of the men. The machine guns having been taken to the corners of the square facing the enemy's fire, the Blue-jackets for a time stood expectant, waiting orders to turn the death-dealing crank handles. General Graham, however, directed that everybody should lie down, and that not a shot was to be fired of any kind till the Arabs could be clearly seen charging the zereba. That night was the only occasion during the campaign the quiet and reticent commander, General Graham, showed signs of annoyance. When the alarm occurred he slowly rose from the ground, drawing himself up to his full height, near six feet three inches, muttered a syllable of which I could only catch the letter d, buckled on his sword, and went off with his Staff to inspect the square. From that hour till reveille very few of the officers got an opportunity for sleep.

CHAPTER XIX.

CONTINUATION OF GENERAL COMMENT.

REVEILLE was sounded at 5.30 a.m., and the clear tones of the bugles re-echoed from the rocky khors and hills around. In a few minutes all were astir, fires were relit, overcoats rolled away, and the good appetites with which the keen morning air had bestowed us, were appeased with coffee, tea, and biscuits. Shortly afterwards a few shots were fired from our 9-pounders at the enemy, just to let them know we were stirring.

By 7.30 a.m., Thursday, 13th March, the cavalry had rejoined us, and by 8 o'clock the infantry were hastily drawn up in precisely the same formation as the day previous, just without the zereba. The scouts had come in and reported the enemy were retiring into the hills, hence the men were hurried out as quickly as possible. The two brigades were now separated by a much wider interval than the twenty-five paces of the day before. ·Indeed, they were placed so as to act as two independent oblongs, the front face or line of each brigade being about 200 yards in length, the sides half that, or 100 yards. The 2nd Brigade was in advance, the 1st Brigade marching on the right rear side of the former, at a distance varying from 600 to 900 yards in an oblique line. In military parlance, the brigades moved in échelon, the 2nd Brigade leading, the object being to expose the enemy to a raking or flank fire if they attempted a charge. This time the main body of the cavalry were écheloned on the left rear of the 2nd Brigade. The Mounted Infantry and Abyssinians again went to the front, and engaged the enemy's advanced pickets and skirmishers. A brisk fire raged between these opponents as the squares quietly, slowly, and steadily marched towards the main body of the Arabs, whom we saw blackening the ridges as they swarmed over them a mile and a half away to the south. Behind them rose grand and large the great red and black slopes of the Soudan ranges, from the vantage of which all our movements must have lain broadly bare to the sharp eyes of their watchers. General Graham and his Staff took up their position within the 2nd Brigade square—General Davis's—with which I also rode, moving about within the square. At first, to avoid some nullahs, the troops made a slight détour to the left, going S.S.W. Bringing their left shoulders up again, the men of the 2nd Brigade faced towards the S.S.E. At our approach the Arab fire quickened, and the Mounted Infantry and Abyssinians, who were "rushed" by small parties of Arabs, had several dashing little hand-to-hand encounters with the natives. As agile and deft with the spear or sword as the Arabs themselves, if not more so, the Abyssinians staunchly met their onrush, bowling over the first comers with rifle bullets, and treating the others to steel for steel. Here it was that several of these fearless hillmen of King John were slain and wounded, as well as of our own men of the Mounted Infantry. We were now drawing close to the enemy, and as the skirmishers would be in the way of the fire of the square, they were ordered to fall back slowly. As they passed by, bearing their wounded comrades, a few cheers were raised in greeting of their gallantry. It was now 8.30 a.m., and the Battle of Tamaai had begun in earnest. The 2nd Brigade was moving slowly towards a rather winding nullah, which extended all along our front, and was 900 or 1,000 yards distant. The 1st Brigade was timing its movements and taking its ground step by step with ours, 700 yards off and to our right rear. The nullah on our front was studded, on its abrupt slopes and crests, with rocks and stones, whilst many bushes and shrubs also increased the excellent cover it afforded.

Probably not more than 5,000 or 6,000 Arabs were visible, and the bulk of these appeared to be on the south side of the nullah, which, in our immediate front, was 50 to 100 yards wide. There were several hundreds of Arabs also among the bushes to our right, as well as our immediate front. When the skirmishers had gone to the rear, the infantry of the 2nd Brigade square began firing. It was not done by volley, but independently, and it scarcely interrupted or checked the tread of the square towards the nullah. The Martini-

Henrys were doing great execution, and the over-eager Arabs, as they rose from their hiding-places, whether to advance or retire, went down like ripe wheat before the sickle. Getting up within 200 yards of the nullah, the enemy became more numerous all along the front and right side of the square. Broken and irregular rushes were made at us by clusters of them; but all these charges ended disastrously for the brave and reckless savages, none of whom at that time got within 20 yards of us; and our front and flanks soon became comparatively clear of foes. There was little wind stirring, but the little there was blew towards our right, causing the smoke of the rifles to hang about the corner of the square in a vexing way. A lull took place for a minute or so—a thing at times which happens in the most desperate of battles. The side of the nullah was but 100 yards away. On our right there was an indent, or pocket, projecting inwards, 30 yards or so, on the side nearest the 65th Regiment. The order was given to charge, and, with many a ringing cheer, down we bore on the nullah's edge. In an instant, black heads popped up in every direction to front and right. The men ran up to within about 30 yards from the nullah's edge, then slackened speed somewhat, and though still advancing, began firing. Somebody ordered "cease firing;" but the men had often heard precisely similar commands at El Teb, as well as on the ridges of Tamaai, and, seeing armed natives flitting all over the place, they were not to be denied their fire. There was much vain endeavour on the part of officers to stop their men cracking away at Arabs not over 100 yards from them, and many were much nearer. The Arabs in question seemed busy running down the slopes of the khor opposite where we stood, and disappearing among the rocks in the little valley. A halt was called a few yards from the edge of the nullah, and whilst the men were sending occasional bullets at the enemy, several of the Gatlings and Gardners were run out a few yards in front of the right corner of the square and turned upon the natives swarming on the ridges opposite. The infantry fire swelled once more as the Arabs again drew closer. At the moment I was alongside Lieut.-Col. Green, who commanded the Black Watch, and was actually speaking about the forbidding nullah and its capacity for affording cover to the enemy. His Highlanders were blazing away smartly and steadily at the Arabs, who were then jumping out of the nullah and charging down to within five yards of us. Glancing to my right, I ejaculated, in language more forcible than choice, that the 65th were giving way, and at once galloped off to their side of the square. The Arabs were all over that side and corner of the square, bounding like deer out of the khor by hundreds, and running at us through the thick smoke. With hair on end, eyes glistening, and their white teeth shining, more like infuriated demons than men, they seemed to bound out of the battle-smoke upon the soldiers like figures in a shadow pantomime. In an instant they were at the guns and among our men, thrusting, cutting, stabbing, with desperate energy. The men recoiled before the avalanche of fierce savages; but to our soldiers' credit, be it ever told, they retired mostly with their faces to the foe, loading and firing with the courage of heroes. The capture of the guns, and the confusion into which the Blue-jackets were thrown were not without their effect upon the 65th, who were now falling back irregularly, more like a confused mass than an orderly line of soldiers. General Graham, Colonel Clery, and others rode about among them striving to re-form the ranks, and get the men to close up and fire steadily. It was a time when one's country was of far greater importance than professional calling, so I did what I could for the former during the surging five minutes that ensued. I rode about in the broken line of the 65th, where General Graham and other officers were, striving to get the soldiers to close up and fire steadily. At the moment we were hardest pushed, I saw an old acquaintance, Captain Rutherford of the 65th, left almost without his company, erect, bareheaded, sword in hand, facing the shouting, jubilant Arabs, and hoarsely calling, "Men of the 65th, close up." I shouted to him, and even in that roar and rush found time to exchange a word or two as to what was best to be done, ere turning again to invite the soldiers, who were showing a bold front to the foe, to aim and fire carefully. As Arab after Arab was knocked over—one almost ought to be ashamed to write it, but truth-telling is above *mauvaise honte*—we laughed and cheered, shouting: "That's the way. Give it them, men!" Still on the enemy came, yelling and screaming with diabolic ferocity. The gaping wounds made by our almost explosive Martini-Henry bullets, scarcely checked the savages in their wild career. It was only when the lead shattered the bone of a leg, or pierced heart or brain, that their mad onrush was instantly stopped. I saw Arab after Arab, through whose bodies our bullets had ploughed their way, charging down on the square, with the blood spouting in pulsating streams from them at every heart-throb. Down they bore on us; some with two or three bullet wounds, reeling like frenzied, drunken men, but still pressing onwards to throw themselves, without attempt at parrying, upon our bayonets, as the surest way to slay or cut one victim before Death's agony stiffened their limbs. Others there were, whose life-blood ebbed ere they reached our men, who fell within a pace or two of the soldiers. The last act of these poor warriors was invariably a despairing effort to hurl the weapon they carried at the moment in their hand— stick, spear, or sword—at their English foemen. A savage gleam shone in their faces, defiant, unrelenting, hating, as they gathered all their strength, to thus make their last blow at us. Who but could admire and applaud such dauntless bravery? Those of us privileged to witness it, and the awful spectacle of those five minutes, can never forget it, or cease to remember the grand self-sacrificing courage of the brave Hadendowas.

As backward the right face and corner of the 65th were borne from the nullah's edge, and the indent or little gully—*see illustration*—the right wing of the 42nd was left exposed, and the savages were among the Highlanders on their flank and rear in a twinkling, cutting and spearing in every direction. Still falling back, in a line to the east of that taken in our advance from the zereba, the Marines who were in rear of the square were wheeled up to support the 65th and close the gaps in our formation. It was too late for the movement to be executed successfully, and they too were thrown into disorder and were borne away from the nullah on the line of retreat.

As that fine body of men were being swept away Major Colwell roared in stentorian tones:

"Men of the Portsmouth division, rally!" Rally they did, about 150 of them closing together in a compact body, forming a little square. These were the last to retire and take up their position in the re-formed line.

In the right corner of the square, or what once was a square, were now inextricably mixed men of the 65th, Blue-jackets, Marines, and a few Highlanders. It was not a rout, but a retreat; for our soldiers kept loading and firing, although there was no semblance at the time of an orderly military line; but in place thereof, facing and fighting the enemy, were an irregular body of men in rather open order on what was the west face of the square. Numerous mêlées occurred, where, with foot and fist, the soldiers mauled the savages. The Arabs threw themselves on our men grasping their rifles, and in one instance actually tearing off a Highlander's kilt in the tussle.

Side by side the best men stood — Blue-jackets, 65th, Highlanders, or Marines—heedless of regimental names, numbers, or order; in places, the rear-ranker six or eight men away from the thoroughly-aroused, enraged Briton in the foremost front, who, battling with sword or bayonet, sought, for country and honour, to beat back the savage horde. Here it was a bold private of the 65th, seeing one of the three or four mounted sheikhs who were hounding on their men, rushed out at him and bayoneted the leader on his horse.

For a brief interval it was the innings of Osman Digna's followers, and they rioted in cutting and slashing for a few minutes. Every soldier who stumbled or fell was done for, the enemy darting in squads for these unlucky ones, thrusting their spears into them. As they followed us closely up, they never missed an opportunity to drive their weapons into the body of any soldier lying on the ground who exhibited the slightest signs of life.

In their first great rush which enabled them to get temporary possession of the Gatlings and Gardners, their success maddened them with joy. In the excess of triumph a sinewy Arab leapt upon one of the machine guns, and capered and yelled in glee not 30 yards from us. In a moment he wilted like a green plant before the leaden hail, and fell headlong to the ground.

Seeing us fall back, many of the Arabs running across the khors to join the main body engaging the 2nd Brigade, streamed off towards the 1st (General Buller's) Brigade, and the zereba. They, no doubt, thought we were quite out of the hunt, and that their fellow-tribesmen were well able to finish us.

As backward the 2nd (General Davis's) Brigade was borne, the enemy continued making desperate onslaughts to shatter and separate the soldiers. Our turn was coming, for every step of ground we gave way increased our favourable chances for dealing death, and lessened theirs. The plain they had to rush across to reach us as we retired, exposed them more and more to our fire which mowed them down as they came on. It was at this juncture also, that General Buller's Brigade, that commander seeing something was wrong, moved up a short distance and began pouring a heavy cross-fire into the Arabs. The Mounted Infantry who had come up on our left did the same from that direction. The situation of the 2nd Brigade was rapidly altered for the better in the next two or three minutes. General Herbert Stewart, who with his cavalry force was on our right rear, 900 yards distant, had determined to come to the rescue, and had actually issued the order for the first of his squadrons to advance. Off they went at a trot, but now the enemy began to thin out and waver, and the squadron dismounted instead of charging over the dangerous broken ground, and commenced firing. The terrible five minutes were over, and Colonel Clery and General Davis galloping off succeeded in halting the retreating troops, and re-forming in line the men on the left front and rear of our aforetime square. As the others fell back, they were assigned to ground to the right of the position thus taken up, and directed to fall into line instead of square. Whilst the 2nd Brigade were being "dressed up" in line with the Marines on the right, the Sixty-fifth in the centre, and the Gordon Highlanders on the left, thus :

42nd	65th	Marines,

the 1st Brigade and the force left at the zereba were sustaining a sharp attack from the enemy. The Arabs had to move across the open ground, and there was no cover or protection beyond what the scant mimosa bush afforded, so the very boldest and luckiest of them never succeeded in getting within five yards of General Buller's square. There was a slight depression in the plain near where the 1st Brigade were halted, and creeping into it the savages tried hard to collect in sufficient force to charge down on that square. Their intention was foreseen by General Buller, who, ordering out the artillery, a few charges of case-shot and inverted shell at short ranges settled adversely for the enemy all possibility of charging in a swarm down on the 1st Brigade square. Of such mettle were these dusky sons of the desert, that nothing daunted by the hopelessness of the task, for nearly a quarter of an hour thereafter, they continued to rush in ones, twos, and sometimes as many as half a score at the orderly and compact British lines, where 1,500 bayonets glistened with a circle of fire environing the bristling steel. They stole to the right, to the left, to the rear faces of the square, and tried by death's hazard to lock with the ranked soldiers. In vain, one after another down they fell, the leaden missiles showing no mercy. Cool and deliberate, our men aimed carefully as the Arabs came running on, and the little puffs and jets of sand thrown up by the striking bullets near the infatuated rushing braves, showed how scant was the likelihood of their career lasting many seconds. The small garrison in the zereba also stood to arms during the peril and excitement, and as the enemy ran past their west and south fronts to attack the squares, they blazed away killing quite a number of the Arabs. It has been said that the enemy seriously threatened the zereba at one portion of the day, but I saw nothing to justify that statement, and could find no fair corroboration of it. Several mounted men, Egyptians and others, and most of the native Egyptians attached to the Transport and Carrier Corps, bolted when the 2nd Brigade gave way. Some of these effective rear-flankers executed very rapid movements towards the cavalry, the new zereba, Baker's zereba, and not a few pushed on without halt into Suakim. Let me add here, *par parenthèse,* although it is mentioned elsewhere, that the latter were nearly all flogged for their celerity.

When the 2nd Brigade was re-formed in line and had been advanced nearly 100 yards, General Graham told the officers the men must retake the guns. After a quarter of an hour's halt the force again moved forward. The 1st Brigade had moved up 200 yards closer to the nullah, and was now halted within 700 yards of the lost Gatlings and Gardners. We were about an equal distance off, the position being thus—

LOST GUNS.

FIRST BRIGADE.

SECOND BRIGADE.

As the 2nd Brigade went once more to the attack I attached myself to the right of the line, as they would have actually to recover the guns, which stood on the brink, some of them just over the nullah's edge where the indent was. Riding alongside of Colonel Tuson, who commanded the Marines, as he had only one mounted officer left, I ventured to offer my services, if they could be of any use. The line was as perfectly kept as if the men were on parade, and marching slowly, the soldiers fired as they advanced, clearing the ground of the enemy, who seemed unprepared or unwilling to mass together to meet our attack.

Here and there Arabs would come running to assail

us, but the rifle fire was now too accurate and sweeping for anyone to survive it. Cheering loudly, our men quickened their pace, carrying their rifles at the charge.

As we neared the nullah's edge numbers of the enemy were seen to move off, trotting across the little valley to the opposite slopes, or running off to the westward. Many others there were who staid to fight to the death, and several hand-to-hand encounters again ensued between Tommy Atkins and these stubborn foes close to the indent.

Another ringing cheer, and with a resistless rush the guns were regained. The right of our line was, when we halted, twenty paces distant from a corner of the indent, so going out with a message for Major Tucker of the Marines to ascertain if the Arabs had collected in that corner of the khor, I met General Buller and his Staff, who were riding over from the 1st Brigade to say that our bullets were occasionally dropping too near that square. Firing in their direction was instantly stopped; and it appeared that the danger came from the men on the left of the 2nd Brigade line shooting at the Arabs who were going off to our right.

The guns having come into our possession again, Commander Rolfe, Lieutenant Graham, and the surviving naval officers with their Blue-jackets instantly hauled them into position, and to see they were all right turned the handles and worked a round or two of shots off at the retreating Arabs.

One of the guns had been run over the nullah's edge down the steep side, as if the enemy had meant to take it away. This was quickly pulled upon the plain by the sailors, who patted and fondled these dread weapons of war as if they had been living things.

Within a radius of 60 yards from the corner where the indent turned at right angles from the nullah, the barren stony upland was thickly carpeted with the slain, Briton and Arab mutually crimsoning the soil with gore. There were 100 of our men and nearly 1,000 savages lying together in that little space.

Not one European who had fallen there from our ranks breathed. All were dead, each with ghastly wounds and livid, bloodless faces; for the deep spear and sword cuts had bereft them of every drop of blood in their veins. The cut hands of several of our dead and the stark, stiff savages lying side by side and around them, proved what fearful struggles had ensued before they had succumbed to the overpowering force of savages.

Dismounting and picking my way carefully among these our honoured dead, many of whom I had known so well and chatted with scarcely half-an-hour before, I roughly estimated their number, and took note of the names of several of the officers. How well memory recalls each particular wound which marred some of the poor fellows! Two or three squads of our men went off, some to search for the dead and wounded, others to see if any wounded or unwounded Arabs were lurking about among the rocks in the khor below.

A fine-looking savage lay half-reclining on the

sloping bank near where the gun had been rolled over. He was badly wounded in the leg, a bullet having shattered his knee. Grasping his heavy broad-bladed spear, he looked defiance and mischief at the soldiers as they approached. A Blue-jacket was the first to venture near him, and although Jack had his rifle and cutlass attached, he liked not the far-reaching, quick-striking spear. The troops were forbidden to fire, and there was nothing for it but to tackle the man with steel. The deft handling of the spear, wounded as the Arab was, made Jack cautious. I looked and watched. A soldier now stole up on the opposite side of the Hadendowa, but even then the savage, like a wounded stag at bay, was not to be trifled with. A mean subterfuge, cunning, stratagem, or what you will you may call it, prevailed. A stone thrown at the Arab's head stunned him for a moment, and before he recovered the Blue-jacket had plunged his cutlass into him, bending the weapon into such a hoop shape he could just barely withdraw it, and so closed the day of another life. But I have already given too many details out of the countless incidents of that battle. Such, however, is war; murderous, cruel at the best wherever I have seen it, no matter whether black or white, savage or civilised man engages in it. Where a war is not dictated by stern duty or necessity, it is absolutely devoid of redeeming feature, except the hardihood and bravery with which some men sacrifice their lives.

Battles, like all mundane things, have an end, and that of Tamaai was nearly over. There were hundreds of shields, spears, swords, knives, and other Arab trophies on the field, samples of which I should like to have possessed myself of, but riding nearly fourteen stone and with a light Arab horse below me, as speed was everything I could not afford to handicap myself. General Graham went with General Buller's Brigade and a portion of the cavalry across the nullah towards the south in the direction taken by the fleeing Arabs, towards the village or huts of Tamaai. Having completed my scrutiny, I rode after the 1st Brigade, catching up with it 500 yards off as the men and artillery were toiling up the hot, rough, steep slopes of the rolling ground to the south. Short as the distance was to be traversed to do so, it was an exceedingly uninviting stretch of ground, for it led down into and across the khor and up the rocky sides of the hillocks opposite, where, had any of the Arabs concealed behind the masses of detached rocks made a dash for me, it would have been very difficult to have got out of their way. Whilst the 2nd Brigade maintained their position at the nullah's edge where the battle had been fought and won, their comrades of the 1st toiled on a mile or so to secure the enemy's villages and the running water to be found in one of the khors. The enemy, now quite broken up, kept moving towards the broken ground to the south and west, some making for the higher mountain ranges to our right. We could see hundreds of their black heads as they stood watching us from spurs of the hills. The men leading the advance kept up a brisk fire at the retreating enemy, which was feebly returned. At length we reached a crest dominating the khors, wherein were the huts and tents of Tamaai. They were quite deserted, but on every side were evidences of the haste with which the occupants had quitted them. Save the wounded negro-woman of whom I have spoken elsewhere (one of the enslaved survivors of the Sinkat garrison), there was not a human being near. She, poor creature! as the cavalry scouts rode down, was standing clinging to the prop at the entrance to a low hut. She might have been a Hadendowa warrior for aught we knew, till with womanly modest grace, as we rode by, she withdrew the cloth covering one of her shoulders disclosing an ugly spearwound. I offered my water-bottle as she looked faint and wan, and she stretched out her hand eagerly for it. A trooper dismounted and gave her a drink, for which she looked thankful.

The troops were following fast, so we pushed forward examining the huts. There were plenty of goats, mostly young kids, and several other animals about, and inside the tents were ample stores of Arab goods and chattels, skins, water-bottles, weapons, rude musical instruments, food, etc. There were also accoutrements and weapons which had been captured from the Egyptians, Remington rifles, bayonets, belts, pouches, and cartridges. The fighting for the day was clearly over, so, riding to where General Graham was, I asked if the force would advance farther. Being assured it would not that day, and that the operations for a time were at an end, my face was set for Suakim. It was then exactly 11.40 a.m. The General asked if I would carry his despatch in, and at once proceeded to write a brief message. He asked me as to the number of dead, and the names of some of the officers killed. These were, of course, given to him, and they were incorporated in the brief despatch which, having been handed to me, I galloped off with from the khor, straight for the sea and Suakim. After going two miles I met four Arabs, on camels, off which they quickly slipped; but whether to make for me or not I know not, as I kept on going with the horse well in hand, ready for a break if necessary. Pulling rein occasionally on the little barren patches, where mimosa and bush were scant, I gave my Arab horse an occasional "breather," walking him over these clear places. By 2 p.m. I was at the telegraph office in Suakim, where, like a dutiful correspondent, I sought to hand in a short message of my own before General Graham's; but Admiral Hewett had given orders that nothing was to go through until the Commanding Officer's message was handed in and despatched. There was no help for it, and so with very bad grace, I yielded the point, handed it in, and followed it instantly up with short and long messages of my own, writing them out in the telegraph office.

CHAPTER XX.

BACK IN SUAKIM.

AFTER the stirring scenes and hardships of the marches, bivouacs, and battle, the troops were glad enough to get back to Suakim, and enjoy a little well-earned rest and improved commons. The following is the record of the events succeeding Tamaai :

Suakim, March 16 (8.55 p.m.)

There was a conference of friendly sheikhs in Suakim this afternoon, to devise ways and means for ending the war.

It was held in the Government House, and attended by General Graham and Staff and Admiral Hewett. Mr. Brewster, Deputy-Governor, acted as interpreter. About thirty sheikhs were present, including Sheikh Morghani. Admiral Hewett said we had conquered Osman Digna, but had no desire to occupy the country, only wishing to restore peace. The English were here, and meant to secure the safe withdrawal of the Soudan

P

garrisons, even if they had to fight again to do so. Could the friendly sheikhs open up the country with their tribes, securing the safety of trade routes? The sheikhs answered that the tribes alone could not do so at present, but could with the help of the British.

A proclamation, offering 5,000 dollars reward for the capture, alive or dead, of Osman Digna as a traitor was submitted by Admiral Hewett, as Commander-in-Chief on the East India station. The sheikhs unanimously approved the proposal to issue it; and to-night it has been posted on the walls of Suakim, and sent outside. Osman Digna is charged with having misled the people of the Soudan by lies and treachery, thereby causing much bloodshed.

This evening General Graham, in General Orders to the army, thanks the officers and men for the great discipline shown and the successful manner in which the operations were carried out; also for their endurance. He draws attention to the want of steadiness displayed in the crisis of Thursday's battle, which led to the death of many of our brave men; but they sold their lives dearly, leaving 400 of the enemy dead around them. He thanks the Naval Brigade for the way they worked their guns, for the defence of which their officers and comrades died so nobly. The men, who displayed want of steadiness at first, finished their work with that discipline and bravery so often shown by the British troops. Osman Digna is described as being now a fugitive in the mountains. General Graham thanks both Brigades, as also all the different Departments, for the manner in which each and all performed their duties.

The small square, composed of two companies of Marines, who kept together throughout Thursday's fight, coming in last, was commanded by Majors Tucker, Schomberg, and Colwell. The Arabs came on like hungry wolves, surging about them on all sides; but, like the small square of Highlanders, they preserved their formation intact until they reached the reconstructed lines of the 2nd Brigade.

Suakim, March 16 (8.20 p.m.)

The *Jumna* sailed at noon to-day for Suez, with 100 wounded and 80 sick. The state of all wounded at starting was satisfactory. Major Dalgetty, of the 65th, Surgeon Cross, R.N., Captain Brophy, Black Watch, and Mr. St. Leger Herbert, are all doing well. Surgeon Prendergast, who received a spear-thrust through his back into the chest whilst attending a wounded man, had a good night, and his condition has improved. Nearly all the slightly wounded left at Suakim have rejoined their regiments.

In view of the dangers and risks the Medical Department and many chaplains have incurred in discharging with efficiency their duties during this trying campaign, they deserve better recognition than the present system admits of.

To-day there are fifty cases in the camp hospital,

principally sufferers from ague, contracted in India, and a few from dysentery. The general health of all the troops is good, but there is deterioration, and the medical authorities state that the resumption of an active campaign would tell heavily.

The embarkation of the wounded was carried out without delay or mishap. The captain of the French war-steamer *Seignelay* offered the services of his men and the boats from his own and sister ship, now in port, to assist in getting the wounded aboard the *Jumna*. They were accepted by Admiral Hewett, and the boats and steam launch were sent from the *Seignelay*. The last boat-load was towed off by the French launch. The wounded were carried to large horse-boats and barges on stretchers, on which they lay till transferred to cots on the hospital ship *Jumna*. One Russian war-ship is also in the harbour, and it is said that her captain also proffered help.

The one wounded Arab who was secured as a prisoner at Tamaai on Friday last, after having lain in the field all night, has become more communicative. The man said to Colonel Ardagh that he alone was left of six brothers, who went into battle with him. He now says that Osman lied, for the English bullets had not been turned aside, but had killed thousands of Hadendowas. Besides, the British were not the terrible cut-throats and beasts they were represented to be. If he recovered he would readily fight for or assist the English in every way.

The Mahdi's General in command during the fight

was Mahmoud Moussa, Osman's cousin. On Friday Mahmoud Ali and some of the friendly sheikhs were allowed to visit the battle-field. Mahmoud identified many of the dead sheikhs, including four principal leaders of the rebels, one of these being a certain Moussa-Ion-Achmet.

On Saturday a reconnoitring party of twenty men from the 10th Hussars, under Major Brabazon, accompanied Major Wood, R.E., from twelve to thirteen miles to Handouk. They returned in the evening, and reported finding plenty of good water there. Numbers of Arabs were seen herding flocks of goats and cattle, but no opposition was shown, the natives talking to the interpreters in a friendly way. If, therefore, an attempt, apparently in contemplation, be made to open the Berber road by force, it will certainly take the caravan route by Handouk and Sibil, thus avoiding the difficult mountain passes. At Sibil the Bishareen Arabs' country begins, and they are reported to be not positively hostile. The infantry would go forward fifty miles into the hills, and a picked force of cavalry, 500 strong, would ride to Berber. To-day preliminary steps, such as issuing supplies and so on, have been taken, so that all is in readiness to move forward.

The details of the advance it would be unwise to give; yet frankly, respecting any further operations here, the greatest dissatisfaction exists among all ranks, particularly among the time-expired men and others, who think that, in common fairness, an arduous campaign like the present should have been reserved for fresh troops. There is more grumbling than I have ever heard among soldiers and officers about the whole business. They are constantly asking, "Why are we here? Why are we killing such brave fellows? Surely not for the sake of wretched Egyptians." It is impossible to magnify the intensity of the feeling thus indicated. They regard any advance to Sinkat, where many think they are going, as fraught with the greatest risk, besides being needless. It is the scarcity of water, whichever way they turn, that troubles them more than the hot weather. Perhaps a week's rest may restore their spirits, but an infusion of new troops would do more.

Our spies say that the sheikhs with Osman Digna are consulting as to what they should do—whether they should fight, or make peace and disgrace him as a false leader. Their attitude, on Friday last, whilst we burned Tamaai, leads me to think, they may risk at least one more battle for the Mahdi's cause. Let us hope they will do it half-heartedly.

I returned to my old quarters in Mr. Levi's, and resumed my former routine of stated visits to the forts and camps to learn what was doing, or was likely to be done. I occasionally visited the wells just beyond the forts, and had a spin on horseback for a short distance outside on the plain. The friendlies by this time were herding their cattle—principally goats and camels—all around Suakim. They chiefly preferred the north-east, or Handouk side, driving the animals out from three to four miles to secure good pasturage of tangle-grass and scrub, which grew on the barren plain. These herdsmen went about armed, carrying the ordinary Hadendowa shield, spear, and bent stick; so that, in taking your canter, you had to be careful not to mistake friend for foe. With a friend or two I went out hunting and exploring occasionally among the nearest small khors.

The variety of rocks and minerals abounding in the neighbourhood was exceptional, and the quest proved most interesting. There were several thick veins of white quartz, and it was from this source the Arabs collected the pretty milky stones and pebbles to decorate the graves of their dead. The Titanic blocks of porphyry, cleft by Nature from the rugged mountain peaks, were piled together sometimes in strange fashion, like the monoliths at Stonehenge, as if by human aid. This was particularly noticeable in places between Handouk and Tambuk, which I afterwards visited. When returning from that expedition with the cavalry I frequently rode apart from the force to either have a closer look at the huge stones, or ride between the columns Nature had so fantastically erected, or under some enormous block resting like a lintel upon them.

The next chapter contains the official reports of the operations leading up to, including, and immediately following the battle of Tamaai.

CHAPTER XXI.

OFFICIAL DESPATCHES, TAMAAI.

THE following are a few of the more important official despatches describing the operations at Tamaai :

" From Sir G. Graham, dated Suakim, 14th (4.40 p.m.)
" Received at the War Office 8.40 p.m.

" In continuation of mine of yesterday actual casualties now stated as follows :

"*Killed*—Lieutenant Montresor, *Euryalus;* Lieutenant Almack, *Briton;* Lieutenant Houston Stewart, *Dryad;* Captain H. G. W. Ford, York and Lancaster; Aitken, Royal Highlanders; and 86 non-commissioned officers and privates, &c., whose names have been verified.

"*Wounded*—Captain Brophy, Lieutenant-Colonel Green, Lieutenant D. A. M'Leod, Royal Highlanders; Major M'Donald, 2nd Highland Light Infantry, attached to Royal Highlanders; Major R. Dalgetty, York and Lancaster; Surgeon H. C. R. Cross, Royal Navy;

Surgeon Prendergast, A.M.D.; M. St. Leger Herbert; and 103 non-commissioned officers and privates."

"From Sir G. Graham, Suakim, 14th (5.10 p.m.)
"Received at War Office, 14th (9.30 p.m.)

"March 14.—Marched whole force to Osman Digna's village, which was burnt, with large stores of ammunition for guns and rifles. One carriage gun removed.

"No opposition from the enemy; a few dropping shots only coming in, by which one man of the King's Royal Rifles was wounded.

"The headquarters and cavalry return to Suakim this evening. Infantry and artillery bivouac at Baker's zereba, and return to Suakim to-morrow.

"The wounded have been moved to Suakim this morning.

"All returned as missing now accounted for as killed."

Continuation of telegram from Sir G. Graham, dated Suakim, 14th, 5.10 p.m., received at War Office 14th, 10.15 p.m. :

"*Killed*—5 officers, 86 men. *Wounded*—8 officers, 103 men. *Missing*—19 men.

"I deeply regret losses, which were mainly caused by 2nd Brigade square being broken by charge of the enemy, who came on regardless of loss, 600 of their dead being counted at that point.

"Three officers and seven men Naval Brigade were killed at their guns, which for a few minutes were in the hands of the enemy, but were retaken.

"The enemy also attacked the 1st Brigade and the zereba at the same time, but were repulsed.

"They were in great force, not less than 10,000 or 12,000, and their loss is estimated at over 2,000 killed.

"I have withdrawn to the zereba occupied on Wednesday, but march on again to Tamaai this morning.

"The wounded are in the tents, with all necessary requirements, and are doing well."

Telegram from Sir G. Graham to Secretary of State for War:

"Suakim, March 15 (5.50 p.m.)

"All the tribes from Sinkat to Tokar were represented at Tamaai, and some men came from near Kasala.

"Osman was in command, but did not appear. Three sheikhs of distinction were killed, and a number of minor ones.

"Enemy's number probably at least 12,000. Impression prevails among Arabs that hostile tribes are losing confidence in Osman, and may soon be induced to treat.

"One hundred and fifty women from Sinkat carried out by Osman, supposed to be in mountains."

From Major-General Sir G. Graham, Commanding Expeditionary Force, to the Secretary of State for War.

"Camp, Suakim, March 15th, 1884.

"MY LORD,

"By my last despatch, posted on 11th March, the operations of this army were related up to the morning of that day.

"At 6 p.m. on the 11th instant, the artillery and infantry advanced to Baker's zereba, about $8\frac{1}{2}$ miles, reaching it about 10.30 p.m. There was a bright moon, and the night air soft and pleasant, so that the march did not distress the men, although it was hard work for the Naval Brigade.

"The strength of the force was as follows:

"ROYAL ARTILLERY.

"6th Batt. 1st Brigade, Scottish Division, 7-pounder camel battery, under Major Lloyd—8 guns, 7 officers, 100 non-commissioned officers and men, with 66 camels, carrying 90 rounds per gun.

"M Battery 1st Brigade, 9-pounder battery, under Major Holley—4 guns, 3 officers, 66 non-commisioned officers and men, with 52 mules, carrying 86 rounds per gun.

"1ST INFANTRY BRIGADE.

"Under Brigadier-General Buller, V.C., K.C.M.G., C.B.

"Royal Engineers, under Major Todd, R.E.— 5 officers, 57 non-commissioned officers and men.

"3rd King's Royal Rifles—19 officers, 546 non-commissioned officers and men.

"1st Gordon Highlanders—23 officers, 689 non-commissioned officers and men.

"2nd Royal Irish Fusiliers—17 officers, 326 non-commissioned officers and men.

"2ND INFANTRY BRIGADE.

"Under Major-General Davis.

"1st Royal Highlanders*—19 officers, 604 non-commissioned officers and men.

"1st York and Lancaster—14 officers, 421 non-commissioned officers and men.

"Royal Marine Artillery and Light Infantry—14 officers, 464 non-commissioned officers and men.

"General total of force of Artillery and Infantry, 116 officers and 3216 non-commissioned officers and men.

"The troops left in camp and garrison at Suakim consisted of the Cavalry Brigade and Mounted Infantry under Brigadier-General Stewart, with orders to join Infantry early next morning, and of the following details left to protect camp and town :

"100 Royal Marines in the fort guarding the town, with five guns in position.

"Sick and weakly men left in charge of the camp, the tents being left standing.

* Already in zereba.

"I appointed Lieutenant-Colonel Gordon, Argyll and Sutherland Highlanders, Commandant of the Base, under the orders of Admiral Hewett.

"At daybreak the Cavalry and Mounted Infantry watered at Suakim, and joined the force at Baker's zereba about 7 a.m. Their strength was as follows :

"10th Hussars—16 officers, 235 non-commissioned officers and men.

"19th Hussars—19 officers, 343 non-commissioned officers and men.

"Mounted Infantry—6 officers, 118 non-commissioned officers and men.

"Total Mounted Troops—41 officers, 696 non-commissioned officers and men.

"On arrival I at once sent the Mounted Infantry to the front accompanied by Colonel Ardagh as Intelligence Officer.

"About 10 a.m. it was reported to me that the enemy was in force some six miles distant. Accordingly I ordered the force to advance as soon as the men had had their dinners, and got in movement about 1 p.m. The afternoon was hot, and frequent halts were necessary. About 5 p.m. the cavalry scouts came in and I received a report in writing from the officer that the enemy was advancing to attack in force. Accordingly I at once formed up the troops in a defensive position on a favourable piece of ground having a clear space in front, and as there was now barely an hour of daylight left I directed the Engineers and pioneers of battalions to form a zereba around the camp by cutting down the prickly mimosa bushes which grew plentifully about.

"About 6 p.m. the Cavalry with Mounted Infantry were sent back to Baker's zereba with instructions to bring in the convoy that had been previously signalled for.

"About half-past 6 p.m. this convoy arrived safely, consisting of 245 camels carrying two days' supplies of water for men, 4,400 rations, forage for 1,200 horses, and reserve ammunition.

"Before this the enemy had fired a few rifle shots at us, and had shown in some numbers on a ridge about 1,000 to 1,200 yards distant. By way of checking this, and to show the power of our guns, I ordered out two of the 9-pounders under Major Holley, R.A., and fired four rounds of shrapnel, two of which burst with great accuracy. Captain Rolfe, R.N., also opened with a Gardner gun, and the enemy disappeared.

"About 11 p.m. Captain Rolfe informed me that he had just returned from an expedition to the front, where he had been to see the effect of our fire. He had found one or two dead bodies, and had come across some of the enemy's sentries fast asleep. Further back the natives were shouting and dancing around fires.

"About a quarter to 1 p.m. there was an alarm,

and the enemy opened a distant dropping fire, which continued throughout the night, causing but few casualties, but disturbing the men's rest.

"I had two of Naval Brigade machine guns run out, but as the range was (by interval between flash and sound) estimated at 1,400 to 1,500 yards, and no men showed themselves, it seemed to me better to treat the enemy's fire with silence, in preference to making an inefficient reply.

"Our casualties were 1 man killed, York and Lancaster; 1 officer and 4 men wounded, besides 2 camel-drivers and some horses struck.

"About 7 a.m. the Cavalry arrived, and at 7.30 Brigadier-General Stewart ordered out the Mounted Infantry to feel the enemy.

"There was a native with us who had lately been a prisoner in Osman Digna's camp, and who informed me that the bulk of their force would be in a deep khor or dry water-course, the sides of which would serve as an entrenchment. I therefore directed the advance to be made to the left of this position, where the ground rose a little, and from whence I hoped to be able to sweep the ravine with Artillery fire before attacking.

"The advance was made by the two Brigades in direct échelon of brigade squares from the left.

"The 2nd Brigade was in the following formation:—On the left flank, four companies of 1st Royal Highlanders, in open column of companies; on front face, three companies of 1st Royal Highlanders, and, at an interval of 30 yards, three companies of 1st York and Lancaster; on right flank, three companies of 1st York and Lancaster; the Royal Marines forming the rear face of square. Inside the square were the guns of the Naval Brigade, ready to run out when required. The 9-pounder battery, with transport animals, moved in rear of the right front of the square.

The 2nd Brigade began to advance from the place of formation about 8.30 a.m., and, owing to some delay in getting the 1st Brigade forward, were somewhat further in advance than I had intended when they first came in contact with the enemy.

"This occurred about 9 a.m., when a large number suddenly appeared from the edge of a ravine in the immediate front of the Brigade. These were soon cleared off; the Royal Highlanders distinguishing themselves by the gallant manner in which they cheered and charged up to the edge of the ravine; but at this moment a more formidable attack came from another direction, and a large body of natives, coming in one continuous stream, charged with reckless determination, utterly regardless of all loss, on the right-hand corner of the square formed by the 1st York and Lancaster. The Brigade fell back in disorder, and the enemy captured the guns of the Naval Brigade, which, however, were locked by officers and men, who stood by them to the last.

"When first coming into action, the 9-pounder

battery of four guns, under Major Holley, R.A., had been ordered outside the square on the right flank, and, when the disordered retirement took place in the 2nd Brigade, this battery was for a time unprotected by Infantry, and exposed to the assault of the enemy now coming on in crowds. Yet officers and men stood firmly to their guns, raking the advancing enemy with case, which told with deadly effect.

"The 1st Brigade was attacked about the same time, but stood firm, and the Cavalry moved up to protect the flank of the 2nd Brigade, which was soon rallied, and advanced to retake the guns of the Naval Brigade.

"The zereba was also threatened, but the little garrison stood to its arms and drove the enemy back.

"After this there was no more serious fighting, and the enemy retreated sullenly, making an occasional stand, towards the camp and village of Tamaai, which was occupied by the 1st Brigade, about 11.40 a.m., when I despatched a telegram to Admiral Hewett announcing the victory.

"The 2nd Brigade held the heights above the springs where the Cavalry watered. Ambulances and mule cacolets were sent for to bring away the dead and wounded, all being brought into the zereba occupied the previous night, where tents and all necessary medical requirements had already been brought up. The Cavalry returned again to Baker's zereba.

"The night was undisturbed by any fire from the enemy, but voices were heard shouting and wailing from the battle-field.

"On the morning of the 14th I sent the Cavalry on at once to the watering-place, where piquets of Mounted Infantry were posted on the heights. The enemy offered no opposition beyond sending a few dropping shots, which were replied to by selected marksmen.

"The whole force was moved out except the Naval Brigade, and the 1st Infantry Brigade crowned the heights above Osman's camp and village, whilst a fatigue party were employed collecting the ammunition preparatory to firing the huts. An escaped Egyptian soldier, one of the garrison of Tokar, informed me of a gun being there, but only the carriage could be found, which was destroyed, together with large quantities of ammunition.

"After the men's dinners the retirement commenced, the Cavalry going straight to Suakim, leaving only a squadron to cover the Infantry, who marched to Baker's zereba.

"The advanced zereba had been cleared. Two hundred sailors of the fleet, who had been promptly sent by Admiral Hewett, and two companies of the 1st Royal Highlanders, together with the ambulance and mule cacolets, being employed to carry the wounded.

"On the 15th the whole force was again concentrated at Suakim.

"In reviewing the operations of the force since landing at Suakim, I beg to record my opinion that the troops of all arms have behaved admirably.

"There has been no crime and no grumbling, even

all through the severe toil of the disembarkation, and of the march in the waterless desert. The absence of scares or panic among the troops during the nights, and especially their silence during the trying ordeal of a dropping fire on the night preceding the battle, all showed a sense of discipline and confidence worthy of the best troops. There was but a temporary check in one portion of the force during the action of Tamaai, and for that many reasons can be given. At the moment of receiving the attack the front face of the square of the 2nd Brigade was slightly disordered, owing to the gallant rush of the Royal Highlanders in charging the enemy to the top of the ravine.

"For this disorder I am to some extent personally responsible, as the charge took place under my eyes, and with my approval. My own observations of the attack were made from the right front angle, formed by the two half battalions of the 1st York and Lancaster, where I posted myself as soon as I saw the enemy's attack, and it was here the main rush came.

"It is the habit of these Arabs to attack the angles of squares, as they know that least fire can be brought to bear on them from these points.

"As the 9-pounder battery was on the right, the sailors' guns were on the left, but I at once sent for them to meet this attack from the right. The Arabs, however, gave no time for further arrangements, but, throwing themselves with desperate determination upon the angle of the square, broke it, carrying all before them. There were many attempted rallies among the

York and Lancaster, and at one time I was almost surrounded by the enemy, one of whom got over my horse's quarter.

"In rear of the square were the Royal Marines, than whom there can be no finer troops, and on whom I calculated as a reserve in the last emergency. Such, however, was the sudden nature of the disorder, and the impetuosity of the rush, that the Royal Marines were for a few minutes swept back, and mixed up in the general confusion.

"Yet, I submit, there was no panic among the men; they had been surprised, attacked suddenly, and driven back by a fanatical and determined enemy, who came on utterly regardless of loss, and who were, as I have since learned, led by their bravest chiefs. As soon as the men had had time to think they rallied and re-formed. This check affected only the 2nd Brigade. The remainder of the force, the Cavalry, the Royal Artillery, and 1st Brigade were firm and perfectly in hand, repulsing all attacks, and co-operating to assist the 2nd Brigade in driving back the enemy, who suffered tremendously for his temporary success, and never charged home again that day.

"Our loss was very grievous, many brave men of the Royal Highlanders and York and Lancaster devoting themselves to certain death in noble efforts to maintain the honour of their regiments.

"The Naval Brigade, too, fought desperately for their guns, 3 officers and 7 men being killed beside them; but they did not abandon them till they were locked, so that the enemy could not turn them against us.

"Many acts of the highest personal courage have come to my notice, and I propose bringing forward at a later period the names of officers and men who distinguished themselves on this occasion, and during the operations subsequent to the landing at Suakim."

The following despatch from Commander Ernest Rolfe, dated Suakim, March 16th, 1884, was forwarded by Rear-Admiral Sir William Hewett, K.C.B., K.C.S.I., V.C., Commander-in-Chief of Her Majesty's ships on the East India Station, has been received at the Admiralty:

"PROCEEDINGS OF NAVAL BRIGADE.

"Suakim, March 16, 1884.

"SIR,

"In compliance with your orders, the Naval Brigade (composed as per margin*) marched from Suakim at 7 p.m., on the 11th instant, arriving at the first zereba at 11.30 p.m., where they bivouacked for the night.

"The Naval Brigade left the zereba on the following day at 1 p.m., and at 5.30 p.m. the enemy was observed, but retired as the force advanced. Another zereba was then formed, where we bivouacked for

---

* One Commander, 5 lieutenants, 1 sub-lieutenant, 1 gunner, 2 midshipmen, 1 surgeon, 1 chaplain, 166 petty officers and seamen, 3 Gardner guns ·45 sec., three Gatling guns, ·45 sec.

the night. At sunset the enemy appeared in large numbers in our front, about 1,400 yards distant.

"Some 9-pounder shells were dropped among them, and two machine guns opened fire, to which the enemy replied. with their rifles. About 7 p.m. the firing ceased, but was renewed soon after midnight, and maintained till daylight.

"At daylight more shell and machine guns were fired; this had the effect of silencing the enemy till 8 a.m. The force advanced from the zereba at 8 a.m., the Naval Brigade being attached to the 2nd Brigade in the form of square, the front of which was formed by half battalions of the 42nd and 65th, the left flank by a half battalion of the 42nd, the right flank by a half battalion of the 65th, the rear brought up by the Royal Marines, the Naval Brigade in rear of the 42nd Regiment in columns of half batteries.

"At twenty minutes past eight the square advanced, and at half-past eight the order was given to charge. The front of the square and the guns advanced at the double till within five yards of a steep nullah; the right half battery was then brought into action on the right of the Black Watch, the left half battery filling up the angle of the square between the half battalions of the 42nd Regiment. Firing was at once commenced, but, the wind being from the north, the smoke from the guns and rifles prevented us in a great measure from seeing the enemy, who appeared to charge the right half battery in large force, which we seemed to be able easily to keep in check; but shortly afterwards a large body of the enemy charged our right flank, and drove the whole force back to the left rear.

"At this time it is with deep regret that I have to report that Lieutenants Almack, Houston Stewart, and Montrésor, as also 7 men, were killed while gallantly defending their guns. Lieutenant Conybeare also received a heavy blow from a club at the same time. After falling back about 200 yards the force formed up, and, advancing, recaptured the guns, which were immediately again placed in action. The enemy then retreated apparently completely routed, and the force proceeded down the right edge of a nullah to the wells at Temanhib, where we remained for dinner, returning to the zereba in the evening. All the wounded were placed under medical care, the dead being buried with funeral rites by the Rev. C. J. Todd, M.A., General Sir Gerald Graham, General Davis, and many officers and soldiers of the force attending. The brigade bivouacked at the zereba for the night.

"Next morning Lieutenants E. C. Moore and J. Brant joined in place of Lieutenants Almack and Montrésor.

"A reconnaisance in force was made, the magazines of the enemy were destroyed, and the village burnt, the troops remaining at the hills of Temanhib for dinner, returning to the first zereba in the evening, and to Suakim on the following day.

"Lieutenant Graham, who acted as my second in command, commanded the right half battery, and rendered me able assistance. He also acted in the same capacity at the battle of El Teb. I cannot represent the conduct of this officer too highly on both these occasions. I wish especially to bring to your notice the conduct of Mr. Edward Tyndale Biscoe and Mr. Edward Matson Hewett, midshipmen of the *Euryalus*, who, in a critical moment, when three lieutenants were killed, took command of the subdivisions, and acted with great coolness and gallantry. I consider these young officers showed a readiness of resource in a moment of danger, which I trust may receive some mark of your approval.

"The Rev. C. J. Todd, M.A., accompanied the force; and I consider the gallantry shown by him in action, when unarmed, and his kindness to the wounded, are beyond praise.

"Dr. Gimlette acted as Medical Officer to the force at both actions. I have already expressed my opinion of this officer's conduct in the first engagement, and need only now say that it was equally meritorious on the second occasion.—I have, etc.,

"E. ROLFE, Commander, R.N.

"Rear-Admiral Sir W. N. W. Hewett, K.C.B.,
"K.C.S.I., V.C., Commander-in-Chief.

"*Euryalus*, Suakim, March 19, 1884.

"NAVAL BRIGADE KILLED AND WOUNDED.
"*Killed*.

"*Euryalus*—W. H. H. Montrésor, Lieutenant.
"*Briton*—W. B. Almack, Lieutenant.

"*Dryad*—Houston Stewart, Lieutenant.
"*Euryalus*—John Strike, Torpedo Instructor.
"*Euryalus*—Thomas O'Brien, A.B.
"*Euryalus*—Benjamin Parrick, A.B.
"*Euryalus*—Richard Nicol, A.B.
"*Euryalus*—Harry Coward, A.B.
"*Briton*—James McLernan, A.B.
"*Dryad*—James L. Howarth, A.B.

"*Wounded.*

"*Hecla*—C. J. M. Conybeare, Lieutenant.
"*Euryalus*—Joseph Chetwin, Coxswain, second class; slightly (hand).
"*Euryalus*—Frank Freeman, Coxswain, second class, dangerously, spear wound.
"*Briton*—William Wood, Gunner's Mate, bullet through thigh.
"*Briton*—Frederick Johnson, Armourers' Crew.
"*Briton*—John Cross, A.B.
"*Sphinx*—William G. Newlove, A.B.
"*Hecla*—William Buckett, A.B.

CHAPTER XXII.

SUAKIM TO HANDOUK.

WHEN the more severely wounded cases had been sent away to the cooler region of Suez, and the troops had enough of idleness and were again longing for action of some kind, or for orders to return home, preparations were begun for another forward movement. The reports daily received from natives indicated that Osman was as recalcitrant and as far from giving in and suing for peace, as ever. Something more had therefore to be done to prove to the Arab mind that while willing to treat with them, we were not afraid to fight. Admiral Hewett was anxious to start on his mission to the capital of Abyssinia to negotiate a treaty with King John, but disinclined to start until matters had quieted down a little more at Suakim. Captain Speedy, the well-known traveller and hunter who had assisted in the expedition against King Theodore and Magdala, was in Suakim waiting to accompany the Admiral. I saw a good deal of him and listened, as everybody else did, with unbounded interest to his capital stories about that country and the black Christians whom we were about to court to enter into an alliance to assist the might of the British empire in withdrawing the Egyptian garrisons and saving General Gordon. Captain Speedy set out a few days later as *avant-courier* to Admiral Hewitt. The advance to Handouk, to which place, as well as beyond there, I accompanied the cavalry is told in the following telegrams and added remarks :

Suakim, Monday, 10.47 a.m.

The *Sphinx* leaves to-morrow for Massowah with a small party to report on defences of that place. She will return in a few days.

Our Arab "friendlies" declare that there will never be peace if the Egyptians are left to govern the country, as the natives have proved their military superiority over them.

They consider that the only chance of restoring order will be by an occupation of the ports by the British friendlies themselves. They would distrust their former rulers.

Suakim, March 17 (7.45 p.m.)

The 19th Hussars, half a company of the Royal Engineers, accompanied by the Mounted Infantry and the Gordon Highlanders, start for Handouk at eight to-morrow morning, General Stewart commanding the force. The animals will draw their water supply from the wells at Handouk, the men getting condensed water. A strong position will be secured for any advance.

The Provost Marshal's Department has had a busy day at Suakim. Sixteen Egyptian camel-drivers, of the Carrier Corps, who, on Thursday last, bolted from the new zereba back to the town, were ordered to receive a flogging. The men were little worse than the rest of the Egyptians of the same corps, all of whom bolted for the rear when the 2nd Brigade began retiring. Some halted at Baker's zereba, doubtless unable to travel further, but sixteen got into the town and spread an alarming story of a disaster to the troops. They were condemned to death, but General Graham substituted flogging. It is worthy of note that these were men represented as volunteers, who at Cairo wept and begged permission to accompany the British force.

This afternoon, a company of Marines, under Captain Baldwin, of the *Euryalus*, marched into the Custom House yard to preserve order and assist at the execution of the sentence on the men of the Carrier Corps, and also thirty-eight Egyptian soldiers who mutinied to-day. The latter refused to work or guard the convicts any longer, and demanded to be sent to Cairo. Instead, they were ordered twenty-four lashes each, and imprisonment at Massowah for a year. This example was thought necessary, as there are 700 Egyptian soldiers at Suakim.

Twelve of the Carrier Corps were first tied to the wheels of wagons, getting several dozen each, and were afterwards cautioned and sent back to duty. The soldiers then had stripes laid on by the Provost-Marshal's men. All of them howled from the first to the last blow, though the flogging was not nearly so severe as the Marines inflicted, at Alexandria, on the looters and incendiaries.

The Abyssinian scouts had a war-dance at their camp to-night, killing an ox in honour of the victory.

Spies report that Osman Digna is at Tamanieb, about nine miles in the hills, west of the late camp, trying to collect more men for further opposition.

To-day there are fifty-seven cases in hospital, all slight. Lord Wolseley telegraphed "Well done, old comrades," to the Black Watch.

Suakim, March 17 (9.15 p.m.)

Admiral Hewett, Deputy-Governor Brewster, and others witnessed the flogging of the Egyptians. The Admiral told the officer supposed to be implicated that if it were proved that he had instigated the mutiny he would be shot, and that only his rank saved him a flogging. The officer was ordered under arrest.

The Egyptians probably bear flogging worse than any people that form of punishment was ever visited upon. They are thorough physical cowards, without a particle of manliness, and the cut of the cat-o'-nine-tails or the thud of the "kurbash"—a thick-looped rope—invariably wrings from them the most terrible wailings and fervent appeals for clemency. Their ejaculations are loud and incessant, and they wring and writhe in a piteous way under the punishment. When it is over they sneak off to weep and lament whilst the sting tingles; but the moment their backs cease to ache and vex them, they are as pert, chatty, and full of vapid laughter as ever, the punishment having no moral degradation for them.

It is sad to have to admit so much against one's common humanity, but it looks as if Ismael Pasha had much to justify him in his oft-quoted remark that Egypt could not be ruled without the "kurbash." Poor wretches! they seem to be so utterly bereft of judgment and common-sense at times, that no appeal short of brute force has the slightest effect upon their understandings.

Handouk (*via* Suakim), March 18 (5.20 p.m.)

General Stewart's force arrived here at one o'clock, without seeing even a single unfriendly native. I went with the troops. The huts here were deserted. Our vedettes occupy the summit of the outlying spurs of the hills, and the enemy is invisible. A laager will be formed at the base of a detached hill, 200 feet high. General Buller accompanied the force as spectator. The infantry remain here; the 19th Hussars and General Stewart go on to Otao, six miles further, returning to the camp here. A squadron, mounted on English horses, led the advance.

The laager, or zereba, which was formed at the

base of the hill, extending to within a few yards of the more permanent wells of water, was triangular-shaped. The apex was at the hill-top, the sides enclosing the west face of the hill, and the base line, at the foot. The latter was protected by a wire entanglement and small iron spikes, called "crows' feet."

Suakim, March 18 (7 p.m.).

A few more malcontent Egyptians were flogged to-day. Admiral Hewett reprimanded and liberated the Egyptian officer imprisoned yesterday.

The small force under General Stewart scouted a few miles beyond Handouk, but no enemy was seen. The troops have encamped at the base of a hill, the top of which and an adjacent hill are held by a company of Gordon Highlanders, who have built a low wall of stones on the summit, behind which they lie. At the base, covering the wells, a strong zereba has been constructed, within which the transport and baggage animals, as well as the rest of this force, are entrenched.

The troops went forward by easy stages, and as a breeze was stirring the men stood the journey well, arriving in good order.

To-morrow morning General Graham intends visiting General Stewart's camp. The last-named General and three squadrons, with the Mounted Infantry, will start at 5 to-morrow morning for a six hours' journey to Otao, and beyond, to ascertain the feeling of the natives.

This evening Mahmoud Ali and 50 of his followers arrived at the Handouk camp. They state that Osman Digna's force is increasing, and that he announces his intention to renew the fighting within ten days. He was twice beaten before, he says, but that this time he will surely win. He has now 2,000 men, and there are a lot of rebels among the hills between Handouk and Suakim. Mahmoud Ali's people add that they will endeavour to cut off any convoys left unguarded beyond Handouk.

Osman Digna is at Tamanieb.

There was an abundant supply of water at Handouk. The well in front of the zereba was simply a round hole 6 or 7 feet deep, and as many wide, dug in the clayey shingle. There were always from 3 to 4 feet of water in it, and no amount of "drawing" for the horses emptied it. If it was plied too industriously the water became muddy, but the supply was not affected. Several barrels and hogsheads were sunk in the plain at the foot of the hill, and in each of these there was also plenty of water. The natives, when they required water, went into the dry bed of the river or khor, and scraping away a foot or two of the loose sand and shingle came upon the water. There were thus ample facilities for baths and morning "tubs," and we made the most of our opportunities in that direction. The troops were ordered to drink the condensed water carried up from the base at Suakim. This they did, but as their thirst was great they superadded to it refreshing draughts of the cool and slightly mineral-tasted waters of Handouk. So far as we could see, no one was any the worse because of these indulgences in good teetotal beverages.

The hills and bushes were full of ringdoves, that kept up a perpetual billing and cooing. There were pigeons flying about the deserted huts of the Arabs, whilst sand-grouse, quail, and bustards could also be found near the camp. For larger game there were gazelle and antelopes, and we used to see the tracks of wild animals, chiefly leopards, along the khors, which they no doubt visited in search of water. We killed a good many doves, and General Stewart had the luck to kill the first bustard (a sort of African wild turkey) and a gazelle.

I went out shooting one day with Lieutenants Payne and Livingstone of the Mounted Infantry, going due west, to get a look at a large mass of white quartz in the mountains immediately opposite the zereba. This quartz was for several days a matter of dispute as to whether it was not smoke, which in its opaque whiteness it exactly resembled, seen through the haze of an African sky. We, however, settled the question that it was a large square vein of quartz jutting out of the mountain side.

That morning, in going out our party saw several bustards and gazelle, without being able to get any with the two carbines and pistol comprising our armament. On returning we met with a small herd of antelope, and Lieutenant Payne wounded a large doe weighing over 75 lb. Having dismounted his horse escaped, and I gave him mine to endeavour to recover it whilst I followed up and despatched the wounded animal. Lieutenant Livingstone had gone away off to the left, to go around an isolated hill, and both he and Payne were soon out of sight and hearing on the rather thickly mimosa-covered plain.

In a moment it flashed upon me that it was not a good spot to be in alone. Arabs might be hiding about in the bush; and, at any rate, I was too near the hills, and so under the watchful eyes of any of their scouts who were sure to be looking down from the height of the mountain crags. Catching the animal by the horns, I thought it wisest to make my way, however slowly, in the direction of the camp; and so started to drag the game home. The day was very warm, and I grew warmer every step I took. At length, after going nearly two miles, my two friends, who had become alarmed and were searching for me, heard my answering halloa and came up. Lieutenant Payne had been unable to recapture his horse, which however trotted back riderless to camp. I remounted my nag, and carrying the venison we soon covered the remaining two miles and got in safe and sound.

The following telegrams describe what afterwards occurred during the cavalry's stay at Handouk:

Suakim, March 19 (3.5 p.m.)

The Handouk force at the zereba were undisturbed during the night.

General Stewart, with two squadrons of the 19th

and Mounted Infantry in advance, left at five this morning for Otao. The route was due west, eight miles, among khors and the dry water-courses of the outlying spurs of the Soudan range.

The country is pretty open, with a few mimosa.

No enemy was seen at Otao. We saw three natives and a sheikh named Hadar Abdullah, a subordinate of Mahmoud Ali. Abdullah said he was coming in with 100 men to-morrow.

Digna was still in the Tamanieb valley, a few miles from Tamaai.

A squadron of the 19th, under Major Flood, also went five miles to-day towards Tamanieb without seeing any one.

All the squadrons returned to camp at noon.

There is but one well at Otao, but water was plentiful, though slightly bitter.

A post will likely be formed there, and to-morrow another squadron will scout as far as Hambuk, eight miles beyond Otao, where the people are friendly.

General Graham visits Handouk to-day.

Suakim, March 19 (7.20 p.m.)

Sir General Graham returned to Suakim at five o'clock.

General Stewart, with a squadron, scouts to-morrow five miles beyond Handouk camp, towards Tamanieb, and on Friday he will move fourteen miles into the hills to Hambuk or Tambuk.

Our spies report that Osman Digna is three miles west of Tamaai.

Suakim, March 20 (1.10 p.m.)

Admiral Hewett to-day issued a notice withdrawing the reward for Osman Digna, adding that in future no money reward will be offered.

Another escaped Egyptian soldier from Sinkat came in to-day, and reports that Osman Digna has 290 wounded. All the sheikhs are still with him.

Osman has asked all the tribes to meet him to-morrow, to arrange for renewing the fighting.

A spy confirms the above.

Suakim, March 20 (5.20 p.m.)

Two batteries of artillery and the 10th Hussars go to Handouk to-morrow morning. The Hussars will return in the evening.

Handouk (*viâ* Suakim), March 21 (5.55 p.m.)

There are no signs of the enemy. The cavalry are reconnoitring in various directions among the hills.

General Buller and the Sheikh Morghani have arrived at Handouk from Suakim.

Morghani has held a durbar with the friendly sheikhs.

Major Wood, with a squadron of the 19th, went towards Tamanieb this morning. He met six Arabs, with camels loaded with grain from Tokar. They reported Tokar almost deserted.

Several squadrons of the 10th left Suakim this morning to intercept a convoy of forty camels carrying grain from Tokar to Digna's camp.

The subjoined telegraphic report will perhaps sufficiently indicate the official anxiety (instigated from London) of the Commanding Officer to meet more than half-way any overtures for alliance with wavering sheikhs or renegade followers of Osman Digna. The gold and presents lavished on Mahmoud Ali and his kidney were to my mind worse than wasted. The brave men who saw that we preferred to buy or bribe, rather than deal firmly, understood and contemned such acts as only indicating fear and weakness on our part.

"From Major-General Sir G. Graham to the Secretary of State for War.

"Suakim, March 20 (4 p.m.)

"Report received from Handouk that three sheikhs of the Samara and Amrar tribes, with 17 followers, have come in to-day. Mahmoud Ali Bey says more will come to-morrow, when the Holy Sheikh and brother are going out to Handouk. The percentage of sick in the whole force is below 2."

Hambuk (*viâ* Suakim), March 22 (3.0 p.m.)

Forty men, women, and children of the Brunoo tribe, Kokabey, Central Africa, have arrived in camp. They have a wretched appearance, and look as if they were slaves. Their leader is Mohammed Zangi. They left their home two years ago, and intended going to Suakim to rest. A party of 200 more are coming in to-morrow.

They had heard nothing of the Mahdi. The road to Berber, from which they had just come, was quite open.

The Arabs were running away westward.

Suakim, March 23 (8 p.m.)

General Stewart left Handouk at half-past three on Saturday morning with the 19th Hussars and Mounted Infantry for Tambuk, on the Berber caravan road, and I accompanied the force. A son of Mahmoud Ali, the friendly chief, and a native acted as guides.

At Otao, eight miles to the westward, there was a brief halt. Thence to Hambuk we saw no enemy, and arrived at nine. There was a good supply of brackish but drinkable water, and a number of natives around the one well at Hambuk, herding camels, sheep, and goats, peaceful and pastoral. The guides said they were of their tribe. The natives reported that the country was rapidly quieting down; that the road to Sinkat, if not to Berber, was quite open; that Digna's men were rapidly deserting; but that Osman himself was still near Tamanieb with about 100 followers. The force started back at eleven in the forenoon, and reached Handouk about three o'clock.

The country slopes gradually upward in a westerly direction, through stony plains, or valleys dotted with mimosa and bunch grass. The hills all rise sharply up from the tableland, so that troops could easily proceed among them from valley to valley, marching through the intervening rolling ground. This seems to be a characteristic of the Soudan; mountain chains, advancing and retiring. The ground for a mile in front and on the flanks was admirably searched by scouts.

Ten days have now elapsed since the battle of Tamaai. Some are chafing at our inaction, and the practice of trusting solely to spies and friendly natives for information. The cavalry will be able to take care of itself.

A movement has at last been ordered. To-day (Sunday) the Gordon Highlanders left Handouk for a point ten miles nearly west by north of Suakim, where a new zereba will be formed near the entrance to the depression leading to the Tamanieb Valley. A company of the 89th left Suakim camp at eight this morning, to effect a junction with the Gordon Highlanders, carrying entrenching tools and guarding a convoy of water and stores. The Gordons missed their way for a time, getting among hills due west, but they saw nobody, and eventually the forces met at the place appointed.

To-morrow General Graham goes forward to

examine this newest zereba, near which water has been found. On Tuesday the whole force will advance thither and bivouac; and on Wednesday will press on towards Osman's present camp, four miles beyond Tamanieb, and about ten miles from the bivouac.

To-day a sheikh of the Samarars, who had left Digna, came into Suakim with 50 followers.

There are 93 men in hospital, but none from sunstroke, and all the cases are slight.

On the way to Hambuk with the cavalry, I climbed the steep sides of a detached conical hill, which was 500 feet above the plain. There were a few natives and cattle visible, but no sign of any force. The annexed map shows the places referred to. Tamanieb is among the hills about 8 miles westward of Tamaai.

HAMBUK TO ES SIBIL.

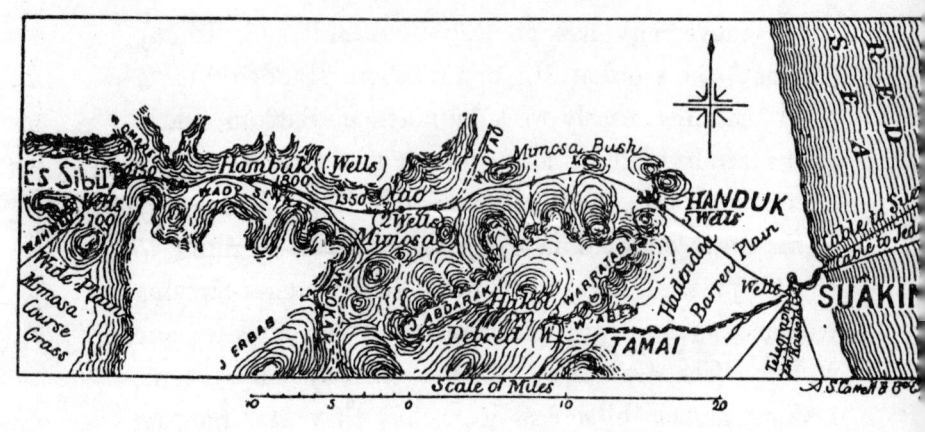

CHAPTER XXIII.

ANOTHER FORWARD MOVEMENT.

EVERYBODY was glad to have something to do and to get within striking distance of Osman Digna once more, and the General Order directing a forward movement was hailed with delight, as it was thought this time, at all events, the campaign would be terminated. The following telegrams show what took place:

Suakim, March 24 (8.45 p.m.)

A General Order to-day directs the advance of the entire force from Suakim camp except a small garrison, as far as zereba No. 4, to-morrow afternoon, at two o'clock. Convoys have been pressed forward all day with water and stores. Water is still the one great obstacle to rapid movement; and, although men are put upon the shortest allowance, and the horses have to drink brackish well water, the reserve increases slowly. The heat to-day has been intense.

General Graham and Staff inspected the new zereba

and afterwards rode four miles towards the north-west. A new zereba (No. 5) was ordered to be formed at the base of the hills, solely for the Cavalry camp. Two companies of the 75th marched and assisted in making the necessary enclosure, whilst a squad of Engineers sank barrels, the ends of which were knocked out, in order to make wells for watering the horses.

To-night spies state that Osman has 700, some say 4,000 men, and that he will certainly fight us. From zerebas 4 and 5, one could plainly see the conical hills, eight miles to the westward, near which Osman is encamped. Small scouting parties of our Cavalry to-day, however, failed to stir up his warriors.

General Graham will bivouac with the troops at zereba No. 4 to-morrow, and early on Wednesday the force will seek and offer battle to Osman's followers. On this occasion, we are not to be accompanied by the Naval Brigade and machine guns; at least, up to to-night no orders to that effect have been issued. The day has passed quietly, the enemy not having in any way attempted to molest the troops or convoys.

The Abyssinians, who have done such excellent service, have had their arms taken from them and been disbanded by Admiral Hewett, for alleged mutinous conduct within the last two days; but they will probably be reorganised to-morrow.

It appears that complaints were preferred against them. They are accused of interfering with, and thrashing, Egyptians on two or three occasions. Their conduct arose chiefly out of their desire to free an enslaved Kasala woman. In fact, the Abyssinians cannot understand why their people should be still kept as slaves by Egyptians, under the English flag, and they have shown, perhaps, a pardonable anxiety to release their enslaved fellow-countrymen. According to the English Consul Baker, and others of our authorities here, the Egyptian Convention is in force, and the British must protect Egyptians who have property in human chattels. We have already sent back several slaves to their Egyptian masters; those masters, speaking of whom the Arabs say, without us they could not remain on the Red Sea coast one day.

Scarcely a week ago, a slave of a local dignitary, Sinawi Bey, who fondly thought the presence of the English freed him, ran away, alleging that his master ill-treated him, and took service with a fellow correspondent. Consul Baker says that the man must be returned to Sinawi, who now has two other unwilling slaves in the police station, where they are being beaten into a tractable condition. I do not regret adding that the correspondent's servant has vanished to a place of safety.

The remarks made at the time by the editor of *The Daily Telegraph*, in connection with the Soudan slave question, are so appropriate that I have here quoted them in full:

"The intelligence furnished in our special correspondent's message regarding the action of the British authorities at Suakim in the matter of runaway slaves brings this question into a new and very perplexing light. Admiral Hewett appears to think himself bound —whether by orders from home, or by reason of General Gordon's proclamation—not only to punish his Abyssinian scouts for setting free their countrywomen, but on his own account to restore escaped slaves to their masters. The 'Hubshees,' who did such good service at Teb and Tamasi, have been degraded and imprisoned because they could not stand seeing Abyssinian women enslaved by the Egyptians, and certain bondsmen who have heard that the British flag was a symbol of freedom have fled, we are told, to its shelter, only to be dragged back again to servitude. It is quite certain that the gallant admiral and his officers would not, of their own accord, carry out such a policy. They must feel the intense absurdity and, what is more, the deep disgrace of patrolling the African coast at Zanzibar to suppress the slave traffic, while at Suakim the British fleet and our land forces thus act as slave-drivers. How this is to be conciliated with the character of Great Britain, how it is to be justified to the Africans, to morality, and to Continental opinion, does not seem at all easy or plain. It is surely one thing for General Gordon to find himself under the urgent necessity of tolerating at Khartoum, and in the "interior of the Soudan," a system of domestic slavery which he has no power to suppress, and quite another to see our representatives in the Eastern Soudan and upon the Red Sea littoral thus adopting a positive reversal of the British habit of enfranchisement as a law binding upon them. If there could be any logic left in so unfortunate a business, it may be presumed that Admiral Hewett will have next to deal by martial law with the correspondent who has afforded shelter to the runaway slave alluded to, and we shall actually hear of an Englishman punished for *not* abetting slavery. Certainly, no more bewildering and disquieting contradiction was ever presented to the British public than in the news of these forcible restorations to slavery at Suakim by the Power which at Zanzibar sinks an Arab dhow with shot and shell if it attempts to carry men and women into enforced servitude."

I have but one statement to add. Despite Parliamentary evasions and equivocations, Admiral Hewett, within two days from the publication of the foregoing, set the Abyssinian woman free from her pretended Egyptian husband, sending her back to Massowah by steamer. She was a native of a village on Kash River, coming from the same place as Tedelar, the leader of the Abyssinian scouts, who personally knew that the Arab slave-hunters had raided the district, killing the woman's husband and carrying her and her two children off into captivity.

Suakim, Tuesday (11.45 a.m.).

Our one wounded rebel prisoner, who was shot in the back and leg at the battle of Tamaai, died in hospital here this forenoon of gangrene.

The utmost care has been taken to disinfect the ward.

General Graham's spies report that Osman Digna's warriors number nearly 1,000, that this force is increasing, and that they will fight.

Suakim, March 25 (2.55 p.m.).

The sheikhs of a number of small tribes, representing in the aggregate about 2,500 men, have intimated their willingness to come in.

Osman's camp is nearly twenty-five miles from Suakim, or thirteen beyond the zereba. The direct road is difficult.

General Graham intends advancing eleven miles to-morrow and making a new zereba. The battle, therefore, would be on Thursday.

Suakim, March 25 (5.35 p.m.).

At four o'clock General Graham and Staff, with the force, left for zereba No. 4. About 300 Marines and Blue-jackets were landed to-day from the *Carysfort* and *Euryalus* to garrison the lines and forts. Preparations, I learn, are being made for Marines to garrison Suez for a year, and Massowah also.

Zereba No. 4, Wednesday Morning (*viâ* Suakim,
March 26, 10.10 a.m.)

Last night's bivouac passed without incident, and the repose of the troops was undisturbed. Yesterday's march from Suakim hither was a trying one on account of the heat, and 300 or 400 fell out through exhaustion. A night's rest has brought the men round, and, with the exception of four, all have returned to duty. Even three of these will go back to the ranks to-day, and the doctors state that only one man will remain unfit for service, because of slight sunstroke.

Zereba No. 4 is square, with sides of 100 yards; and, the enclosure being too small to hold the total force, only the ammunition, stores, water, and the 75th Regiment were inside it. The rest of the troops bivouacked on the rear face of the zereba. The infantry were formed, as at Tamaai, in two brigades, first and second, Buller's, Davis'; and the men lay down with their arms. General Graham also withdrew the outlying cavalry, and General Stewart's command was encamped close behind the oblong formed by the infantry brigades. A double line of sentries was thrown forward, supported by strong pickets, to guard against the possibility of a surprise. The men soon had fires lit and supper ready, after which nearly everybody, tired out with the day's work, lay down for the night.

Yesterday the infantry carried fifty rounds per man only, and, perhaps, much of the falling out on the march was due in some degree to the fact that the men had dined, and that many had drunk copious draughts of canteen beer before starting, that beverage evidently overheating them.

During the night Major Chermside, R.E., came

in along with a party of natives, recruited during the afternoon in Suakim. They included 7 minor sheikhs and 161 men, all armed with their own weapons, swords and spears. Sheikh Morghani accompanied them, some of the Arabs acting as his bodyguard. In order to distinguish them from the enemy, each man wears a piece of red calico round his head or neck.

The scouts having reported last night their inability to find out either the enemy's exact position or force, General Graham has determined on resting the infantry here to-day, and on sending General Stewart forward with the entire cavalry force to ascertain Osman's whereabouts. The troopers are to be accompanied by our new native auxiliaries, who are, by General Graham's orders, to scout, not to fight. They leave this place at 9 a.m., and, of course, I go with them. Sheikh Morghani says there will be no more fighting; that when we go forward the sheikhs in the mountains, all of whom are tired of the war, will give in their submission, and that Osman Digna will run. He was mistaken, however, before about the end of the fighting, and may be so again. We are off.

CHAPTER XXIV.

THE SKIRMISH AT TAMANIEB.

THE last act of the campaign was fairly entered upon, and the events which transpired are detailed in the following despatches and notes thereon:

Near Tamanieb, Wednesday Night (viâ Suakim), March 26, 9.5 p.m.

General Stewart's Brigade of Cavalry, after leaving zereba 4, proceeded at a walk towards Tamanieb. General Graham's orders were that operations should be confined to reconnoitring, the troops to fall back on learning the enemy's actual position. The cavalry went forward in échelon of troops from the right of brigade, the 10th Hussars leading. The front of the advance was covered by scouts drawn from the 10th Hussars, under the command of Major Gough, and the flanks and rear by troopers from the 19th Hussars. The Mounted Infantry, under Captain Humphreys, for a time marched in rear of the Hussar regiments. For the first four or five miles it was easy going along the plain through mimosa sparsely growing, and occasionally over bare patches of sand, gravel, and small stones.

When we got to the foot hills, the ground became very rough, full of sharp pieces of splintered gneiss, granite, and green stone, making the horses walk as gingerly as cats on a broken glass wall, and laming several, despite the utmost care. It was the worst piece of ground we have as yet traversed in the campaign. For about five miles our 168 native auxiliaries, under Major Chermside, moved in a line, parallel with the right of the 10th Hussars. The force held to the left in order to get the benefit of the light sea-breeze, which otherwise would have been at our backs, and to enable us to turn the right flank of the enemy's position and have our rifle smoke carried away from our lines.

Just at the entrance to the foot-hills we noticed small parties of Arabs on our front and flanks. They were mostly on foot, but about half a dozen were seen on fleet-footed dromedaries watching us. One and all retired as we moved on, taking a westerly course. Finding an isolated, conical hill about 600 feet high, General Stewart established a heliographic station, signalling therefrom back to the zereba, five miles in our rear.

Still pushing along over rough ground, a slight change was effected in the line of advance. The native auxiliaries were all sent to the rear of the cavalry, except six, who, with Major Chermside, went to the front, with instructions to tell all Arabs that the

THE PRELIMINARY SKIRMISH.

English troops had no quarrel against them, and would not injure anyone unless fired upon; whilst, as to Osman Digna, if he would surrender and come in, his life would be spared. Three of the natives were mounted, and they galloped about, trying to communicate these tidings to their fellow Hadendowa tribesmen who had espoused the Mahdi's cause. They were invariably distanced by the enemy's outlying scouts, and never had a chance even to shout their message of peace. The Mounted Infantry were also sent in advance that the enemy might have a taste, if necessary, of accurate shooting from long rifles instead of carbines.

Five miles more we got over, and the cavalry were now among the hills, which surrounded them on every side. The higher peaks were between 3,000 and 4,000 feet. Here a second signal station was placed on a boldly defined hill, 600 feet high.

From the top could be seen the enemy's position at the foot of a bold range of white hills, streaked with quartz. It was a little over two miles distant. The Arabs were standing along the crest of a nullah singly and in groups of ten to twenty. About 200 in all were visible along the line, a mile in extent. Behind them were the wells and running waters of Tamanieb khor. Heaps of stones, like Highland cairns, had marked the nullah ridges for miles. Monuments and graves to departed sheikhs stood clearly up against the sky-line where the enemy were gathered. Major Chermside and two of his natives went to within 800 yards to talk with the Arabs, but his overtures were received with a volley from their Remingtons, and that, in an instant, put to flight all hope of their submission.

It was now about half-past one o'clock, and in a few minutes our Mounted Infantry, pressing up to within 700 yards of the enemy, who was keeping up a sharp rifle fire at our advance, replied with telling effect. Several volleys were fired at the Arabs where they had gathered thickest on the crest of the nullah, and a few of them were seen to drop. Until three o'clock a lively skirmish was carried on between the Mounted Infantry and the enemy, the latter soon showing very little of their swarthy bodies, but firing from behind rocks.

The object of the reconnaissance having been secured, General Stewart directed the withdrawal of the troops. As the Mounted Infantry fell back at a slow walk, the Arabs jeered at us. I was with the men, and heard them distinctly enough; but, all the same, the enemy seemed chary either of showing himself or pushing the men as they retired.

Evidently the enemy have a very strong position, out of which only infantry can turn them. They, however, showed little of their former eagerness for battle, and during our fire many of them were seen to move off to the hills on their right. Our loss was but one horse killed, shot through the head. General Stewart and the troops returned to the first signal station, five miles from zereba No. 4, and there he was met by General Buller, who had advanced with the 75th and 89th, having left the camp in the forenoon.

The news from the front, also, had the effect of bringing General Graham and his staff out; and, in the afternoon, orders were issued directing the whole force, except the 65th and sick or invalid men, to move out, together with all necessary supplies, and join General Buller. The 42nd, Marines, and 60th set out about five o'clock, and two hours later all were safely encamped five miles south-west of zereba No. 4. Bushes were cut and a new zereba made, and there the troops will bivouac to-night, advancing early to-morrow to drive Osman out of his last stronghold. zereba No. 4 will be held as a base for the troops who are at the front.

The enemy number probably 3,000. They have plenty of cattle.

I rode forward during the skirmish, joining the Mounted Infantry engaged in that work. The Arabs fired from behind rocks, often aiming their Remingtons through crevices at our men. One or two of our fellows, in order to draw the enemy's fire, and ascertain their exact whereabout, used to rise and look at the Arabs, who then were from 400 to 600 yards distant. Bang! the Arab guns went, and at the flash and smoke they made our fellows, who were lying down to watch their opportunity, sharply replied. I saw a rock crevice through which an Arab had fired for an hour, the front of which for a space of one yard was plastered with the splash from lead bullets.

Tamanieb (*viâ* Suakim), March 27.

General Graham's force made an early start this morning for Osman Digna's camp, so as to avoid marching during the heat of the day.

A pleasant night was spent at the advanced zereba. It was cool, and there were no sick. The Cavalry bivouacked in the rear of the zereba, within which both brigades lay down beside their arms. There were no alarms to disturb their rest.

Everybody fell in at 5 a.m., and by 5.40 we were again on the march.

The Cavalry and Mounted Infantry went to the front, followed by the Infantry in échelon of brigade square—General Buller's Brigade, the 1st, leading, the six guns of the camel battery and four 9-pounders of R.A., under Major Holley, moving between the squares.

The 1st Brigade was composed as follows: 75th, 89th, and 60th Regiments.

The 2nd Brigade included the Black Watch and Marines, with a few detailed men from the 65th.

Major Chermside, with his Native Auxiliaries, moved on the left flank of the 2nd Brigade.

In advancing our front and flanks were finely covered and protected by General Stewart's Cavalry.

The total of our force was about 3,000 men, the reduction being due to the absence of the Naval Brigade, casualties, invalided and weak men left behind.

The troops went forward very slowly, the Cavalry proceeding along the crests of the nullahs and ridges, and the Infantry taking the best ground obtainable, sometimes walking in the khors, and occasionally skirting the high ground. Short halts were made from time to time to breathe men and horses, the rough ground proving very trying.

All were in the best of spirits, not so much at the prospect of another brush with the enemy, but because it was understood to-day was to end the campaign for the season.

As we came near the enemy's position, General Stewart sent the Mounted Infantry, under Captain Humphreys, and a squadron of the 10th Hussars, under Major Gough, three miles in advance of the Infantry brigades, to occupy the ground held during yesterday's skirmish. The enemy opened a sharp rifle fire upon the troopers, who were going forward, firing as they went at every 100 yards.

It was exactly half-past seven when the fusillade began. Apparently Osman Digna's followers had thrown out their right flank somewhat since yesterday, for it was from a mass of rocks on our left, close to which the Mounted Infantry got yesterday, that the heaviest firing came. The enemy were also showing in greater numbers on the ridge in front of the villages and wells. Leaving the slowly-moving Infantry behind, I had joined the Cavalry to witness the opening of the day's struggle, intending, of course, to return to the squares when the more serious business of the assault began.

The troopers kept creeping forward under cover of the rocks and ridges, cracking away at the enemy from every point. After half an hour's firing General Stewart ordered the Mounted Infantry to move to our left, leaving the centre of the position to the Hussars. The object of this change was to get around the enemy's right flank, opening up to an enfilading fire the khor in which Digna had ensconced himself and his men.

We were without further accurate information as to the enemy's numbers beyond what has been already communicated. They were anything, we were told, from 500 to 5,000 strong.

Whilst the troopers moved to the left, the Arab fire grew livelier, and our men replied quite as sharply, firing occasional volleys. Still our men pressed on. By 9.10 a.m. General Graham and Staff had come up with the reserve of the Mounted Infantry, leaving the infantry of the 1st Brigade behind.

Shortly after the enemy's fire slackened. Getting within 600 yards of the khor the firing quickened, the ping and crack of the rifles re-echoing from hundreds of surrounding crags and rocks.

By 9.50 the cavalry skirmishers were within 100 yards of Tamanieb khor. Below us we could see a small stream of running water, some 4 feet wide and 6 inches deep.

The enemy were making off in small numbers to our left and right. Indeed, all the morning but comparatively few of them were seen.

The men and horses brightened at the sight of the water, for the morning was very warm. As for the horses, some of the poor brutes had drunk no water for twenty-four hours. Thirst had actually disabled half-a-score of them, and these were lying down in the bottom of the khors along our route, gasping and with parched tongues.

By this time the 1st Brigade had got up to within 800 yards, and two shells from the 9-pounders were sent hurtling among the rocks, bursting close to the flying Arabs. The khor was now clear, and down into it everybody went, making straight for the water.

For the second time since our arrival in Soudan, man and horse had an unrestricted and unlimited supply, and the best use was made of the opportunity. The soldiers not only drank copiously, but laved faces and hands in the clear, cool running stream. A few bathed under a pretty little cascade that fell from a low ledge of rocks.

After a quarter of an hour's halt, the cavalry formed up and moved to the right and left along the the stream. To our right was a green grove of trees and a village. The latter was burned.

I close this despatch at 11.50, and will send you further particulars later.

General Graham has decided that, after thoroughly exploring the vicinity, everybody shall return towards Suakim to-night. The campaign is over.

We have no casualties except amongst the horses. Several of the enemy were hit.

Suakim, March 27 (5.30 p.m.)

At 12 o'clock I sent in a runner with the result of the day's operations. He arrived two hours ago, and I have myself just galloped in from the front, leaving General Graham and his forces well on their way back.

We scoured the khor of Tamanieb, following up the running stream several miles to its source. We found it disappeared in places underneath soft sand and gravel, reappearing here and there. The advance was again led by the Mounted Infantry and Major Gough's squadron of the 10th, on whom all the honour and burden of the day's work fell. As they moved up the khor to the north-west, they were supported by the Black Watch and Marines, who, however, were a long distance in the rear.

By noon, on a high conical hill, two or three of the enemy fired upon us from behind huge detached rocks, resting their rifles in the crevices. A little later a few more of the enemy fired at us from the right. Squads of our troopers were sent up the hillsides, and volleys were fired at these snugly-secured followers of Digna. The shots generally were so well aimed that the Arabs either bolted or lay hid until our fire ceased. There were evidently not many about.

Following the tracks of the footprints, as well as the marks of their camels and cattle, I could see there had been a large force lodged in the fertile, though narrow, winding valley. Stupendous rocks and hills rose at sharp angles from the sides of the valley, affording splendid cover for an enemy who wished to form an ambuscade; but there was no sign of anything of the kind, and the enemy's fire was too irresolute and scattering to lead us after them in any direction. Besides, vedettes and scouts were perched, by General Stewart, on every vantage-point, and, had an ambush been intended, timely warning would have been given us. The Arabs took pot-shots at us, but their marksmanship, though unpleasant, was poor.

Passing up the khor, in front of our skirmish line, one of them had a point-blank shot at me, at 90 yards, but he might as well have been two miles away. They fired and dodged, and it was often only by the ping of the passing bullet and the puff of white smoke from their rifles that we could tell where they were screened. I looked at one rock behind which three Arabs had lain for two hours, blazing away at us. More than thirty bullets from the Mounted Infantry had spattered their lead over the granite rock to within a few inches of the natural loophole from which the enemy had aimed.

There being no more to do, General Graham ordered the firing of the huts. The troopers set to work with a will, and in a quarter of an hour some 300 Arabs' huts were sending up long forks of flame and volumes of smoke to show that English soldiers had actually put their feet in the village of Tamanieb.

It was now 1 o'clock, and the following of Osman's force, or the catching of that rebel, being as problematic as finding a needle in a bottle of hay, the General Commanding directed the troops to return towards Suakim. A start was soon made, and in a long sinuous line of cavalry, infantry, and baggage animals, our forces moved up and out of the valley and back towards the sea.

General Graham purposes that the men shall rest to-night at zereba No. 4; coming in here to-morrow or next day. Notwithstanding the great heat, there were few cases of sunstroke or heat exhaustion.

Suakim, March 27 (7.45 p.m.)

I understand that the contractors are still busily engaged in purchasing camels, in order to despatch a caravan to Berber. The matter has been taken up by the English authorities, and the present plan is to send an Egyptian force of about 1,500 men and camels. The road to Berber is, no doubt, open to ten or twenty good men, and, if a caravan is sent on, attended by friendly Arabs, it is pretty safe to get through. Digna's power must be completely broken, now that he has run into the hills without offering a fair stand-up battle. His brother Arabs will soon dispose of him, and, at any rate, the Eastern Soudan difficulty is practically settled.

The troops will probably embark for Egypt and England next week. I may add that the enemy even fired a few shots as we left.

[NOTE.—Had an expedition been sent I believe Osman Digna would never have recovered from his defeats, and Berber would have been reached and saved, if not Khartoum.]

CHAPTER XXV.

THE END OF THE CAMPAIGN.

THERE being no more Arabs in the immediate vicinity of Suakim, who cared to yield us further victories, or who were "spoiling for a fight," my occupation in the Eastern Soudan was gone. All that now remained, was to chronicle the everyday events of Suakim life, and ware the increasing heat of the noonday sun. General Stewart and his cavalry were longing to ride to Berber, and General Graham, I believe, advised the authorities at home, that no obstacle of a serious nature interposed to stop them on the way. Still that journey was not to be just then, so we were told the troops were to be sent away from Suakim, and only a small garrison left in the place, till September or October next, when possibly more marching and fighting would be undertaken from that base. The few telegrams that follow, speak of the departure of the troops. I shook the dust of Suakim off my clothes, out of my pockets and watch-case about the time the last of the force had embarked, returning to Lower Egypt, and thence home to England.

Suakim, March 28 (3.15 p.m.)

The 65th, 89th, and 10th Hussars embark to-morrow, on board the *Jumna*, for England, with M-1 battery. The vessel sails on Sunday.

At Massowah, according to news received to-day, all was quiet. The Egyptian soldiers were anxious to leave the place.

Suakim, March 28 (7.20 p.m.)

General Graham and Admiral Hewett met a number of sheikhs in durbar this afternoon at Government House and discussed the situation. They agreed to assist in keeping the Berber road open, and in maintaining the peace against the rebels. The sheikh of the Gherib tribe, just in, attended. Osman's power is broken, but he means robbing caravans.

A score of Egyptian soldiers, belonging to the Tokar garrison, who came in yesterday from down the coast, allege that they were compelled to fight against us.

Admiral Hewett sails on Tuesday for Massowah, and everybody is getting ready to leave. To-day the Custom House and other points were turned over to the Egyptians to guard. As the Arabs despise them fresh trouble is thereby assured.

Suakim, March 28 (7.40 p.m.)

At Massowah the big drum has been beaten. The Abyssinian warriors are flocking to the King to receive Admiral Hewett. Ras Aloula, the Prime Minister, will escort the Admiral to Adytiklai. The King will await him at Adowa with an army 25,000 strong.

Suakim, March 30 (7.50 p.m.)

Major Chermside's plan is first to establish communications with the tribes outside, controlling stations on the Berber road, step by step. This may take a month, before which no caravan will start. A junction also would be effected with a caravan from Berber, midway.

Several minor rebel sheikhs are still coming in. Osman Digna is said to have returned to Tamanieb.

General Graham, in General Orders issued on Saturday, said that operations appear now to have terminated. The last was a bloodless victory, but was not gained without hardship. The toilsome march, he adds, was borne cheerfully, the troops moving with a confident spirit that augured of victory. Too high praise cannot be accorded to the cavalry and Mounted Infantry, who bore the brunt of the action, the horses going twenty-four hours without water. The General concluded by warmly praising all the troops and Departments, and congratulating the forces on the result.

It is reported that Sheikh Tahel has left Osman for Berber, preaching a Jehad (holy war).

Sunday's orders are that to-morrow morning early part of the 19th Hussars, with the Mounted Infantry, shall embark on the *Rinaldo*, including General Stewart and Staff. On the *Osiris* the remainder of the 19th will embark, on the *Utopia* General Buller and Staff, and the Gordon Highlanders on the *Northumbria*. The *Gilsand, Teddington,* and other transports take stores, etc. The Black Watch will probably embark on Tuesday. The *Orontes*, with the rest of the troops, will follow immediately.

Suakim, Tuesday (8.40 a.m.)

The transports *Utopia, Rinaldo, Osiris,* sail hence to-day for Suez, with troops and stores; Generals Graham and Davis, with the Staff and the Black Watch, embarking in the *Orontes*, which starts to-morrow.

Next week the *Utopia* will return here to remove the last of the British expedition—the 60th, a portion of the Marines, and some stores.

From Major-General Sir G. Graham to the Secretary of State for War.

(Despatched Suakim, March 26, 7.45 p.m.; received 7.50 p.m.)

"Near Tamanieb, March 26, 1884, 4 p.m.

"Day being cooler, one brigade of infantry followed cavalry, starting at 11 a.m. About 50 men fell out from heat, and were brought on in ambulances. No serious cases. Infantry have arrived at entrance of broad rocky valley, very difficult, if not impassable for wheels. Cavalry 7 or 8 miles in front in heliographic communication.

"Message received from General Stewart at 3.50 p.m., March 26: 'Pushed on towards enemy, who opened fire from position over a mile long. Difficult to estimate strength, but drove back several lots of 20 or 30. Ground bad, so shall fall back gently on you.'

"I am concentrating in zereba, and will advance to-morrow on enemy's position if, by report of cavalry, it is practicable."

From Major-General Sir G. Graham to the Secretary of State for War.

(Despatched Suakim, March 27, 11.10 a.m.; received 11.30 a.m.)

"Zereba near Tamanieb, March 27, 1884, 5 a.m."

"Yesterday, Gordon Highlanders and Irish Fusiliers, with 9-pounder battery, 4 guns, advanced at 11 a.m., followed by convoy with camel battery, six guns, and Royal Marines, at noon.

"At 4 p.m., on receipt of message from Stewart telegraphed to you yesterday, I formed zereba here, and heliographed for Royal Highlanders and Rifles, who arrived at 8 p.m. in excellent condition, not a man having fallen out. Evening cool. Reveille sounded this morning at 3.30, and troops are now in formation for advancing upon Tamanieb—cavalry in front, infantry in échelon of brigade squares, guns between brigades. Colonel Colvile has returned to duty. No men sick in advanced zereba."

From Major-General Sir G. Graham to the Secretary of State for War.

(Despatched Suakim, March 27, 4.30 p.m.; received 5.15 p.m.)

"Tamanieb, March 27, 1884, 1.30 p.m.

"Force returning to zereba occupied last night after burning Osman Digna's villages, having met with no opposition worth mentioning. Two horses killed Mounted Infantry."

From Sir G. Graham to Secretary of State for War.

(Despatched Suakim, March 27, 4.30 a.m.; received 5.30 p.m.)

"Valley of Tamanieb, March 27, 1884, 10 a.m.

"Have occupied enemy's position and springs without serious opposition; enemy firing a few shots and retiring on approach of infantry. No casualties. Ground very rocky, unfit for cavalry, very difficult for artillery. Cavalry and Mounted Infantry had no water since yesterday morning, and have worked splendidly. After watering shall reconnoitre up valley and retire on zereba occupied last night. Water supply. Troops in excellent condition. As yet see no signs of friendly tribes, and consider this position unfit for occupation."

From Major-General Sir G. Graham, to the Secretary of State for War.

"Suakim, March 28 (7 a.m.)

"Arrived here with Staff and cavalry last night. Infantry bivouacked at advanced zereba seventeen miles to front, excepting York and Lancaster, left in near zereba ten miles to front; whole move at daybreak this morning towards Suakim. Sun powerful, but there is a fresh north breeze which blows in the men's faces returning and makes heat endurable. Officers commanding brigades, acting on medical reports, will keep all weakly men at nearest zereba for to-night. Orders have been given for frequent and long halts, and plenty of water will be taken."

From Major-General Sir G. Graham.

"Suakim, March 29, 1884, (1 p.m.)

"The troops marched in yesterday, leaving a rear guard in nearest zereba with stores. Rear guard marched in this morning, and all stores cleared. Troops came in cheerfully, scarcely a man falling out, though the distance from advanced zereba is nearly seventeen miles. Abundance of water was supplied from stores on the road. The following troops from India have embarked this day in the *Jumna*, which sails to-morrow. 10th Hussars, M-1 Battery Royal Artillery, 1st York and Lancaster, 2nd Royal Irish Fusiliers, details of Staff and Departments. The following sick will embark this evening in the *Jumna*: 5 officers, 69 non-commissioned officers and men, 11 Royal Marines. All sick doing well, including three cases of sunstroke. General health of troops very good. Sick rate below 2 per cent."

The following is from the columns of the *Daily Telegraph*, and in clear, terse style, presents a retrospect of the campaign. Only one or two unimportant alterations have been made in the text:

"Now that the campaign in the Eastern Soudan is over it will be interesting to glance backward upon its moving and sanguinary incidents. Nearly two months have passed by since Baker Pasha and the wretched levies which it was his ill-luck to command were routed near El Teb in an attempt to relieve Tokar. After that shocking incident the Egyptian garrison in Tokar made some sort of arrangement with their adversaries; yet it was held that Suakim would not be safe from attack or insults unless the malcontents in arms were compelled to disperse. Accordingly, the British Government got together from various quarters a little army, appointed General Sir Gerald Graham to command it, and sent out from England Sir Redvers Buller and Colonel Herbert Stewart to assist him. The troops were taken from the army occupying Egypt, from Aden, from the Mediterranean garrisons, from Chatham, and from the fleet. One battalion, the 65th, was on its way home after long service in India, as were the 10th Hussars, who had to obtain horses in

Egypt. For artillery, the General had to rely on the war-ships, which supplied him with 9-pounders, Gatlings and Gardners. An Egyptian camel battery was also sent, and was of some service. Trinkitat, an inlet south of Suakim, and well adapted for the purpose, was selected for a landing-place, and the total force gathered there late in February amounted in round numbers to nearly 5,000 men.

"With this composite and hastily-collected body, suddenly drawn together from points between the Thames and Aden, General Graham advanced upon the enemy, who had assembled near the wells of El Teb, halfway from the shore to Tokar. Before starting, in deference to orders from home, a letter, directing them to disperse, was stuck on a spear or pole and left in the desert; but the Arabs merely fired upon it and the bearer, and showed no disposition whatever to yield. The General, therefore, marched upon their position, which, he discovered, was entrenched near a village and an abandoned mill. He moved upon the foe in an oblong formation, covered by cavalry scouts, and supported by a body of regular cavalry, the 10th and 19th Hussars. Instead of assailing the front, General Graham swept round the position, and fell upon the rear and left flank. His adversaries, in no way disconcerted, delivered a daring charge upon the face and angle nearest to them, fighting stoutly and striving hard to break in. It was here that Captain Wilson, of the *Hecla*, fought with his fists after breaking his sword. The onset was repelled, and the troops pressed on into the very heart of the position, emerging on the Trinkitat side. After the first rush, the combat resolved itself into a close fight with men who leaped out of hiding-places or holes in the ground, and the number of killed—the Arabs neither gave nor took quarter—shows with what bravery they maintained the battle. Nevertheless, a large mass sullenly retreated towards Tokar, and they were so little disposed to fly that the cavalry, whose time for action had come, plunged through them thrice before they were dispersed. The gallant blacks fought the cavalry, evading the horses, and spearing the men. The resolution with which they endured the infantry attack, and the valour exhibited during the cavalry charges, won the admiration of all. But they paid dearly—nearly 3,000 dead being left on the plain of El Teb.

"General Graham moved on to Tokar, which he 'relieved,' and there he halted. Before quitting the neighbourhood he searched several villages, destroyed there hundreds of Remingtons and much ammunition, and brought away relics of the officers who fell when Baker's Egyptians were routed. Then the army retired upon the sea-shore, and were quickly transported to Suakim. The English loss in this battle and march was a little over 3 per cent. of the troops.

"Although a lesson so drastic had been read to the 'rebels,' neither they nor their chiefs exhibited the least inclination to submit. Osman Digna, especially, remained, and still remains, firm to the Mahdi—and himself. He still had with him thousands of Arabs, whom he had collected at Tamaai wells, near the mountain range west of Suakim. What should be done with him? The British army was encamped near that town which Osman, for nearly a month past, had been daily threatening, and the leader of the hostile natives replied to a demand that he should disperse his gathering by a threat that he would drive the English into the Red Sea. In any case, so long as he remained in the field, the caravan route to Berber could not be opened, nor were even the environs of Suakim safe. It was useless to expect that the so-called friendly tribes would 'come in' while Osman was in arms. The British Government, therefore, sanctioned further operations against this intractable malcontent. He was again formally required to submit, and once more he sent back an answer of defiance to Admiral Hewett, the Governor of Suakim. Sir Gerald Graham forthwith made preparations for a fresh movement, with the same force, a 9-pounder battery, borrowed from the fleet, being the sole additions to his corps. He first moved out on to the plain, and established a depôt for water and stores in Baker's old zereba. There the entire force assembled, so soon as enough water could be deposited in the enclosure. Then he marched upon Tamaai on the 12th, and, having ascertained by means of cavalry scouts the exact position occupied by the enemy, he daringly took up a position on the bare upland, threw up a temporary bush enclosure, sent back his cavalry to

Baker's zereba for water, and spent the night under arms, within two miles of the foe. A bright moonlight alone saved him from a night attack; but of course the General took the moon into account when he boldly settled down so near his adversary.

"The next morning the horsemen rejoined the infantry betimes; and at an early hour the two Brigades, in oblong formation, one in rear but on the flank and not immediately behind the other, advanced on Osman's army. The cavalry were on the left flank, but the nature of the ground prevented them from repeating the dashing charges delivered at El Teb. General Davis's Brigade led the way, and, with great resolution, went straight at the enemy, who had posted themselves behind bushes and on the inner slope of a nullah, or ravine. By some mischance, the front battalions had moved quicker than the flank; there was a great smoke from firing, and a gap at the angle where the Bluejackets plied their machine guns. With a desperate and swift rush, into this opening the enemy poured. They came on fiercely, were not kept back by shot or bayonet, and the sudden impact forced the front battalions back upon the others, so that in a few moments the Brigade fell into confusion and receded several hundred yards. Many squads, however, held together and retired facing the foe; but, for a few moments, the disorder was serious. Then was seen the power of discipline and the strength of a formation which preserved a redoubtable flanking fire. General Buller's

Brigade, assailed but compact, and the cannon swept away the raging multitude of spearmen, and during the brief interval Davis's Brigade, with whom was Sir Gerald himself, regained its ordered ranks, and burned with ardour to renew the combat. The Blue-jackets had been obliged to leave their guns, which they disabled, and how they fought for them is shown by the lamentable loss of their officers. By the second advance the battle was decided. Failing in a first dash the Arab is slow to come on again. At Tamaai he fell back slowly but continuously, and the Brigade recovered the guns and drove the enemy from hill and valley until Osman's headquarters were in possession of our troops. It should not be forgotten that the cavalry, at the critical moment, did excellent service by dismounting and opening fire.

"Routed from his camp, Osman took to the hills, fixing himself at Tamanieb, several miles from Tamaai. General Graham marched his troops back to Suakim, and then sent out a party to Handouk, while the cavalry rode several miles on the Berber road, meeting with no opponents. A price was put on Osman's head by proclamation; but the British Government directed Admiral Hewett to withdraw it, which he did in the plainest terms. The result of various scouting operations was the information that the northern Berber road was free to a considerable distance; but no use could be made of it so long as Osman lingered in the hills, and continued defiant. A few days ago our special correspondent reported the movements which had been made and the ulterior designs of General Graham. The infantry were drawn from Handouk, a fresh zereba was established, and the entire force marched out towards Osman's hill fastness. The upshot of this operation we published yesterday. By forming zerebas, employing the cavalry, using the heliograph or some method of signalling, the skilful General was able to keep his men to the front and act on the intelligence signalled from the hills. The horsemen detected the enemy's position, and yesterday the army entered the stony valleys, expelled a foe who, although he fired long shots, was plainly unwilling to risk close battle, and penetrated several miles into the range. These operations are admirably described in our telegrams, and the return of the troops to Suakim to-day will end the Soudan campaign.

"It has been eventful, and not without vicissitudes which put the mettle of our soldiers to rough tests. They had to adapt themselves to a novel method of fighting—that is, acquire new habits in front of the enemy—and no one can truly say that they did not perform this task with rapidity and effect. They had to recover from a check; they did so splendidly in the heat of combat. They have also had to endure severe privations, especially the want of water, and we have heard no murmur, certainly seen no failure of hardihood and discipline. The General has shown that he is a resolute and skilful commander. Aided by Admiral

Hewett, who has worked so ably and heartily ashore and afloat, he has overcome that immense difficulty, the provisioning of an army in a desert. General Graham may be proud of his soldiers, and they may be proud of him."

CHAPTER XXI.

THE FINAL OFFICIAL REPORTS.

I ALSO append the final official reports, prefixing them by the sad commentary on the whole expedition, Tewfik Bey's last despatch. May there not be a similar message of General Gordon's to insert before the final reports on the expedition to relieve Khartoum as there was to that to relieve Sinkat!

The last communication forwarded by Tewfik Bey, the hero of Sinkat, to the Governor of the Eastern Soudan, runs thus:

"I am obliged to reduce the soldiers' rations to what is strictly necessary, so as to run as little risk as possible of starvation. If our provisions were to be exhausted before assistance should arrive (which God forbid!) we shall attempt a collective sortie, and endeavour to reach Suakim. We prefer death to surrender. I might easily save my own life, but military honour makes it my duty to share the fate of those placed under my command. We trust in God and await His decision—life or death."

OFFICIAL REPORT ON THE VALOUR OF OFFICERS AND MEN.

From the General Commanding in Egypt to the Under-Secretary of State for War.

Headquarters, Army of Occupation,
Cairo, April 14, 1884.

SIR,
I have the honour to forward herewith, by Captain Baynes, 1st Battalion Cameron Highlanders, who acted as Assistant Military Secretary to Major-General Sir Gerald Graham, V.C., K.C.B., during the late expedition, a despatch mentioning officers, non-commissioned officers, and men who have distinguished themselves during the late campaign in the Soudan.

I have, &c.,
FREDK. STEPHENSON,
Lieutenant-General, Commanding in Egypt.

From Major-General Sir G. Graham, V.C., K.C.B., Commanding Expeditionary Force, to Lieutenant-General Stephenson, C.B., Commanding Troops in Egypt.

Suakim, March 31, 1884.

SIR,
The military operations being now completed, I have the honour to bring to your notice the names of officers, non-commissioned officers, and men of the force under my command who have distinguished themselves during or in connection with these operations.

STAFF.

I must record my thanks for the services rendered by the Staff, who are all good officers, carefully selected, and who all worked loyally and well. The share of work that fell to the General Staff was heavy, and after Captain Wauchope was wounded at El Teb, Lieutenant-Colonel Gordon was the only officer available for the duties of embarkation and disembarkation. When the base was changed from Trinkitat to Suakim this work was proceeding at two ports at the same time, and on three occasions we advanced over sixteen miles from our base—once over twenty—and were dependent on large convoys for our supplies.

My personal Staff consisted of Captain Baynes, Cameron Highlanders, Assistant Military Secretary; Lieutenant Romilly, Scots Guards, Lieutenant Scott, Cameron Highlanders, and Lieutenant Lindsay, R.N., H.M.S. *Euryalus*, Aides-de-Camp. Where all worked so well it appears invidious to make distinctions, but I cannot help recording my sense of the zeal displayed by Captain Baynes, my Assistant Military Secretary, and of the ever-ready, intelligent activity shown by Lieutenant Lindsay, R.N., my Naval Aide-de-Camp, whose services were kindly placed at my disposal by Admiral Sir W. Hewett.

In my despatch of March 3, I recorded my opinion of the value of Lieutenant-Colonel Clery's services as Assistant Adjutant-General, and further experience has only served to confirm and deepen my sense of his worth. Conspicuous by a red coat, in a force where officers and men usually wore kharki, Lieutenant-Colonel Clery could always be recognised from a distance, and when at any critical period I saw his red coat I knew that there matters would be going well, or if wrong would soon be rectified, and turned my attention to another part of the field.

Brevet Lieutenant-Colonel Gordon, Argyll and Sutherland Highlanders, D.A.A.G., has shown throughout his well-known devotion to duty, and his services as Staff officer in disembarking and embarking troops at Trinkitat and Suakim were very valuable.

At El Teb Lieutenant-Colonel Gordon was present on my Staff. During the advance on Tamaai I required a thoroughly trustworthy officer at the base, and selected Lieutenant-Colonel Gordon for that duty.

Captain Wauchope, C.M.G., Royal Highlanders, was

severely wounded at El Teb. Both before and during the action—even after receiving his wound—he did good service, and would not go on the sick list until compelled to do so.

Captain Williams-Freeman, Sussex Regiment, did service as Provost-Marshal to my satisfaction.

Lieutenant Beaumont, 3rd King's Royal Rifles, was in charge of signallers, who proved most useful—I may say indispensable—in sending messages along the line of communications, and, in one instance, to the front.

In my previous despatch I brought to your notice the valuable services rendered by Brevet Lieutenant-Colonel Ardagh, as head of the Intelligence Staff and as Commanding Royal Engineers. The following officers served in the Intelligence Department under Lieutenant-Colonel Ardagh, C.B., R.E.: Major Wood, Royal Engineers; Captain Green, Royal Engineers (wounded at El Teb); Captain Slade, Royal Artillery; Lieutenant-Colonel Colvile, Grenadier Guards. All these officers have rendered most valuable service during the operations, having shown great zeal, energy, and capacity for work, combined with thorough technical knowledge in carrying out the important duties of collecting information, surveying, making reconnaissances, &c.

In my previous despatch of March 3 I mentioned the services rendered by General Baker, and I must beg to bring to notice the coolness and gallantry of Colonel Burnaby, Royal Horse Guards, who was attached to the Intelligence Department during the first part of the operations, and who, although severely wounded at El Teb, continued to do duty until the end of the action.

The officers under Lieutenant-Colonel Ardagh were frequently employed on General Staff duties in addition to their special work in the Intelligence Department. Major Wood rendered good service in charge of water supply. Captain Slade in scouting and leading troops, &c., also did duty as Deputy Assistant-Adjutant-General at the action of Tamaai.

Sergt-Major Bure, Military Police, displayed great steadiness and coolness when under fire. He carried the headquarters flag, which he made as conspicuous as possible, and also rendered good service throughout the operations in camp duties. Sergeant Sherwood, of the Signalling Department, is also favourably mentioned for zeal and efficiency.

CAVALRY BRIGADE.

The Cavalry Brigade was commanded by Brigadier-General H. Stewart, C.B., A.D.C., who has shown all the qualifications of a good leader of cavalry, being cool and daring, or cautious, as required in action, also skilful and careful in reconnaissance and outpost duties. Brigadier-General Stewart speaks highly of the services rendered by Lieutenant-Colonel Taylor, the Brigade Major, and by Lieutenant Rhodes, of the 1st Royal Dragoons, Aide-de-Camp.

10th Hussars.—Colonel Wood, who commanded the 10th Hussars, is an excellent cavalry officer, as evinced by the energy and ability with which he equipped his splendid regiment from local sources, so as to make it fit to take the field, and by the manner he handled it in action. Brigadier-General Stewart reports Colonel Wood as having rendered him invaluable assistance. Lieutenant-Colonel Liddell and Major Gough have also done good service. I regret to have had as yet no report from Colonel Wood of the non-commissioned officers and men of the 10th Hussars who distinguished themselves.

19th Hussars.—Lieutenant-Colonel Webster commanded the 19th Hussars, and gave every assistance in his power to secure the success of the brigade. Lieutenant-Colonel Barrow, C.M.G., 19th Hussars, is a most valuable officer, and his leading of the second line at El Teb, until he was wounded, is reported by Brigadier-General Stewart as beyond praise. Captain Jenkins took command of the left wing after Colonel Barrow was wounded. He led the first squadron in the charge, and was personally engaged with three of the enemy at one time, and his horse was wounded in three places with assegais. By his gallantry and conduct this officer set a good example to all under his command. Regimental Sergeant-Major Lima and Quartermaster-Sergeant Marshall, 19th Hussars, set a good example of coolness and courage. The latter is mentioned for his devotion shown in saving the life of Colonel Barrow when that officer was wounded, and I beg to enclose [see enclosure marked A] evidence reporting this non-commissioned officer's conduct on this occasion, which, I submit, should place him among the candidates for the Victoria Cross. Sergeant Phipps, who was twice badly wounded, refused to leave the field, and remained with his troop till he fainted from loss of blood. Troop Sergeant-Major Taylor, Sergeant Fenton, and Private Bosely, 19th Hussars, are also favourably mentioned for gallantry.

MOUNTED INFANTRY.

The Mounted Infantry was most efficiently handled on all occasions by Lieutenant and Local Captain Humphreys, the Welsh Regiment. Brigadier-General Stewart reports of this officer that he cannot speak of him too highly. He was ably assisted by Lieutenant C. H. Payne, of the 1st Gordon Highlanders. All ranks of the Mounted Infantry displayed great coolness and readiness under fire. In a letter marked "B" attached, Brigadier-General Stewart mentions the gallant conduct of Lieutenant Marling, 3rd King's Royal Rifles, of the Mounted Infantry, whom he recommends for the distinction of the Victoria Cross. Privates George Hunter, 3rd King's Royal Rifles, and Joseph Clift, Sussex Regiment, are mentioned for gallantry and devotion at Tamaai on March 13, 1884.

ROYAL ARTILLERY.

The Royal Artillery at El Teb consisted of eight 7-pounder naval guns with camel transport, and were commanded by

Major F. T. Lloyd, an officer whose professional knowledge, energy, and judgment have been most valuable. On return to Suakim four 9-pounder guns were equipped as a mule battery by M Battery 1st Brigade Royal Artillery, commanded by Major E. H. Holley, R.A. Major Lloyd specially mentions Major Holley for the ability and energy with which he equipped this 9-pounder battery, entirely from naval sources, for the field, under exceptionally difficult circumstances. These guns were of great service, and Major Holley has proved himself an excellent artillery officer in the field.

Captain J. H. Wodehouse, R.A., of the Egyptian Army, who was attached to the camel battery, made himself conspicuous by his energy and ability. Surgeon Lucas and Veterinary-Surgeon Beech are also favourably mentioned. Major Lloyd brings specially to my notice the conduct of Gunner W. Hanson, of M Battery 1st Brigade Royal Artillery, at the action of Tamaai, who, when the enemy made a rush upon his gun, knocked down one of them with his rammer thereby saving the life of a comrade.

In my despatch of March 3 I have referred to the cool deliberation and remarkable efficiency with which the 7-pounder naval guns were worked at El Teb by the 6th Battery 1st Brigade Scottish Royal Artillery, when opposed to the heavier Krupp guns of the enemy. These guns advanced with the infantry, and sustained several of the enemy's desperate charges. On one occasion those brave blacks succeeded, in spite of a storm of fire from artillery and infantry, in charging up to the guns and penetrating among the gun detachments. One was knocked down by Gunner Isaac Phipps with a rammer, another by Gunner James Adan with a blow on the face from a round of case which he was carrying in his hand, and a third was shot by Bombardier Treadwell with a revolver. At Tamaai, on March 13, the 7-pounder camel battery was attached to the 1st Brigade, and did good service at close range with case on the enemy. In this action M Battery 1st Brigade of four 9-pounders distinguished itself by the steady way in which it stood and plied the enemy with case during the attack on the 2nd Brigade, although during the retirement there was no infantry to protect it.

ROYAL ENGINEERS.

The Royal Engineers have worked to my entire satisfaction throughout the expedition. On them devolved the arduous duties connected with the disembarkation and water supply. They had also to provide for entrenching the depôts at Fort Baker and El Teb. This work had to be undertaken with a very insufficient Engineer force and equipment, a portion of the latter having been lost in the *Neera*. The 26th Company numbered in all on disembarkation 5 officers and 86 non-commissioned officers and men, of whom 26 were drivers, leaving only about 50 artificers available for works and camp duties. The officers and men worked with the greatest zeal.

Major Todd made excellent arrangements for supplying the deficiencies in materials, and Captain Dorward showed great practical ability in the construction of jetties, etc., and the other officers all had hard work and did good service. Major Todd brings specially to my notice the following non-commissioned officers and men of 26th Company Royal Engineers, for zeal and efficiency in their work, particularly in the construction of piers, which exposed them to great fatigue and to blistering by the sun while working naked in the water, viz.: Second Corporals Bruce and Martin, Lance-Corporal Jones, Sappers Brown and Kirwan.

1ST INFANTRY BRIGADE.

The 1st Infantry Brigade was commanded by Brigadier-General Sir Redvers Buller, V.C., K.C.M.G., C.B., A.D.C., who, by his coolness in action, his knowledge of soldiers, and experience in the field, combined with his great personal ascendency over both officers and men, has been most valuable.

Besides the ordinary command of his brigade, Brigadier-General Buller was in charge, as senior military officer, of the re-embarkation at Trinkitat, a laborious and responsible duty, which he performed to my entire satisfaction.

Brigadier-General Buller reports that he has received every assistance from his Staff: Captain Kelly, Sussex Regiment, brigade-major, and Lieutenant St. Aubyn, Grenadier Guards, aide-de-camp. Captain Kelly was severely contused by a spent case-shot at El Teb, but remained at his duties.

KING'S ROYAL RIFLES.

The 3rd Battalion of the King's Royal Rifles was commanded by Colonel Sir Cromer Ashburnham, K.C.B., A.D.C., an officer of well-tried capacity for leading troops in the field. At El Teb, the 3rd King's Royal Rifles were in reserve, but at Tamaai they assisted in repulsing the attack of the enemy on the 1st Brigade, and delivered their fire with great coolness and steadiness.

The names of the following officers are submitted for favourable notice: Lieutenant-Colonel Ogilvy and Major Fraser. Sir Cromer Ashburnham has also submitted to me that No. 2213, Sergeant William Nix, is deserving of notice for his conduct in action.

1ST GORDON HIGHLANDERS.

The 1st Gordon Highlanders were commanded by Lieutenant-Colonel Hammill, C.B., and showed great steadiness on all occasions. Colonel Hammill mentions Major Cross and Captain Menzies as having specially distinguished themselves. Private Daniel M'Pherson received a spear-wound in the face at El Teb, and after being taken to the hospital was, at his own urgent request, allowed to march with his battalion next morning to Tokar.

2ND ROYAL IRISH FUSILIERS.

The 2nd Royal Irish Fusiliers were commanded by Lieutenant-Colonel Robinson, and were conspicuous for steadiness in formation during action, and for good discipline on the march. Captain Gordon performed duty as major at action of Tamaai, and commanded the battalion during advance on Tamanieb, when the senior officers of the battalion were on the sick list; and I beg to recommend this officer to your notice for the zeal and ability displayed by him. Captain and Adjutant Rogers is also favourably mentioned; and Surgeon Pedlow, A.M.D., showed great devotion to duty.

2ND INFANTRY BRIGADE.

The 2nd Infantry Brigade was commanded by Major-General Davis, who has done his utmost to preserve steadiness and good discipline on all occasions. Major-General Davis, as senior military officer, superintended the disembarkations at Trinkitat and at Suakim, both which operations were very successfully carried out.

2ND BRIGADE STAFF.

Major-General Davis wishes to bring to notice his staff—Captain Hitchcock, Shropshire Light Infantry, brigade-major, and Lieut. C. C. Douglas, Scottish Rifles, aide-de-camp.

1ST ROYAL HIGHLANDERS.

The 1st Royal Highlanders were commanded by Lieutenant-Colonel Green, whom I noticed exerting himself to keep order and discipline at both the actions of El Teb and Tamaai. In my despatch of March 2, I referred to the 1st Royal Highlanders as having been somewhat out of hand at El Teb, by their over-eagerness to fire on the enemy. I have now, however, the satisfaction of reporting that since that action this fine battalion has shown an excellent spirit and a determination to prove itself worthy of the high reputation earned by a century and a half of splendid service in all parts of the world.

At Tamaai the Black Watch charged most gallantly, only fell back when forced to do so, losing more men in close fighting than any other battalion, and rallying to a man when the opportunity offered.

The following officers have been specially brought to my notice for coolness and gallantry in action: Major Eden, Captain Brophy, and Lieutenant Norman Macleod. Surgeon Treherne is specially mentioned for attention to the wounded in action.

The following non-commissioned officers and men have been specially noticed, viz.: Sergeant J. Sutherland, Private Henry Shires, and Drummer Henry Mumford, for distinguished coolness, and for encouraging their comrades at Tamaai. Hospital-Sergeant W. Davidson is mentioned for his devotion in attending to the wounded in action. Private Thomas Edwards especially distinguished himself in defence of one of the naval guns at Tamaai. Commander Rolfe, in a letter marked "C," annexed, states that he saw Private Edwards besides the gun, with Lieutenant Almack, R.N., and a Blue-jacket. "Both the latter were killed, and Edwards after bayoneting two Arabs, receiving a cut on the knuckles from a spear, and rejoined the ranks." I beg to concur in Colonel Green's recommendation of Private Edwards for the Victoria Cross.

1st YORK AND LANCASTER.

The 1st York and Lancaster were commanded by Lieutenant-Colonel Byam. This fine battalion of seasoned soldiers only landed on the evening of our march to Fort Baker, on Feb. 28. During the action on Feb. 29, in which they took a prominent share, being in the fighting line, the

THE FINAL OFFICIAL REPORTS. 295

York and Lancaster gave me great satisfaction by their steadiness, and by the firmness with which they met and repulsed the charges of the enemy. When advancing on the first battery captured, Captain Littledale rushed in front of his company, and had a hand-to-hand encounter with several of the enemy. He was knocked down, receiving a severe spear-wound in the left shoulder, but was rescued by his men coming up. He then rose, and although bleeding profusely, continued to lead his company throughout the engagement. Major Dalgetty, although injured by the fragments of a shell at El Teb, continued to lead his men; and at Tamaai displayed the utmost gallantry in rallying his men until severely wounded. Several other officers distinguished themselves at El Teb, and especially at Tamaai. Among them was Quartermaster Mahony, who also attended to the supply of ammunition, and proved himself a very efficient officer.

Of the non-commissioned officers and rank and file, the following are mentioned by their commanding officer as distinguished for gallantry at El Teb: Colour-sergeant Wake (badly wounded), Colour-sergeant Hayward, Sergeant Doyle, Sergeant Webb, Lance-sergeants Haycock and James, Corporals Baxter and Dossett; also Privates Edwards and Callanan, who were both killed. Sergeant Howell and Private P. Foy are also mentioned for their coolness and gallantry at Tamaai.

It is on occasions of repulse and retreat, such as that which temporarily befell the 2nd Brigade at Tamaai, that the individual efforts of officers and men show most clearly and are of greatest value, and it is on this account that I have so many names to mention in the two leading battalions of the 2nd Brigade—the 1st Royal Highlanders and 1st York and Lancaster. The men who died nobly doing their duty to the last, I submit, also deserve the tribute of having their names recorded.

The 1st Royal Highlanders lost a good officer in Major Aitken, who had been previously mentioned for his gallantry at El Teb, and who fell fighting bravely at Tamaai. With him fell Sergeant Ronald Fraser and Lance-Corporal Percy Finlay, who nobly went back to assist their officer. Colour-Sergeant Michael Johnston and Sergeant William Campbell, and many others, all of the Royal Highlanders, were seen bravely fighting to the last.

One officer and fifteen men of the 1st York and Lancaster were killed at the right front corner of the square, where the storm first burst upon them. These men, as Lieutenant-Colonel Byam (who was himself in the thick of it) reports, "stood their ground and would not be forced back."

Their bodies were afterwards picked up on the margin of the ravine where they fell. Their names are: Captain H. G. W. Ford, Corporal W. Maynard, Lance-Corporal R. Mayors, Private W. Webb, Private J. Richards, Private J. Roy, Private S. LeBlancq, Private G. Higginson, Private W. West, Private J. Brophy, Private R. Cripps, Private I. Hope, Private P. Molloy, Private J. Pilbeam, Private C. Read, and Private C. Rookyard.

ROYAL MARINES.

The Royal Marines, under Colonel Tuson, C.B., A.D.C., Royal Marine Artillery, were in the fighting line at El Teb, and by their steadiness and gallantry contributed largely to the success of that day's operations. At Tamaai they were in the square of the 2nd Brigade, and assisted in forming the rallying line.

Brevet-Major Tucker, Royal Marine Artillery, showed great readiness and intelligence in at once turning the captured Krupp guns, taken in the first position at El Teb, on the enemy's remaining battery, thereby facilitating the advance of the infantry.

Staff-Surgeon Martin, R.N., is favourably mentioned for attention to wounded in the field.

The following officers, non-commissioned officers, and men have been specially brought to my notice: Major Colwell,

Royal Marine Light Artillery; Surgeon Cross; Sergeant-Major J. Hurst, Royal Marine Light Infantry, H.M.S. *Téméraire*; Private J. Birstwhistle, Royal Marine Light Infantry, H.M.S. *Téméraire*; Private Yerbury, Royal Marine Light Infantry, H.M.S. *Téméraire*; Gunner Rolf, Royal Marine Artillery; Private F. Patterson, Royal Marine Artillery; Private J. Davis, Royal Marine Artillery; Gunner A. Bretwell, Royal Marine Artillery; and Private D. Brady, Royal Marines.

ARMY MEDICAL DEPARTMENT.

The Army Medical Department, under Deputy-Surgeon-General M'Dowell, was most ably administered, and the wants of the wounded carefully provided for, and promptly attended to. As soon as we were in possession of the position at El Teb on Feburary 29, about 4.25 p.m., I signalled to Fort Baker, at the instance of Deputy-Surgeon-General M'Dowell, for tents, medical comforts, &c., to be sent on immediately. As mules had been kept ready laden, the convoy, under Surgeon Prendergast, arrived at 6 p.m., and the serious cases were at once placed under cover for the night. Additional blankets were provided for the slighter cases, which were kept in the open. Immediately after the action Surgeon-Major Connolly, who was principal medical officer of the Cavalry Brigade, by my orders took out eight mule cacolets with a cavalry escort, and proceeded over the ground where the cavalry had charged, to make sure that no wounded were left, and, as far as possible, to bring in the dead. After the action of Tamaai the wounded were at once brought into the zereba, and promptly attended to. As the Surgeon-General remarks in his report: "Though many of the wounded had injuries of the severest form, still we had no deaths from hæmorrhage, a fact which exhibits in the strongest light the skill and attention of the medical officers working under the most trying circumstances."

The following medical officers are especially brought to

your notice for their care and attention to their important duties in the field on the occasion of the actions at El Teb and Tamaai: Surgeon-Major Wilson, principal medical officer of the Infantry Brigade; Surgeon-Major Connolly, principal medical officer, Cavalry Brigade; Surgeon Prendergast, who was badly wounded while attending a wounded man at Tamaai; Surgeon-Major Catherwood, principal medical officer at the base, and Surgeon-Major Greene, at El Teb; Surgeon-Major Venour had charge of the sick on hospital ship at the base (Her Majesty's ship *Jumna*), and, assisted by a detachment of Army Hospital Corps, made every possible provision for the care of the wounded on their passage to Suez.

I also beg to bring to your notice the services rendered by the Army Hospital Corps. Quartermaster Enright, Army Hospital Corps, is reported as having carried out his duties with indefatigable energy and devotion. Staff-Sergeants Clarke and Genese, also Sergeant A. G. Chalk (whose leg was broken by a fall from a mule), are favourably mentioned. The names given are those of officers whose conduct came most prominently to notice, but all the medical officers attached to the force have contributed to the excellent results attained.

COMMISSARIAT AND TRANSPORT CORPS.

The Commissariat and Transport Department under Assistant Commissary-General Nugent have given me very great satisfaction by the indefatigable zeal and intelligence with which they have worked to bring up supplies to the front. The task before this department was a very difficult one. The supply of food, water, and ammunition in a waterless country with no roads required a good organisation, abundant means of transport, and great energy in working it. The water transport alone required incessant watching, as many of the skins supplied from stores were found to leak so much as to be worthless. Fortunately Egyptian camel tanks had been brought, and the navy furnished some breakers. The greatest vigilance had to be exercised to prevent the native camel drivers and soldiers from drinking and wasting the water on the road. The storage of the water at the base, and at the advanced depôts or zerebas, was of vital importance. Here again the navy came to our assistance, with empty barrels and large canvas tanks, which latter proved invaluable. I must, in connection with this subject, acknowledge my sense of the great service rendered to the expedition by Mr. Crook, Chief Engineer of Her Majesty's ship *Euryalus*, and those under him. Nothing could exceed the ability and devotion with which Assistant Commissary-General Nugent threw himself into his work, and he was ably supported by those under him, who literally worked night and day when the service required it. I must especially mention Deputy Assistant-Commissary-Generals Rainsford and Hamilton, who proved themselves most valuable officers. Major Forster, Duke of Cornwall's Light Infantry, Lieutenant Turner, Shropshire Light Infantry, and Lieutenant Bower, 3rd King's Royal Rifles, employed on transport duties, and Conductor Hickie, also deserve mention for their zeal and energy.

ORDNANCE STORE DEPARTMENT.

The Ordnance Store Department, under Assistant Commissary-General of Ordnance Mills, has worked most satisfactorily. The supplies of reserve ammunition have come up without any delay. The organisation for storage and transport was good, while officers and men worked hard to meet all requirements. I have especially to bring to notice Deputy-Assistant Commissary-General of Ordnance Houghton for his zeal and intelligence.

ARMY CHAPLAINS.

I have to record my sense of the services of the Army Chaplains attached to the force. The following Chaplains—

The Revs. G. Smith, Church of England; J. McTaggart, Presbyterian; and R. Brindle, Roman Catholic, were present in the field, and assiduous in their attention to the wounded. The Rev. J. Webster, Wesleyan, also accompanied the expedition.

ARMY VETERINARY DEPARTMENT.

The duties of the Veterinary Department were satisfactorily carried on by Principal Veterinary-Sergeon Clayton and those under him.

ARMY PAY DEPARTMENT.

The Army Pay Department was well administered by Major Farwell. I have also to express my thanks to Mr. Wyld (now at the head of the police of Suakim) for the services rendered by him to the expedition when giving information as to the locality, and when in charge of the Abyssinian scouts, on March 12 and 13.

NAVAL BRIGADE.

In my previous despatch I have already mentioned the splendid services of the Naval Brigade. At El Teb they fought under the eyes of their admiral, who accompanied the force into the field, and cheerfully bore his share of danger when the square came under fire. With Admiral Hewett was Captain Wilson, commanding Her Majesty's ship *Hecla*, who was not content with the position of a spectator, but took such an active share in the defence of the sailors' guns in a hand-to-hand combat that I have, in my report to the Admiral, recommended this officer for the distinction of the Victoria Cross. The Naval Brigade suffered severely in the actions of El Teb and Tamaai. Lieutenant Royds (a most promising officer, since dead) was dangerously wounded at El Teb, and, by the direction of the Admiral, Surgeon Gimlette, R.N., and twelve men were told off to carry Lieutenant Royds back to the fleet. These men, who had been previously dragging their guns over heavy ground and then through the three hours' fight, arrived with their wounded officer about eleven o'clock that night at Trinkitat. So anxious were they not to miss the advance on Tokar that they started off again about four o'clock the next morning, arriving at El Teb in good time to take their share in the severe toils of that day. This is merely an illustration of the gallant spirit that animated the entire Naval Brigade, from its commander to the last man.

I beg to be allowed to express my high admiration, and that of the force I have had the honour to command, at the thoroughly cordial co-operation of the Royal Navy throughout the expedition. Nothing could exceed the courtesy and readiness of Admiral Sir W. Hewett to meet all our requirements; and the work of loading and unloading the ships under Captain Andoe, R.N., proceeded smoothly and swiftly, the officers and men of both services working cordially together. I beg to attach to this despatch a letter received from Admiral Sir W. Hewett, in reply to one of mine thanking him for the great services rendered by the Royal Navy to the expedition.

In concluding this despatch, I wish to express my deep sense of the admirable spirit in which the duties that have fallen to the officers and men have been carried out during this short but arduous campaign. The shifting of the base from Trinkitat to Suakim entailed severe fatigues and labours, as, owing to the dangerous character of the coast, ships could only move by day, and the time at my disposal being short it was necessary to hurry on the operation of embarking and disembarking men, horses, camels, stores, etc., so that the work had to be carried on day and night. Officers and men understood this and worked cheerfully. They also bore the toils and privations of long marches in the desert under a burning sun with a necessarily short supply of water. On the night preceding the action at Tamaai there was little sleep, as the enemy were firing on us continuously from past midnight to dawn. This, too, was borne silently and without flinching. As regards strength and endurance, I beg to point to the remarkably low sick-rate (less than 2 per cent.), and to the fact that not one man was lost by sickness. The distances marched under a burning sun were also creditable. On the return from Tokar to Trinkitat the distance marched was about sixteen miles, and the two return marches to Suakim from the front were about the same distance. On all these occasions the troops marched in easily with scarcely a man falling out, though there were many cases of blistered feet from the burning sand. It is true that many men were prostrated by the intense heat during the march out on the first day of the last advance, yet the same men, with few exceptions, advanced cheerfully the next day towards Tamanieb. Late that afternoon I had to call up the Royal Highlanders and Royal Rifles in expectation of resistance, and the men marched cheerily to the sound of song and pipe, not a man falling out when the next move was to bring them in presence of the enemy. This could not have been accomplished without a thoroughly sound system of interior economy in the regiments, battalions, and corps composing the force; and the greatest credit is due to the regimental officers who kept their men in such a high state of efficiency. Considering the way in which the hardships were borne, and the obstacles overcome, also that the foe was far from being a despicable one, it is in no spirit of boasting I venture to submit that, although containing many young soldiers in the ranks, and although hurriedly got together, partly composed of troops on passage home from India, who had to be equipped from local sources, the force sent on this expedition has shown itself worthy of the British Army.—I have, etc.,

G. GRAHAM,
Major-General, Commanding Expeditionary Force.

SUB-ENCLOSURE NO. 1.

Evidence of Lieut.-Colonel Barrow, 19th Hussars: Having been wounded through my left arm and side, and my horse having been killed, I found myself on the ground surrounded by the enemy and by my own men, who were charging, and passed quickly over me. I held out my right hand, which was seized by Quartermaster-Sergeant Marshall, who stayed behind with me, and dragged me through the enemy, and took me back to the regiment. Had I been left behind I must have been killed.

Evidence of Officer Commanding E Troop, 19th Hussars.— I have the honour to bring to notice the name of the under-mentioned non-commissioned officer, who distinguished himself at the battle of El Teb: No. 1,384, Quartermaster-Sergeant Marshall, "For leading Lieutenant-Colonel Barrow out of action under a heavy fire and frequent charges of the enemy, Lieutenant-Colonel Barrow being severely wounded at the time."

J. C. A. WALKER,
Lieutenant, commanding E Troop, 19th Hussars.

True copy—K. S. BAYNES,
Captain, Assistant Military Secretary.

I concur with the above remarks.—D. R. APTHORP,
Captain, commanding 2nd Squadron, 19th Hussars.

SUB-ENCLOSURE NO. 2.

From the Brigadier-General Commanding the Troops, Handoub, to the Chief of the Staff, Headquarters.

Handoub, March 21, 1884.

SIR,
With reference to your memo., dated Camp, Suakim March 19, 1884, I have the honour to forward the attached return of officers, non-commissioned officers and men of the troops under my command, who have distinguished themselves

in the field since landing at Suakim. I beg to bring to your notice the gallant conduct of Lieutenant P. S. Marling, of the King's Royal Rifles, during the battle of Tamaai. In my humble opinion the attached evidence proves this officer to have behaved in a manner entitling him to the reward of the Victoria Cross, and I beg, therefore, most favourably to recommend him to the notice of the General Officer Commanding for this distinction.—I have, etc.,

HERBERT STEWART,
Brigadier-General, Commanding Cavalry Brigade and Troops, Handoub.

1166, Private Joseph Clift, 1st Battalion Royal Sussex Regiment, states: "I was present with my division at the battle of Tamaai on March 13, 1884. Just before the enemy made their attack on the squares, Private Morley, of my division, was shot and fell. The order had just been given to us to retire, and the men were running to their horses. I remained to assist Private Morley, and Lieutenant Marling, and Private Hunter, of No. 1 Division (3rd Battalion King's Royal Rifles), immediately came up. Private Hunter dismounted, and we put Morley on the horse, in front of Lieutenant Marling, but he slipped off almost directly. Seeing this, Lieutenant Marling dismounted, and we put him (Morley) across Lieutenant Marling's saddle. Lieutenant Marling and myself held him on, and Private Hunter led the horse. We succeeded in bringing him away towards the square, which was then coming up. We placed him near a bush, and I remained with him for a short time, until a stretcher was brought and he was taken into the square.

JOSEPH CLIFT,
Private, 1st Battalion Royal Sussex Regiment.

Statement of Lieutenant Todd Thornton:

At the battle of Tamaai, on 13th inst., I was sent by Captain Humphreys to support Lieutenant Marling on the right of the position which we had taken up. On my arrival at the place where Lieutenant Marling's division was engaged, I found the fire of the enemy was very hot both on our left flank and in front, and as it gradually became hotter, and the square was by this time close up, within about 200 yards, Lieutenant Marling gave the order to the men, "To your horses." Just as this occurred, Private Morley of my division was shot on my right; he was lifted up by Private Hunter of the Rifles, and Clift, of the Sussex, and placed in front of Lieutenant Marling on his horse; he, however, fell off almost immediately; Lieutenant Marling then dismounted and gave his horse up for the purpose of carrying off Private Morley, the enemy pressing close on to them, and they succeeded in carrying him about eighty yards towards the square, by which time the fire had slackened, and we were all in comparative safety.

F. DODD THORNTON,
Lieutenant, 1st Battalion Royal Sussex Regiment, Mounted Infantry.

April 11, 1884.

No. 3356, Private George Hunter, 3rd King's Royal Rifles, states:

I was present at the battle of Tamaai on March 13, 1884, with my division. No. 4 Division (1st Royal Sussex) was also with us. We were under a very hot fire just before the attack on the square by the rebels, and were just on the point of retiring to get out of the way of the square, when I saw Private Morley, of the Sussex Division, fall wounded. The order, "To your horses," had been given, and we were all going to our horses. I went back to his (Private Morley's) assistance, and Lieutenant Marling also went and got off his horse, and we put Morley across the horse to bring him away. After a few yards he slipped off, and we picked him up and put him on again. Private Clift, 1st Battalion Royal Sussex, also remained with his comrade and assisted us. We succeeded in carrying him to a place of safety near the square. While we were doing this, the rebels made their attack on the square, and were close upon us. The fire from the square and the Abyssinians, who were acting with us and behaved very well, alone saved us from being cut off.

G. HUNTER,
Private, 3rd Battalion King's Royal Rifles.

April 11th, 1884.

SUB-ENCLOSURE NO. 3.

To the Brigade-Major, 2nd Brigade, Suakim Field Force.

Suakim, March 31, 1884.

SIR,

With reference to the attached correspondence regarding the gallant conduct of No. 235, Private Thomas Edwards, of the battalion under my command, I am of opinion, on the evidence advanced, that he deserves the Victoria Cross, and I would solicit the favour of the Major-General Commanding the Brigade interesting himself in obtaining for Private Edwards this coveted reward.

I have, &c.,
WILLIAM GREEN,
Colonel, Commanding 1st Battalion The Black Watch, A.A.G.

Major-General J. Davis, Commanding 2nd Brigade, concurs in the above opinion as regards Private Edwards.

From Commander E. Rolfe to Rear-Admiral Sir W. Hewett, Commander-in-Chief, East Indies.

Suakim, March 24, 1884.

SIR,

I beg to bring to your most favourable notice the gallant conduct of Private Thomas Edwards, 235 H Company Royal Highlanders, who was doing duty as mule driver with the Royal Naval Brigade, and attached to No. 4 Gatling gun with supply of spare ammunition. I was informed by the armourer of Her Majesty's ship *Hecla* that he saw this man beside the gun with Lieutenant Almack and a Blue-jacket. Both the latter were killed, and Edwards, after bayoneting two Arabs, received a cut on the knuckles with a spear, and rejoined the ranks with his mules. Lieutenant Ballard, officer in charge of the transport, has informed me, and I myself can testify to his doing good service subsequently, and he remained by his gun throughout the action.

I have, etc.,
E. ROLFE,
Commander.

From Rear-Admiral Sir William Hewett to Major-General Sir G. Graham, Commanding Expeditionary Force.

H.M.S. *Euryalus*, Suakim, March 21, 1884.

SIR,

I have to acknowledge the receipt of your despatch of yesterday's date, and in reply thereto, I need hardly tell you what deep gratification it has afforded me to hear of the high praise which you accord to the officers and men of the Royal Navy; and although we have suffered the loss of some gallant officers and men, I rest satisfied that the example of their devotion can never be lost to our service, accompanied by such a tribute as you have deemed fit to pay them. Allow me, sir, to express to you how I have esteemed the value of your cordial co-operation with me at all times, and from my experience of, I may now say, many campaigns, it is only another instance which shows what thorough cordiality exists between Army and Navy, and so long as that continues we may look for similar success to that your forces have obtained here.

I have, etc.,
W. HEWETT,
Rear-Admiral.

April 11, 1884.

CAN GORDON BE SAVED?

In conclusion I trespass further upon the reader's patience by asking leave to insert the following letter published in the *Daily Telegraph* and from my pen upon a subject now exciting the attention of millions of my countrymen and countrywomen.

To the Editor of " The Daily Telegraph."

SIR,
　　The question, "Can General Gordon be saved, and how?" is one of deep concern at the present moment to millions of his countrymen. Mr. Gladstone's Government, at whose request General Gordon went to the Soudan, to assist in carrying out their declared policy, but yesterday most properly expressed their interest in that gallant officer's safety. In the Premier's own words: "The country feels a profound interest, and likewise a sense of obligation incumbent upon it with regard to the safety of General Gordon. That feeling of interest, and that strong sense of obligation with regard to the safety of that gallant and heroic

officer, Her Majesty's Government have fully shared from the first, and they will be careful to put themselves in a position to fulfil those obligations in the sense in which they believe that the country, in common with themselves, recognise them. It would not be compatible with our duty, having made that statement, which I hope is sufficiently explicit and significant, to enter upon any further explanation."

Mr. Gladstone vouchsafes, therefore, no information as to how General Gordon is to be rescued or the garrisons he was sent to save withdrawn. As that brave man has lost all hope in getting help from the Government, perhaps I may be pardoned if I myself lack implicit faith in their foresight, vigour, and fixity of purpose. General Gordon has appealed from the Government to the people of England and America for help, and, to my mind, the act is another instance of his quick and sound judgment. Having some slight knowledge of the Soudan, from which I have just returned, I would like to show why it strikes me that the situation is one in which the people can render Gordon substantial aid if not actual deliverance. Sir Edward Watkin and others have generously offered large sums towards the £200,000 Gordon asks for to equip a relief expedition. That amount in cash probably would suffice for carrying out the plan the outline of which I now propose to lay before your readers; but nominally the sum required would be nearer half a million. To relieve Gordon I would expend the money in constructing a narrow-gauge railway from Suakim to Berber. The distance is about 250 miles. No serious engineering difficulties bar the way, and there are a score of contractors, any one of whom would, I am sure, undertake to put down a road that would answer all the purposes needed within six months from to-day. In Woolwich, at the present moment, I learn from the best authority, there is plant and material for laying and operating fifty miles of narrow-gauge railway, which could all be put on shipboard within forty-eight hours, and twenty days more should take it to Suakim to start the work. Surely the Government would sell or lend the material to forward such an enterprise. I have gone over about twenty-five miles of the ground—or from Suakim, Handouk, Otao, to Tambouk—with General Stewart's cavalry, and I never saw any country better adapted for rapidly putting down a first-rate road. From Tambouk to Berber, I have been told by those who have passed repeatedly over the road, it is no worse at any point than between Otao and Tambouk. The ascent to the passes through the Soudan mountain ranges are at an easy gradient, and neither rock cutting nor tunnelling is necessary. A few short-span trestle bridges would be needed to cross the narrow khors, or usually dry watercourses, but even these should not prevent the track-laying going on at the rate of two miles a day. The Arabs or Egyptian fellaheen would supply the navvies, and with the stimulus of good wages, and under the direction of European foremen, the work could be rapidly hurried onward day and night. The first eight miles laid would secure the wells at Handouk, where there is plenty of water. A further eight miles would take the road to Otao, and so on, by similar stages, till the last well was reached at Obach. From there, at certain seasons, a waterless waste of about fifty miles interposes to within three miles of Berber. That, however, is a difficulty a locomotive and water tanks would at once remove.

As to the opposition from the Arabs, Hadendowas, or Bishareen, need that be considered after the successful manner in which the Americans have laid and run their Western and Pacific Railroads through a country of daring and fierce savages, possessing, moreover, arms of precision? The Sioux, Modocs, Comanches, Apaches, and others had the advantage of living by the chase, and dwelling in a green and well-watered land; whereas the poor Arab's sole dependence is on his herds and scant store of grain. His herds cannot be driven over twenty miles in a day without injury; and were it clearly made known to the Hadendowas, Bishareen, or other Arabs, that interference with the railway would lead to their flocks being driven from the wells, raided upon, houghed, or killed, the road would be absolutely safe from their hands. In the Soudan they fought like heroes, but they never once seriously threatened our numerous convoys, many of which might easily have been captured. I am even inclined to think that they would welcome the advent of the iron horse, as they have keen trader instincts, and would speedily realise it meant cheaper goods and grain, and a better price for skins and other articles they have to sell. However that may be, half a score of armed men in a blockhouse or iron hut, some iron-covered waggons to protect the navvies in an emergency, and a regiment of mounted police, would amply ensure the safety of the Suakim and Berber railway. It takes weeks for boats to pass from Assouan, with its intervening five cataracts, to Berber. A railway from Suakim to Berber could cover the distance in a single day. One cataract only interposes between Khartoum and Berber, and Gordon, once knowing that the English were at the latter place, could, with a little help from below, cut his way down the river. Once let some 'John Company' be formed to carry out the relief scheme, by building this railway, and they will not only tap and command the trade of the whole of Equatorial Africa, with its chains of great lakes, but outstrip in friendly rivalry Stanley's International African Association. The cost of freighting from Suakim to Berber is now from £8 to £12 a ton, and nothing weighing over 500 lbs. can be carried in one parcel. Over 100,000 tons of freight, Mr. Wyld, of Suakim, has assured me, annually has to find its way down the Nile to the sea-board. It is not my province to make calculations showing whether such a road would pay or prove a sound or permanent investment; it is enough if I can point out it would help to rescue General Gordon. Before the first fifty miles were laid the news would have spread all over the Soudan that the English had taken a firm hold on the land, and meant to succour their countryman in Khartoum. The wavering, the timid, and the freebooters attracted to the Mahdi's standard, would slip away from him as the steam-engine advanced yard by yard into the country.

Let the friends of Gordon Pasha take heart; for the ensuring of his safety, and the putting an effectual stop for ever to the African slave trade, are in their own hands.

I am, Sir, yours sincerely,

YOUR SPECIAL CORRESPONDENT.

London.

SUPPLEMENTAL.

MILITARY honours and emoluments have been awarded to the officers and men. These, as the official records themselves show, are on a most niggardly scale, as compared with former recognitions of services rendered by British forces fighting abroad. Mr. Gladstone's Government accorded far higher honours, together with medals and the usual "thanks of Parliament," to those who passed through the much less hazardous and trying campaign that terminated at Tel-el-Kebir in September, 1882.

The reason assigned by Government why no vote of thanks was to be proposed in Parliament was the fewness of the force comprising the expedition. That seems an absurd contention, which would equally militate against the recognition of individual acts of bravery or the devotion and heroism displayed by a British battalion in some terrible crisis. It furthermore has not the respectability of consistency attaching to it, as medals and clasps have been given in very recent times in Africa and India, where the British forces actually engaged were less in number than those who fought at El Teb and Tamaai. General Graham and his men deserved better of their country. The Commanding Officer, hampered as he and every general ever has been by rules, orders, and appointments made in London, laboured incessantly, never sparing himself, in field or camp, to secure the successes which crowned the work of the expedition. Brave and generous to a fault, General Graham has frequently assumed the responsibility for orders and movements directed by subordinates, and which he did not and could not approve of.

The following are the official notifications of honours, promotions, and emoluments :

THE VICTORIA CROSS AND SPECIAL REWARDS.

War Office.

The Queen has been graciously pleased to give orders for the following promotions in, and appointments to, the Most Honourable Order of the Bath:

To be Extra Members of the Military Division of the Second Class, or Knights Commanders of the said Most Honourable Order, viz.: Lieutenant-General Frederick Charles Arthur Stephenson, C.B.; Colonel Herbert Stewart, C.B., Aide-de-Camp to the Queen.

To be Ordinary Members of the Military Division of the Third Class, or Companions of the said Most Honourable Order, viz.: Major-General John Davis; Captain Hilary Gustavus Andoe, R.N.; Colonel Edward Alexander Wood, 10th Hussars; Colonel Barnes Slyfield Robinson, Princess Victoria's (Royal Irish Fusiliers); Colonel Cornelius Francis Clery, half-pay; Brigade Surgeon Edmund Greswold M'Dowell, Army Medical Department; Lieutenant-Colonel

William Green, the Black Watch (Royal Highlanders); Lieutenant-Colonel William Byam, York and Lancaster Regiment; Lieutenant-Colonel Arthur George Webster, 19th Hussars; Lieutenant-Colonel John Charles Ardagh, C.B. (Civil), Royal Engineers; Lieutenant-Colonel Percy Harry Stanley Barrow, C.M.G., 19th Hussars; Captain Ernest Neville Rolfe, R.N.: Assistant Commissary-General Robert Arthur Nugent, Commissariat and Transport Staff.

The Queen has been graciously pleased to signify her intention to confer the decoration of the Victoria Cross upon the undermentioned officers, non-commissioned officer, and private soldier, whose claims have been submitted for Her Majesty's approval, for their conspicuous bravery during the recent operations in the Soudan, as recorded against their names:

Captain Arthur Knyvet Wilson, Royal Navy.—Lieutenant Percival Scrope Marling, 3rd Battalion, King's Royal Rifle Corps, late Mounted Infantry.—Quartermaster-Sergeant William Marshall, 19th Hussars.—Private Thomas Edwards, 1st Battalion, Royal Highlanders.

Admiralty.

Rear-Admiral Sir William Nathan Wrighte Hewett, V.C., K.C.B., K.C.S.I., to be Vice-Admiral whilst in command of Her Majesty's ships and vessels employed on the East Indian Station.

The following promotions have been made in Her Majesty's Fleet for services rendered with the Naval Brigade forming part of the Soudan Expeditionary Force. Dated May 20, 1884:

Commander E. N. Rolfe to be Captain; Lieutenants W. H. B. Graham and C. J. M. Conybeare to be Commanders; Sub-Lieut. P. D. M. Henderson to be Lieutenant; Staff Surgeon J. H. Martin to be Fleet Surgeon; Surgeon H. E. F. Cross to be Staff Surgeon; Surgeon T. D. Gimlette will be promoted to Staff Surgeon on April 1, 1885. The following promotions have also been made for services rendered in the Red Sea in connection with the Soudan Expeditionary Force. Dated May 20, 1884:

Lieutenants H. C. Bigge and W. D. Morrish to be Commanders; Navigating-Lieutenant F. Hire to be Staff-Commander; Chief Engineer George T. Crook to be Inspector of Machinery; Assistant-Paymaster James A. Bell to be Paymaster. The Lords Commissioners of the Admiralty have been pleased, under the terms of Her Majesty's Order in Council of Jan. 15, 1878, to promote Captain and Brevet Major William G. Tucker, Royal Marine Artillery, to be Major, in recognition of his meritorious service at the engagement of El Teb. Dated May 21.

War Office.

The Queen has been graciously pleased to approve of the following promotions being conferred upon the undermentioned Officers and Warrant Officer, in recognition of their services during the recent operations in the Soudan. Dated May 21.

BREVET.

To be Lieutenant-General (for distinguished service in the field).—Major-General Sir General Graham, V.C., K.C.B., Royal Engineers.

To be Major-General (for distinguished service in the field).—Major and Colonel Sir Redvers H. Buller, V.C. K.C.M.G., C.B. Aide-de-Camp to the Queen, half-pay.

To be Colonels.—Major and Brevet Lieutenant-Colonel Cornelius Francis Clery, half-pay; Lieutenant-Colonel Denzil Hammill, C.B., Gordon Highlanders.

TO BE LIEUTENANT-COLONELS.

Major Francis T. Lloyd, Royal Artillery; Major Edmund L. Fraser, the King's Royal Rifle Corps; Captain and Brevet Major John P. Brabazon, 10th Hussars; Major Edmund H. Holley, Royal Artillery; Major George H. T. Colwell, Royal

Marine Light Infantry; Major Reginald W. Dalgetty, the York and Lancaster Regiment; Major Alaric E. A. Cross, the Gordon Highlanders; Major Hugh S. Gough, 10th Hussars; Major Elliot Wood, Royal Engineers; Major Killingworth R. Todd, Royal Engineers; Major Charles J. Eden, the Black Watch (Royal Highlanders); Major Andrew G. Wauchope, C.M.G., the Black Watch (Royal Highlanders). Memorandum.—Major Walker Aitken, the Black Watch (Royal Highlanders), would have been recommended to Her Majesty for promotion had he not been killed in action at Tamaai.

TO BE MAJORS.

Captain Thomas B. Hitchcock, the King's (Shropshire Light Infantry); Captain Nicholas W. P. Brophy, the Black Watch (Royal Highlanders); Captain William F. Kelly, the Royal Sussex Regiment; Captain John Gordon, Princess Victoria's (Royal Irish Fusiliers); Captain Arthur O. Green, Royal Engineers; Captain James J. B. Menzies, the Gordon Highlanders: Captain William H. Poë, Royal Marine Light Infantry; Captain Charles B. H. Jenkins, 19th Hussars; Captain Frederick G. Slade, Royal Artillery; Captain Josceline H. Wodehouse, Royal Artillery; Captain Herbert C. T. Littledale, the York and Lancaster Regiment; Captain Kenneth S. Baynes, the Queen's Own Cameron Highlanders; Captain Edward William Herbert, the King's Royal Rifle Corps.

Chaplains' Department.—The Rev. Robert Brindle, Chaplain to the Forces of the Third Class, to be Chaplain to the Forces of the Second Class.

Commissariat and Transport Staff.—To be Assistant Commissaries-General: Deputy Assistant Commissary-General Marcus E. R. Rainsford; Deputy Assistant Commissary-General George V. Hamilton. To be Quartermaster: Conductor of Supplies Henry Hickie.

Medical Department.—To be Surgeons-Major, with the relative rank of Lieut-Colonel: Surgeon-Major, with relative rank of Major, William A. Catherwood, M.D.; Surgeon-Major, with relative rank of Major, William D. Wilson, M.D.

Ordnance Store Department.—Assistant Commissary-General of Ordnance, with relative rank of Major, Herbert J. Mills, to be Assistant Commissary-General of Ordnance, with the relative rank of Lieutenant-Colonel.

Army Pay Department.—Staff-Paymaster and Honorary Major Robert B. Farwell to be Chief-Paymaster, with the honorary rank of Lieutenant-Colonel in the army.

Veterinary Department.—To be Veterinary Surgeons' First Class, ranking with Majors, but junior of that rank except for choice of quarters: First Class Veterinary-Surgeon, ranking with Captain, Charles Clayton.

First Class Veterinary-Surgeon, ranking with Captain, Henry Thomson.

Honorary Rank.—To be Captains: Quartermaster Edward Enright, Army Hospital Corps. Quartermaster Frederick H. Mahony, the York and Lancaster Regiment.

GRATUITY TO THE TROOPS.

The following Special Circular has been issued from the War Office:

1. A gratuity will be issued to the European troops engaged in the recent operations in the Soudan. Every officer, warrant officer, non-commissioned officer, and private who was serving at Suakim or Trinkitat between 19th February and 26th March last (both dates inclusive) will be entitled to participate in the grant.

2. The gratuity will be issued according to the rank or relative rank of the recipient upon the following scale:— General, 400 shares, with 100 shares extra if in chief command; Lieutenant-General, 152 shares, with 100 shares extra if in chief command; Major-General, 76 shares, with 100 shares extra if in chief command; Brigadier-General, 57 shares, with 50 shares extra if in chief command; Colonel —Staff or Departmental Officers, or Officers having regimental

rank of Colonel, 40 shares; Colonel, except as above defined, and Lieutenant-Colonel, 32 shares; Major, 15 shares; Captain, 12 shares; Lieutenant, 7½ shares; Warrant Officer, 4 shares. Non-commissioned officers and men, according to classification, contained in Article 1032, Royal Warrant of 11th March, 1882, *i.e.*:—Class 1, 3 shares; Class 2, 2½ shares; Class 3, 2 shares; Class 4, 1½ share; Class 5, 1 share.

3. The amount of each share be £2.

Admiral Sir John Hay, M.P. has given notice in Parliament, that he will move a vote of thanks to Admiral Hewett, General Graham, and the officers and men of the Expedition. The result, at this writing of the motion, is unknown.

THE END.